Sweet Home

チーズ スイートホーム

1

Konami Kanata

contents
homemade 1~20

1 a cat is lost   3

2 a cat is found   11

3 a cat is given a hard
   time   19

4 a cat forgets   27

5 a cat begins   35

6 a cat is disappointed
                               43

7 a cat understands   51

8 a cat remembers   59

9 a cat dreams   67

10 a cat is fired up   75

11 a cat plays   83

12 a cat is lost... again   91

13 a cat fights!   99

14 a cat goes to the vet
   (part 1)   107

15 a cat goes to the vet
   (part 2)   115

16 a cat fears   123

17 a cat discovers   131

18 a cat is discovered   139

19 a cat obsesses   147

20 a cat is home alone
                               155

   Introducing Chi's Home
   Sweer Home   163

homemade 1: a cat is lost

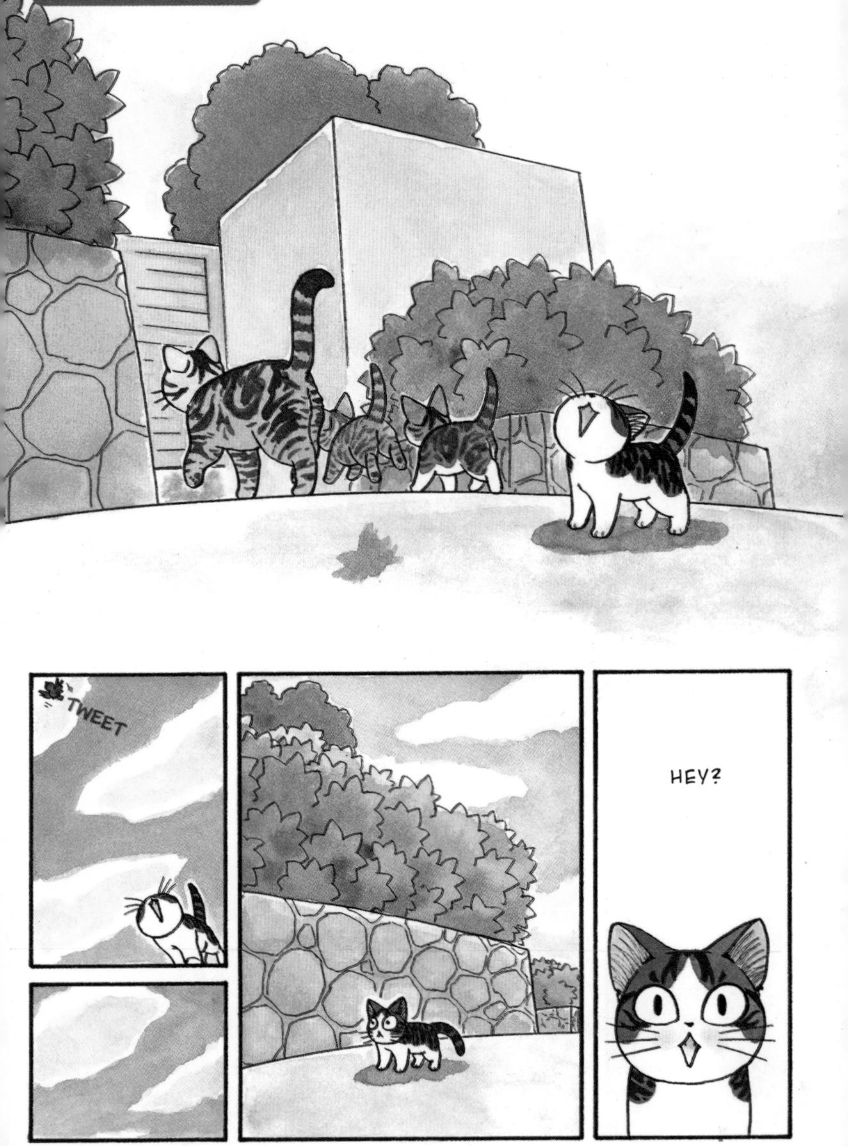
TWEET
HEY?

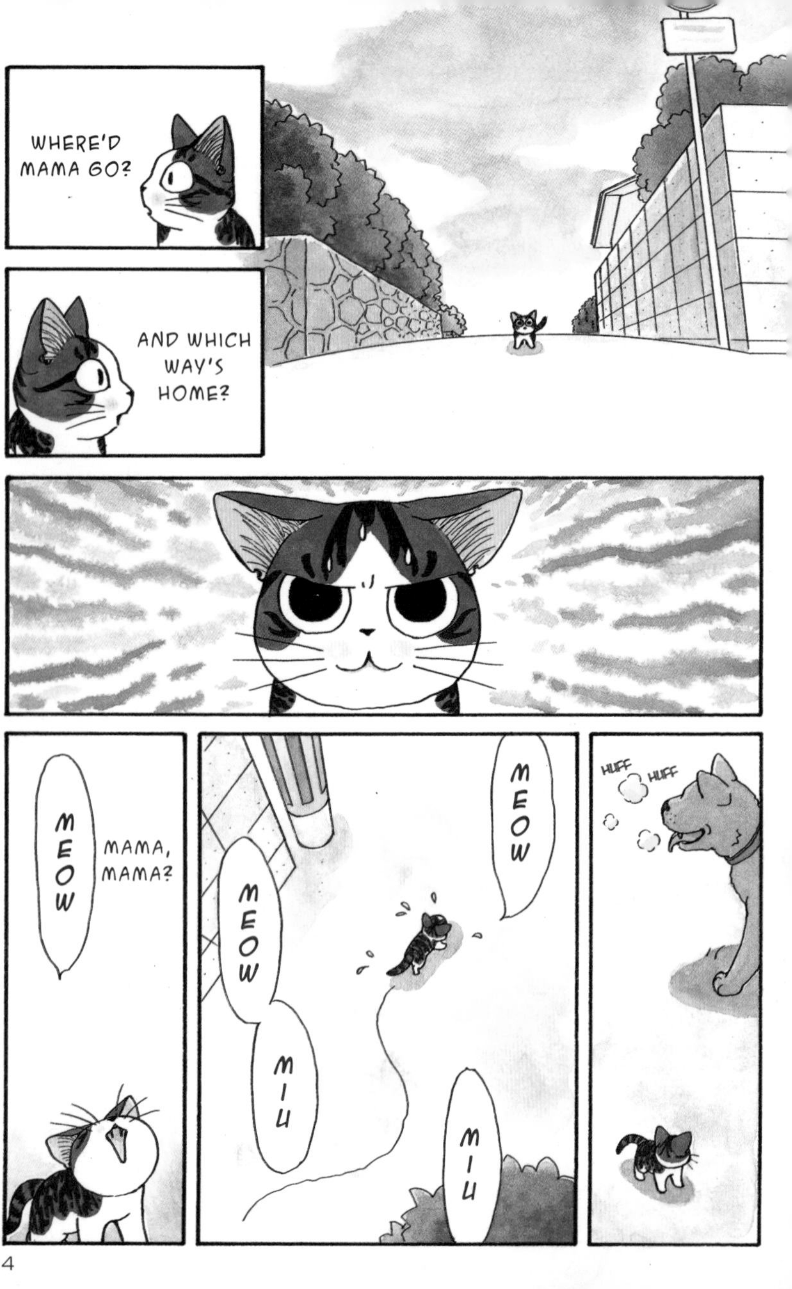
WHERE'D MAMA GO?
AND WHICH WAY'S HOME?
MEOW
MAMA, MAMA?
MEOW
MEOW
MIU
MIU
HUFF
HUFF

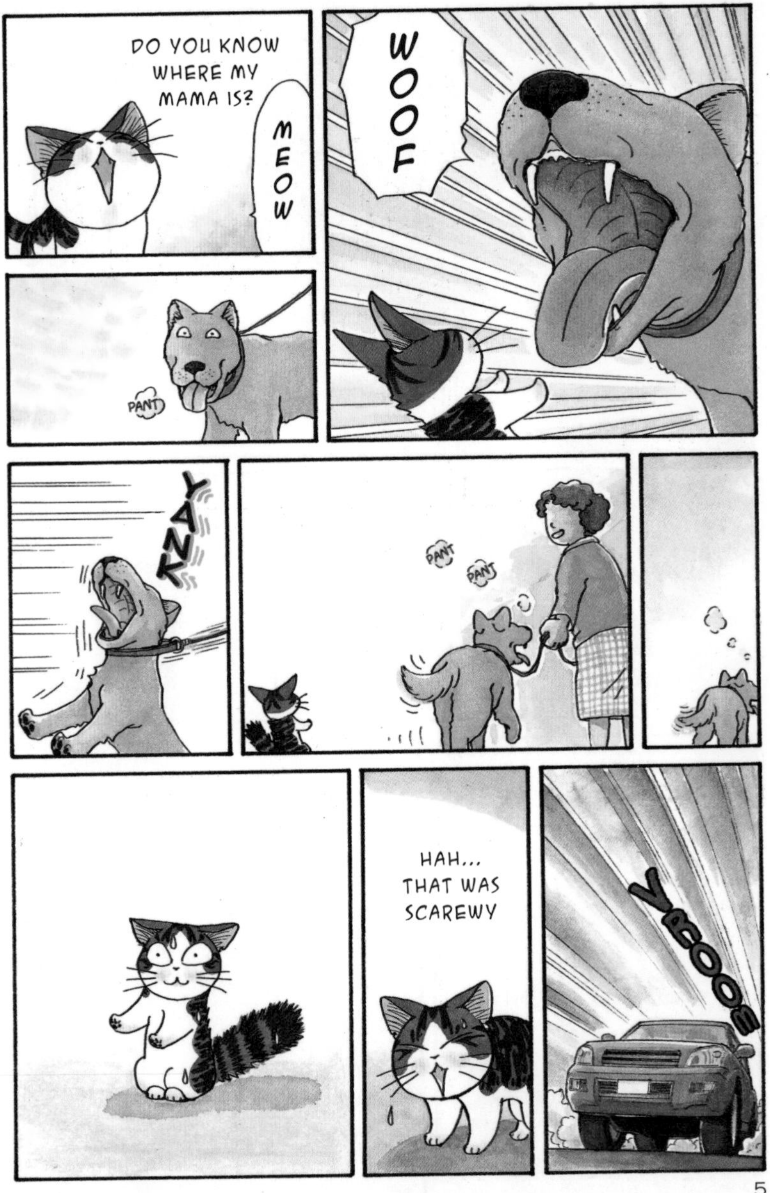

DO YOU KNOW WHERE MY MAMA IS?
MEOW
PANT
WOOF
YANK
PANT
PANT
HAH... THAT WAS SCAREWY
VROOOM

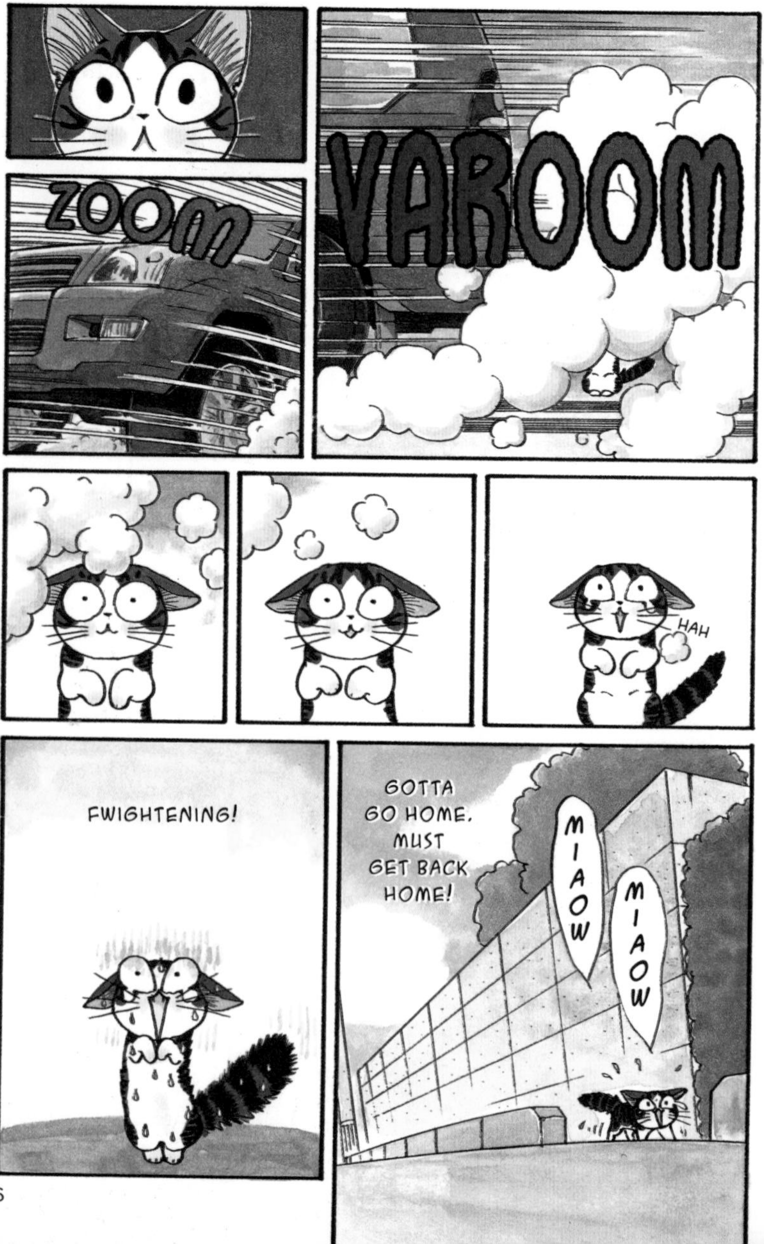
ZOOM
VAROOM
HAH
FWIGHTENING!
GOTTA GO HOME. MUST GET BACK HOME!
MIAOW
MIAOW

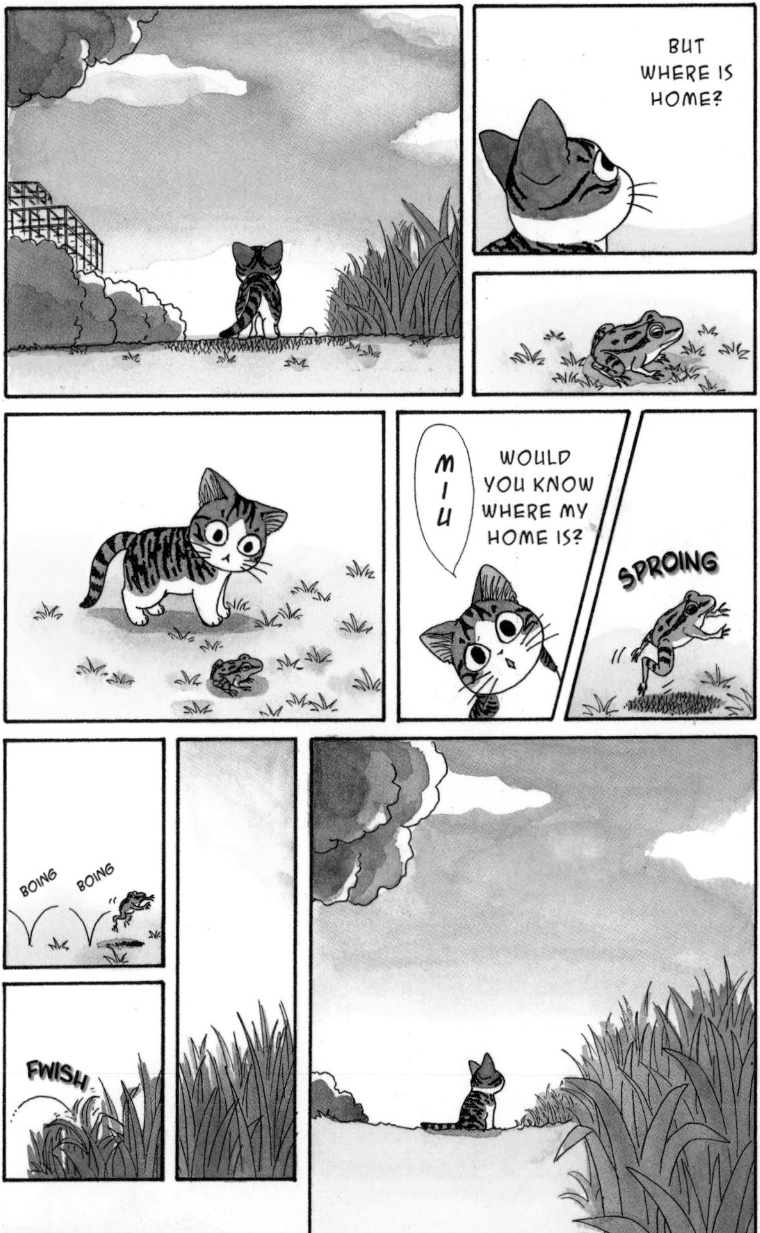
BUT WHERE IS HOME?
MIU
WOULD YOU KNOW WHERE MY HOME IS?
SPROING
BOING
BOING
FWISH

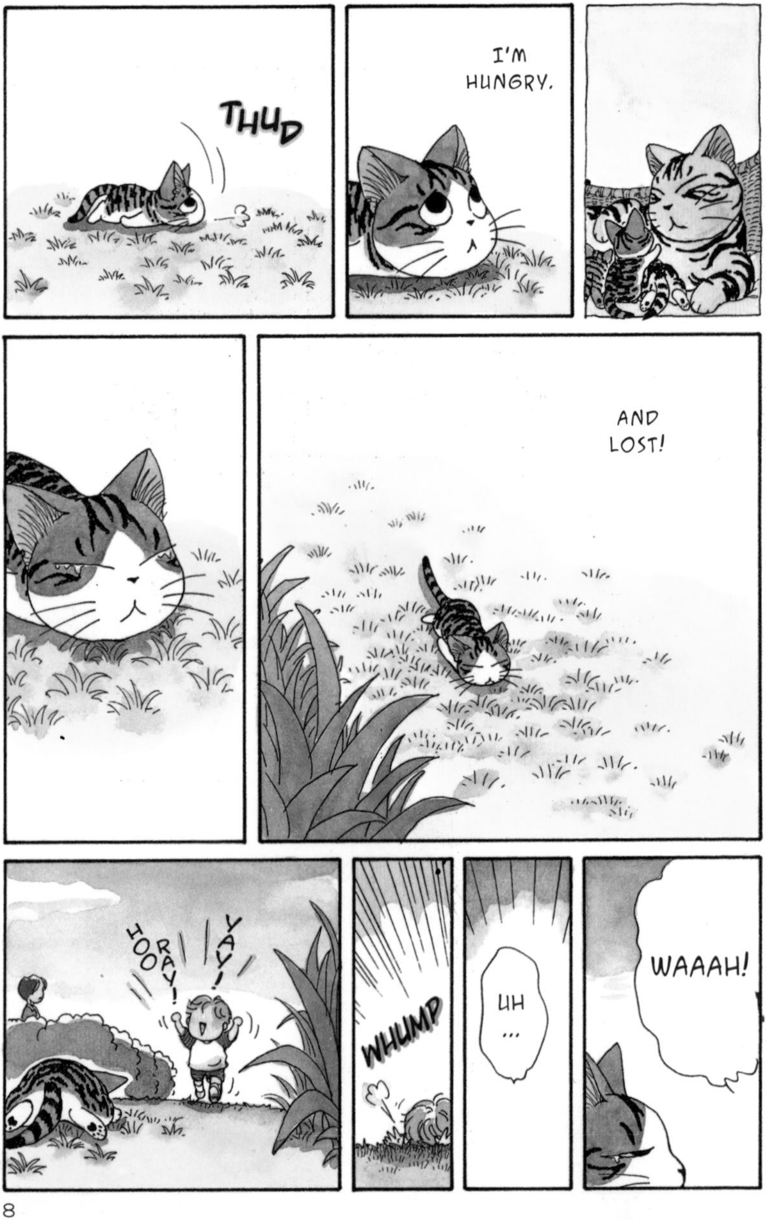
THUD
I'M HUNGRY.
AND LOST!
HOORAY!
YAY!
WHUMP
UH ...
WAAAH!

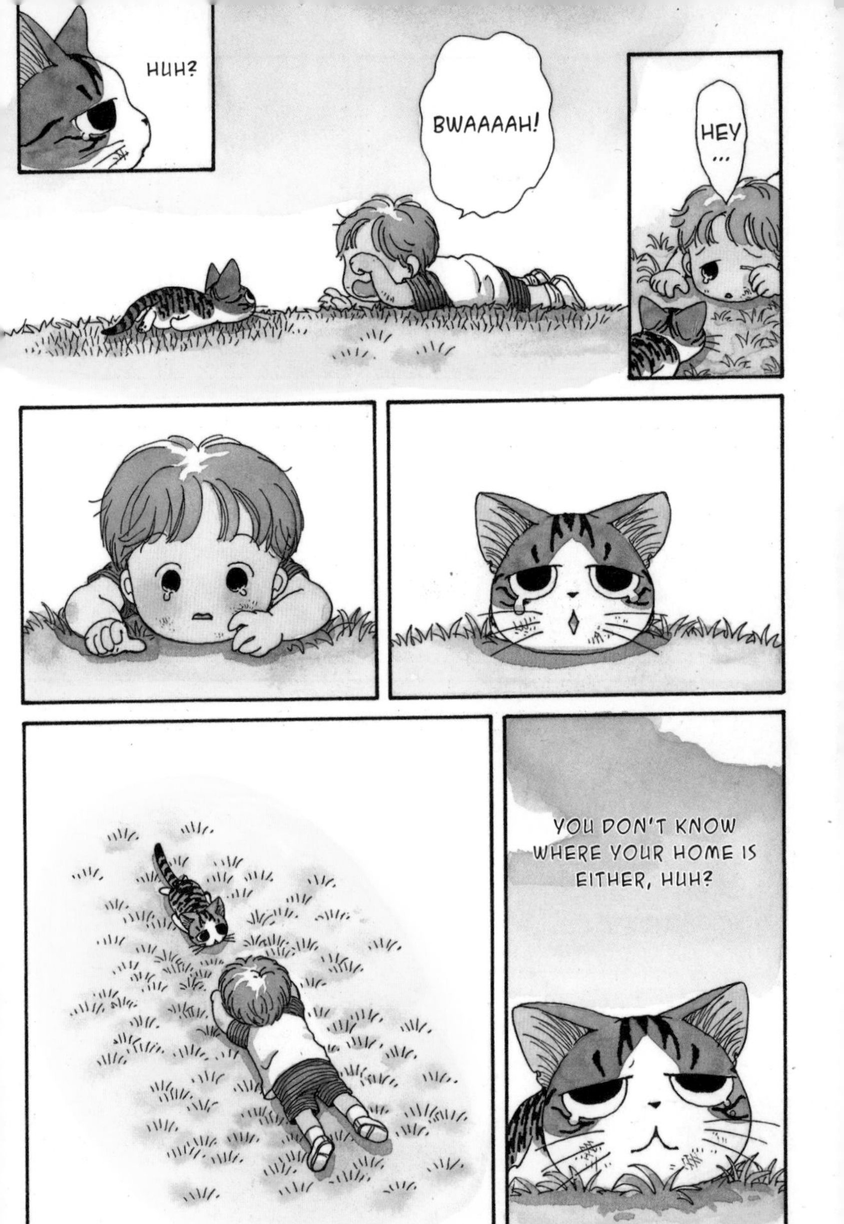
HUH?
BWAAAAH!
HEY ...
YOU DON'T KNOW WHERE YOUR HOME IS EITHER, HUH?

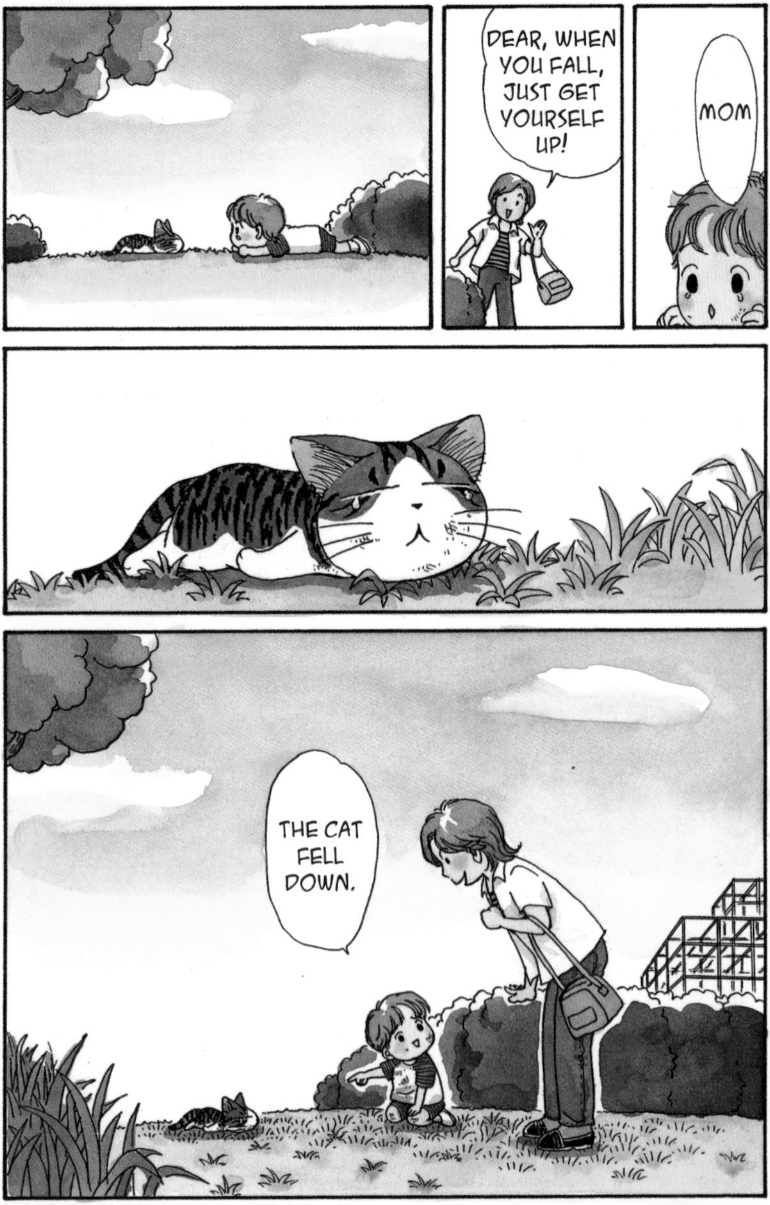
DEAR, WHEN YOU FALL, JUST GET YOURSELF UP!
MOM
THE CAT FELL DOWN.

the end

homemade 2: a cat is found

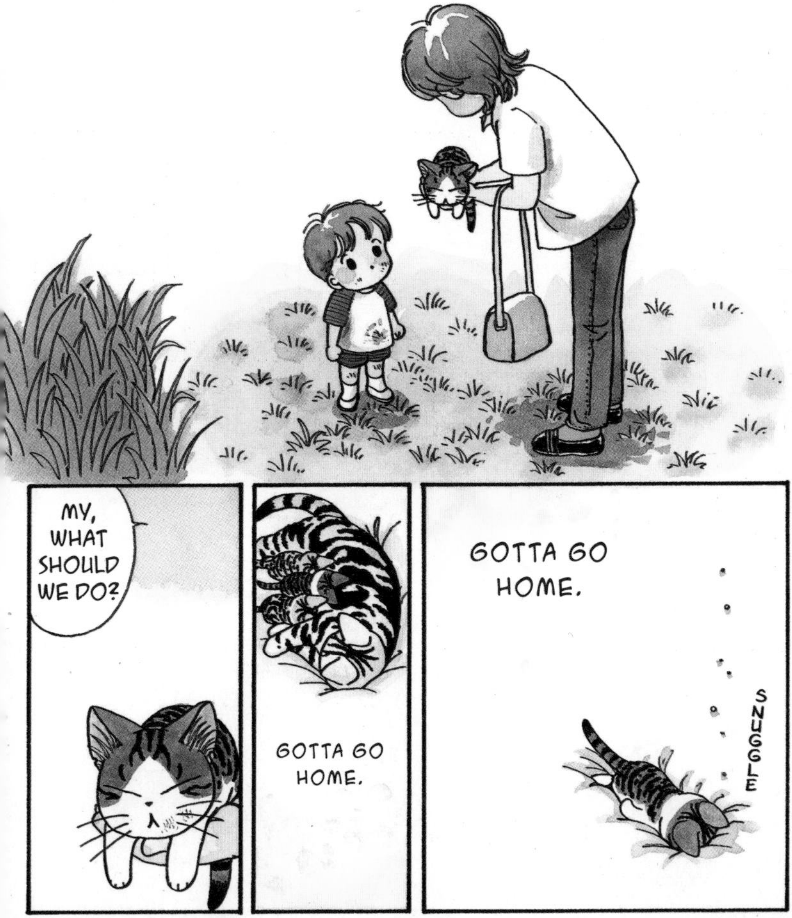
MY, WHAT SHOULD WE DO?
GOTTA GO HOME.
GOTTA GO HOME.
SNUGGLE

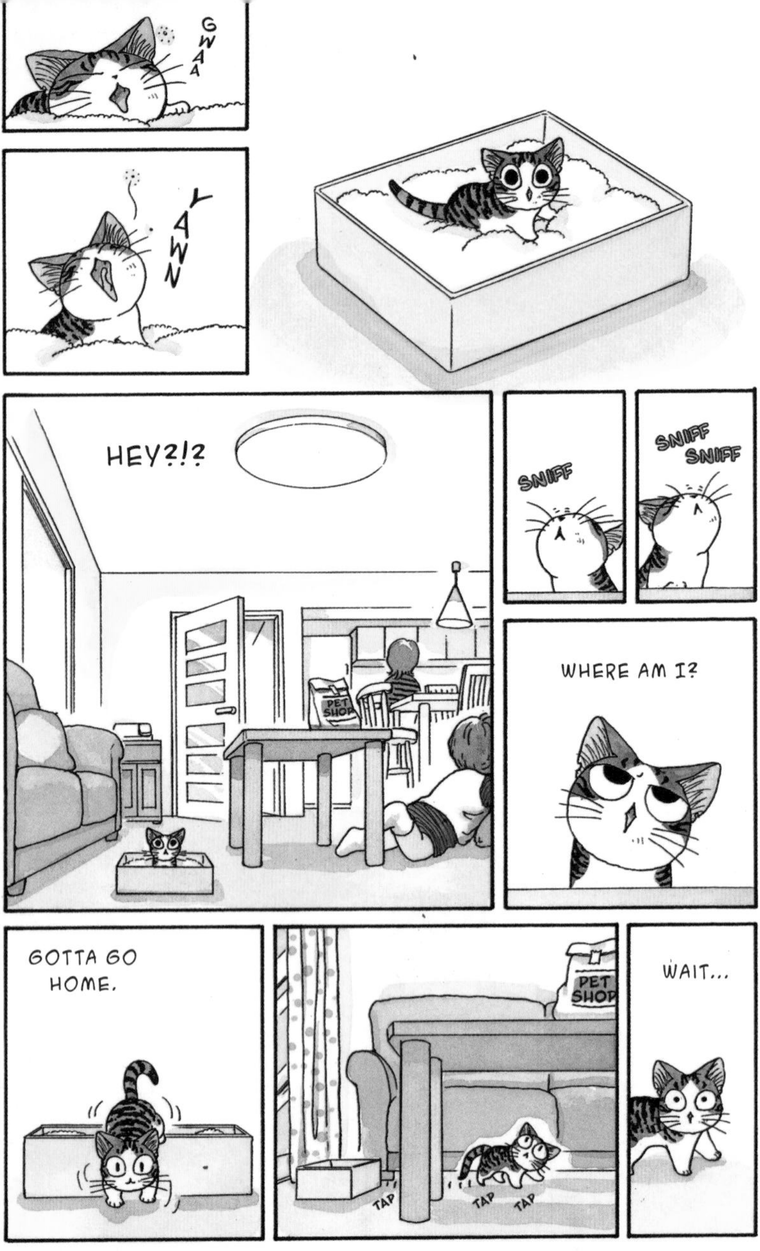
GWAA
YAWN
HEY?!?
SNIFF
SNIFF SNIFF
WHERE AM I?
PET SHOP
GOTTA GO HOME.
PET SHOP
TAP
TAP
TAP
WAIT...

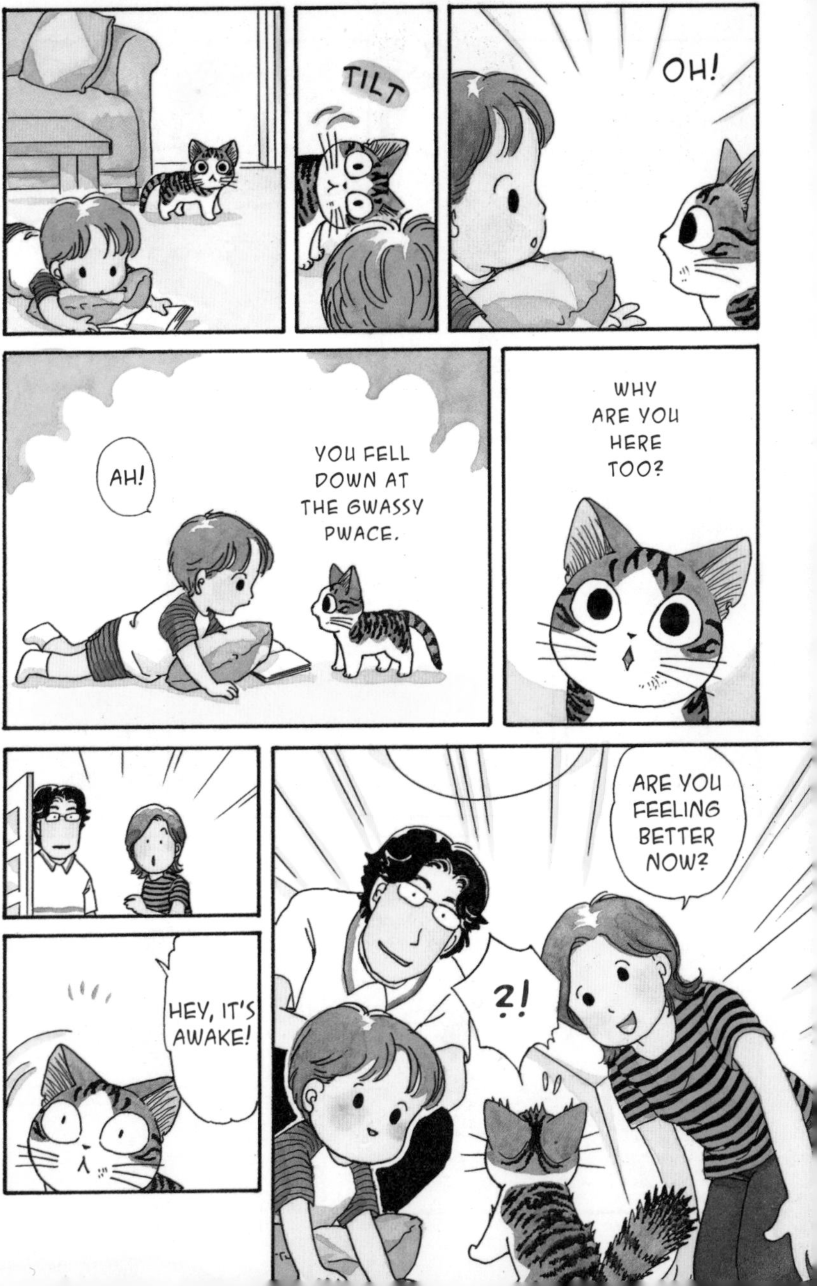
TILT
OH!
AH!
YOU FELL DOWN AT THE GWASSY PWACE.
WHY ARE YOU HERE TOO?
HEY, IT'S AWAKE!
ARE YOU FEELING BETTER NOW?
?!

ISN'T THAT A SHAME.

LITTLE ONES LIKE THIS CAN'T MAKE IT ON THEIR OWN.

WHAT'S THE KITTY GONNA DO?

SCAMPER

I'M GOING HOME!

UM

WANNA GO HOME!!

GOTTA GO HOME!!

HEY, WHAT'S THAT?

IT'S KITTEN MILK. THE STORE SUGGESTED IT.

KITTEN MILK

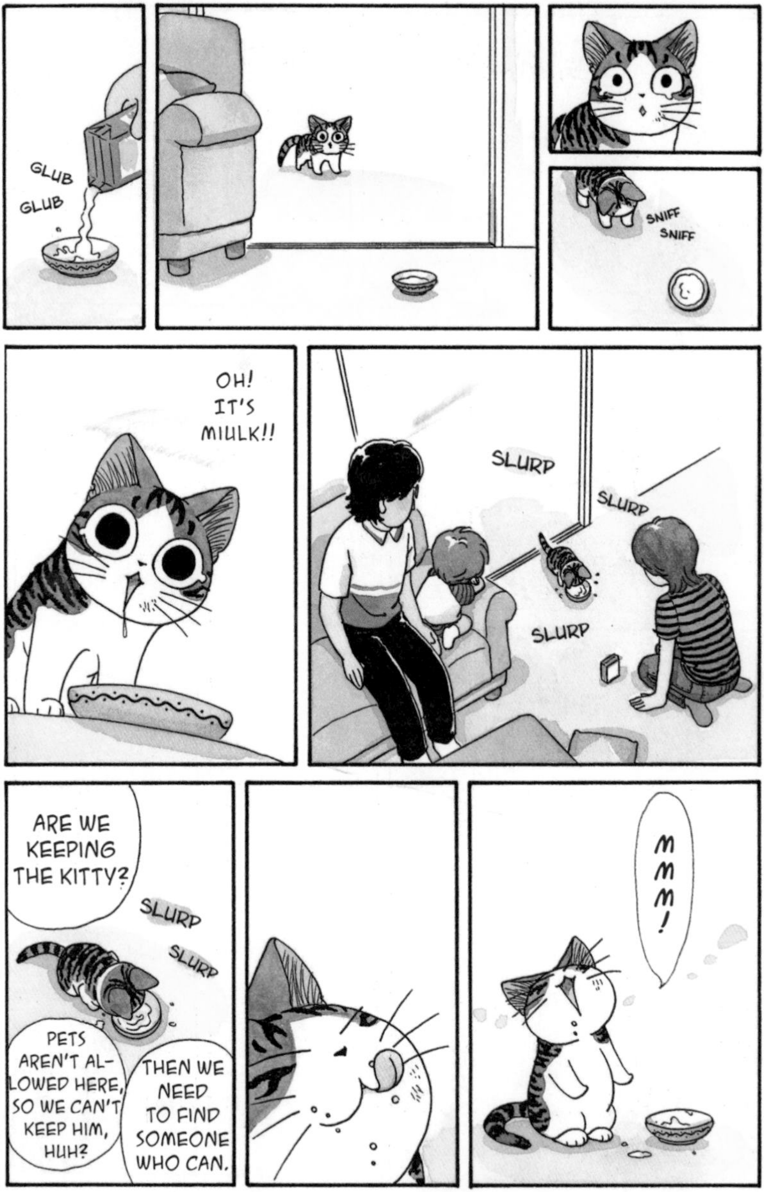
GLUB
GLUB
SNIFF
SNIFF
OH! IT'S MIULK!!
SLURP
SLURP
SLURP
ARE WE KEEPING THE KITTY?
SLURP
SLURP
PETS AREN'T AL-LOWED HERE, SO WE CAN'T KEEP HIM, HUH?
THEN WE NEED TO FIND SOMEONE WHO CAN.
MMM!

I'M STUFFED! **SHWUMP**

HOME!!

FLIT
FLIT
FLIT

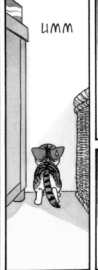
UMM

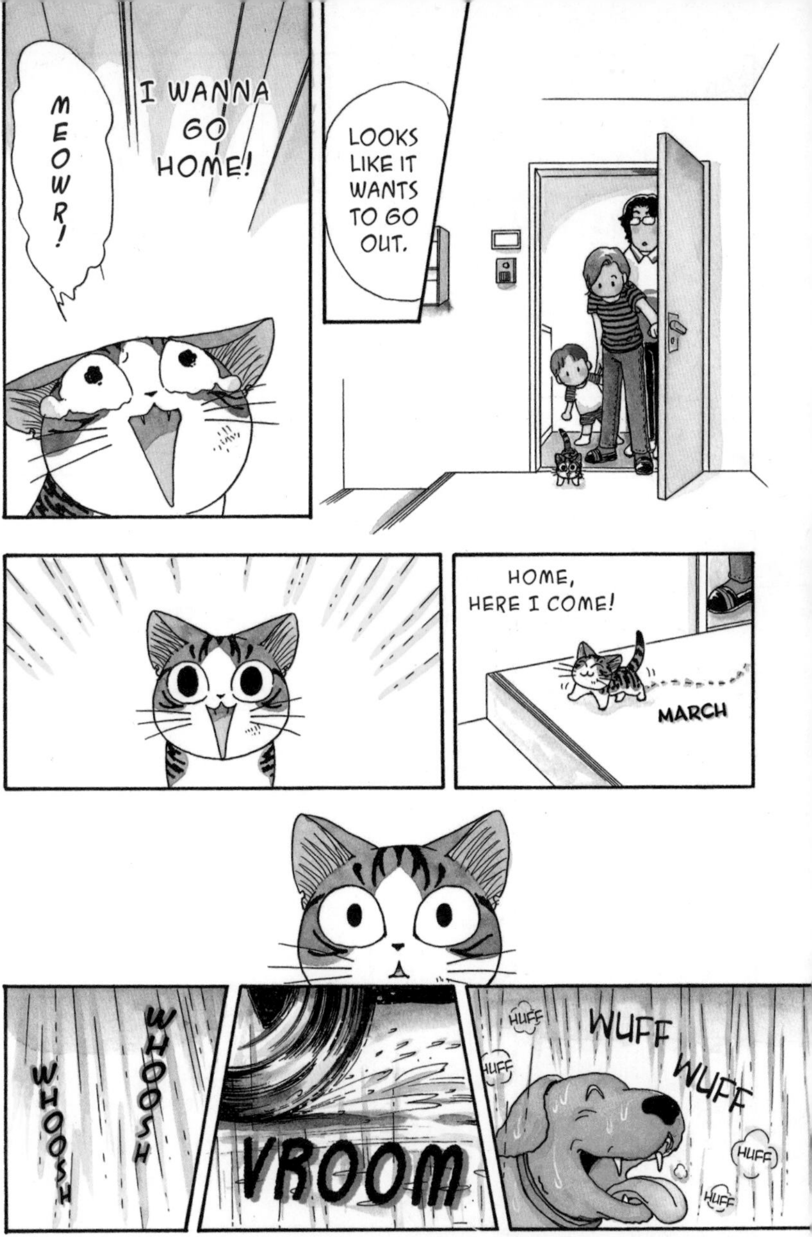

MEOWR!
I WANNA GO HOME!
LOOKS LIKE IT WANTS TO GO OUT.
HOME, HERE I COME!
MARCH
WHOOSH
WHOOSH
VROOM
HUFF
HUFF
WUFF
WUFF
HUFF
HUFF

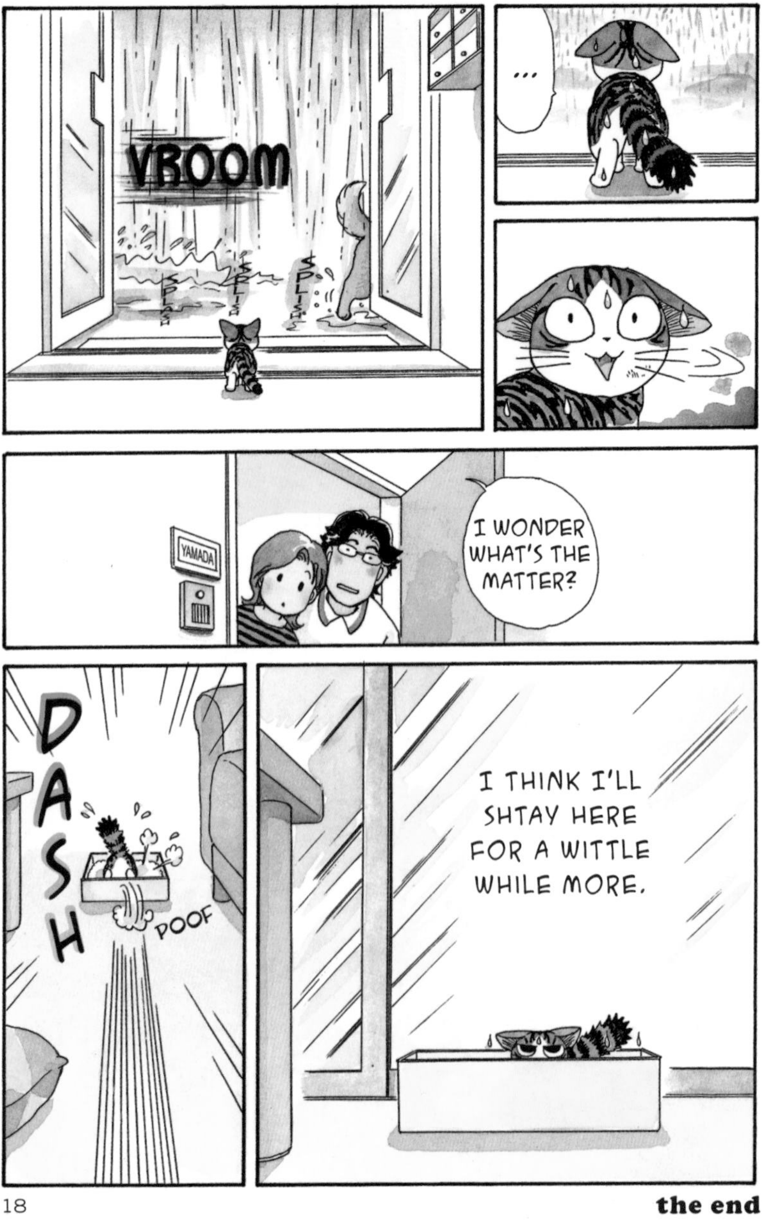
VROOM
SPLASH
SPLISH
SPLISH
...
YAMADA
I WONDER WHAT'S THE MATTER?
DASH
POOF
I THINK I'LL SHTAY HERE FOR A WITTLE WHILE MORE.

the end

homemade 3: a cat is given a hard time

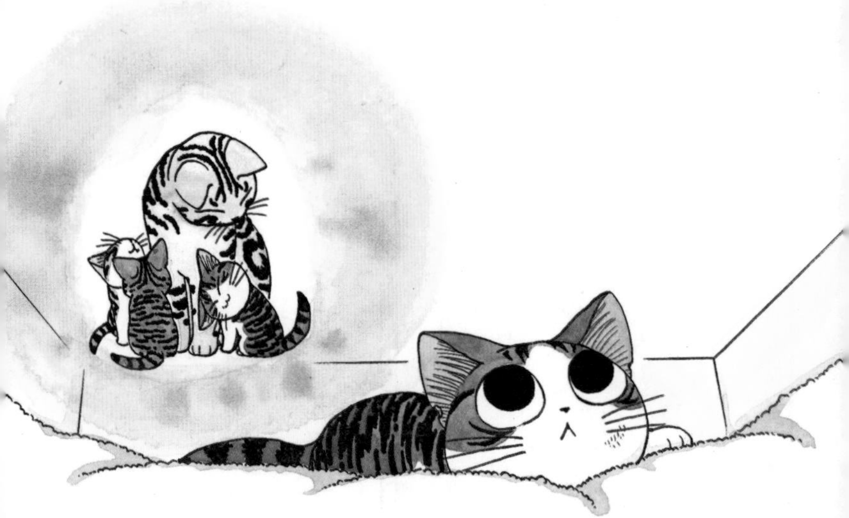

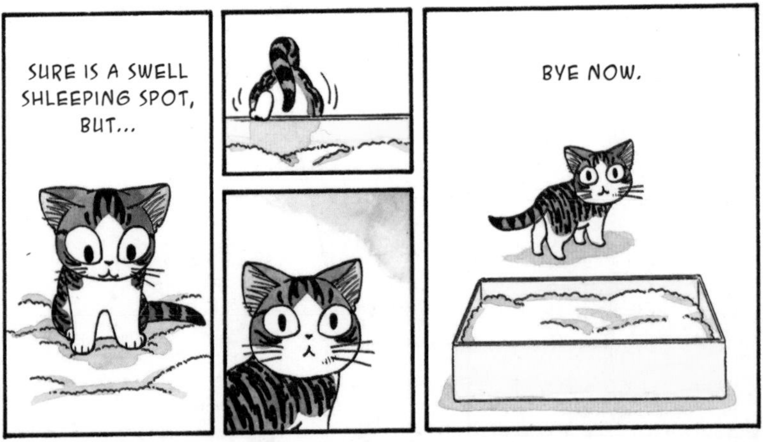
SURE IS A SWELL SHLEEPING SPOT, BUT...
BYE NOW.

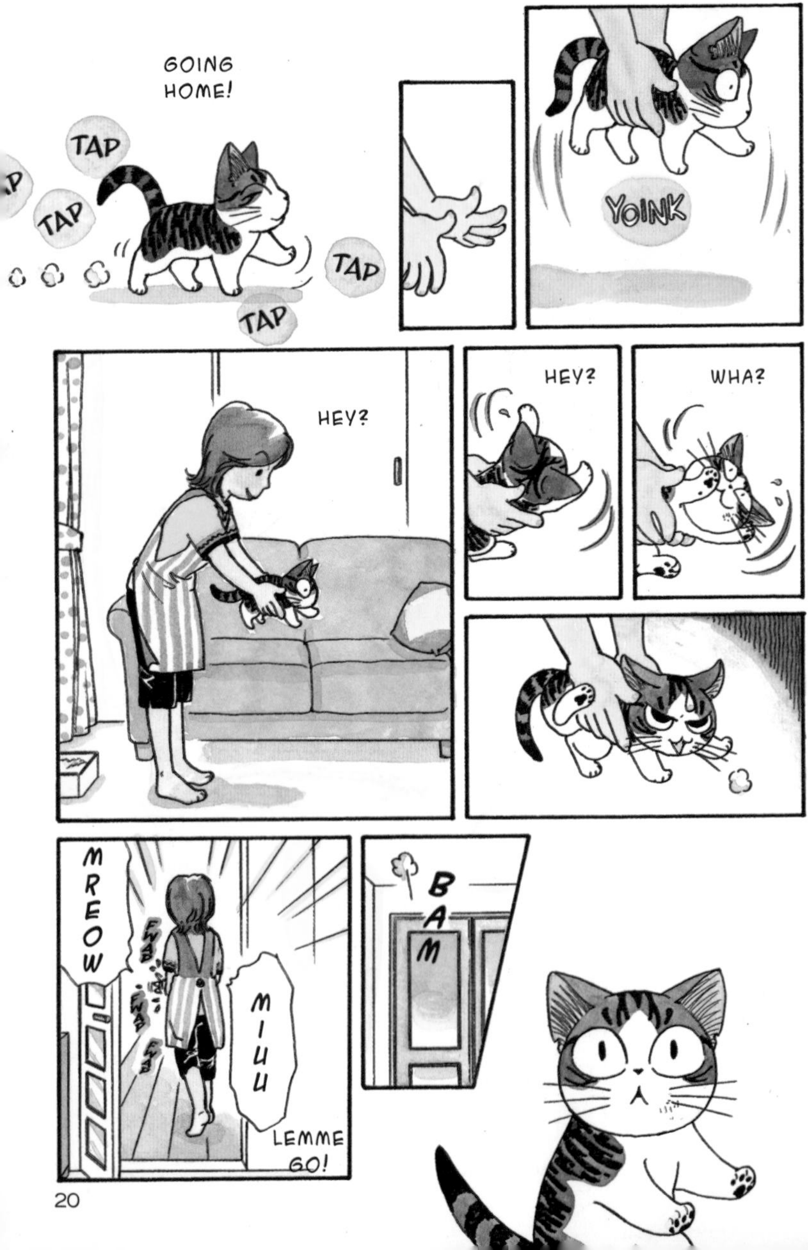
GOING HOME!
TAP
TAP
TAP
TAP
TAP
YOINK
HEY?
HEY?
WHA?
MREOW
MIUU
LEMME GO!
BAM

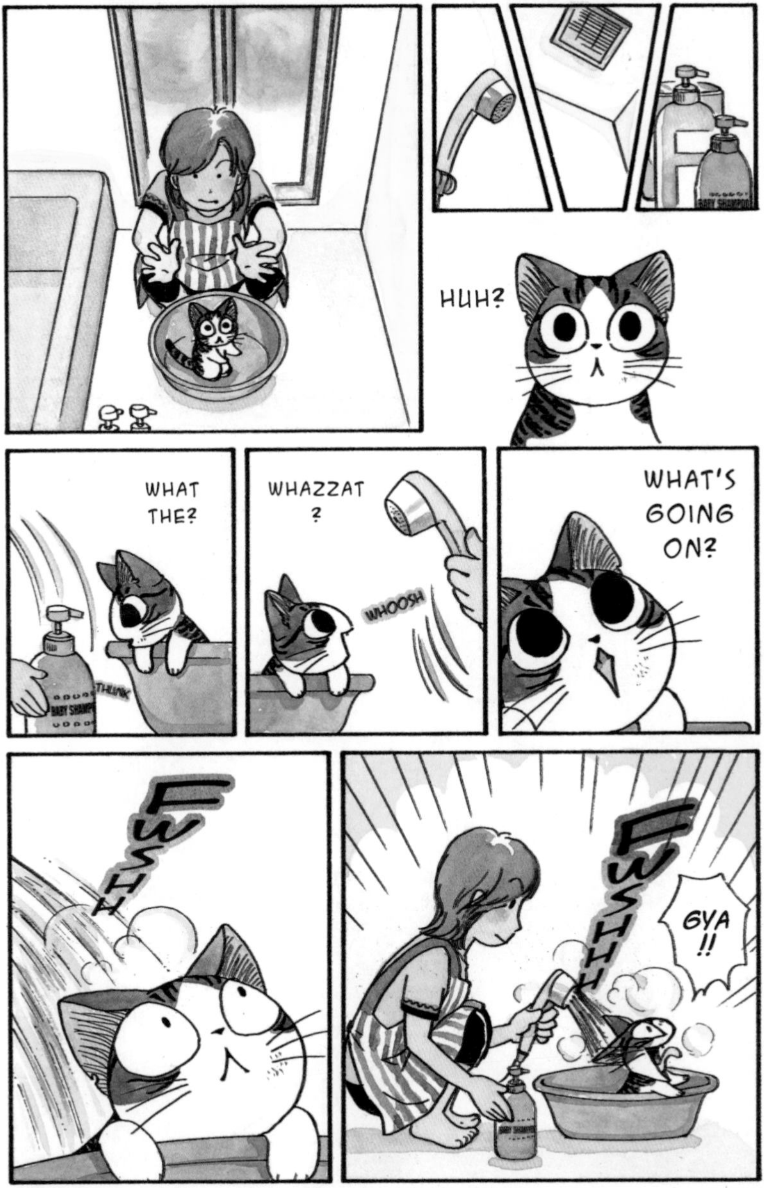
HUH?
WHAT THE?
THUNK
WHAZZAT ?
WHOOSH
WHAT'S GOING ON?
FWSHH
FWSHH
GYA !!

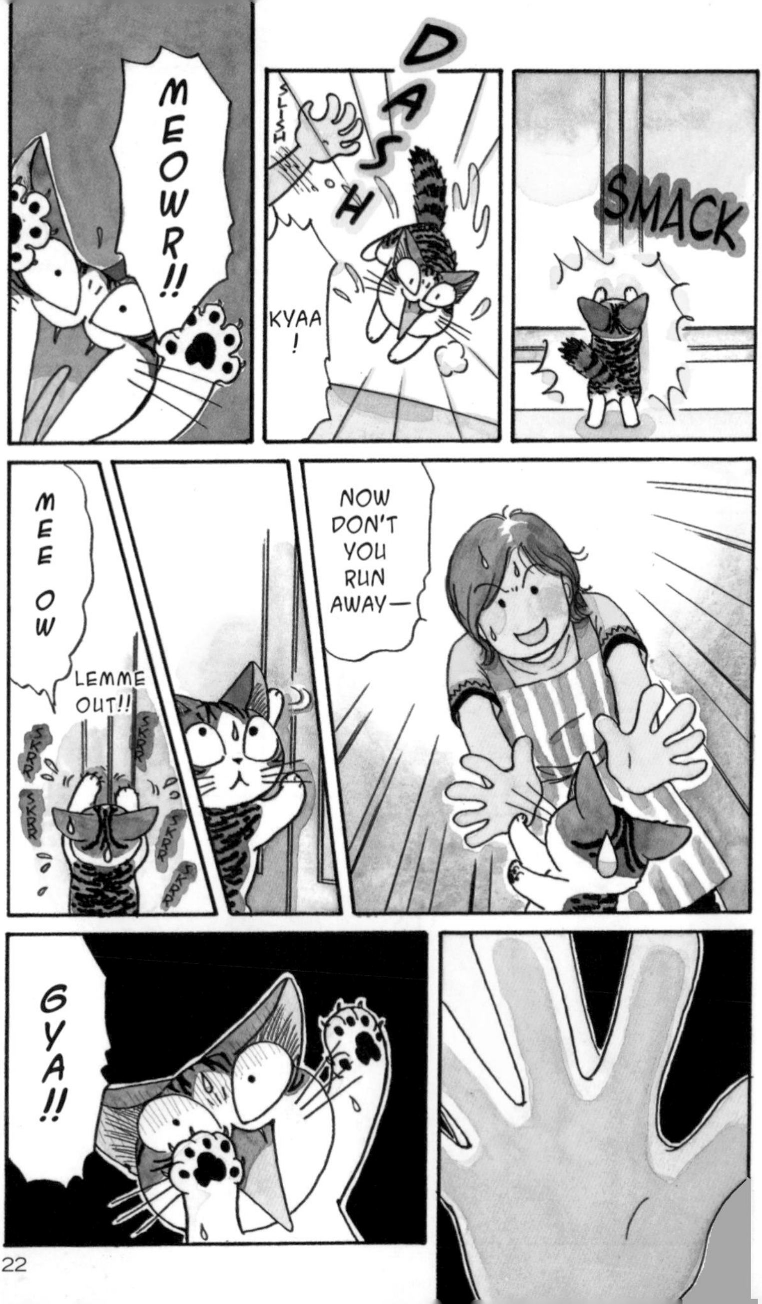
MEOWR!!
SLISH
DASH
KYAA!
SMACK
MEE OW
LEMME OUT!!
SKRR SKRR
SKRR SKRR SKRR
NOW DON'T YOU RUN AWAY—
GYA!!

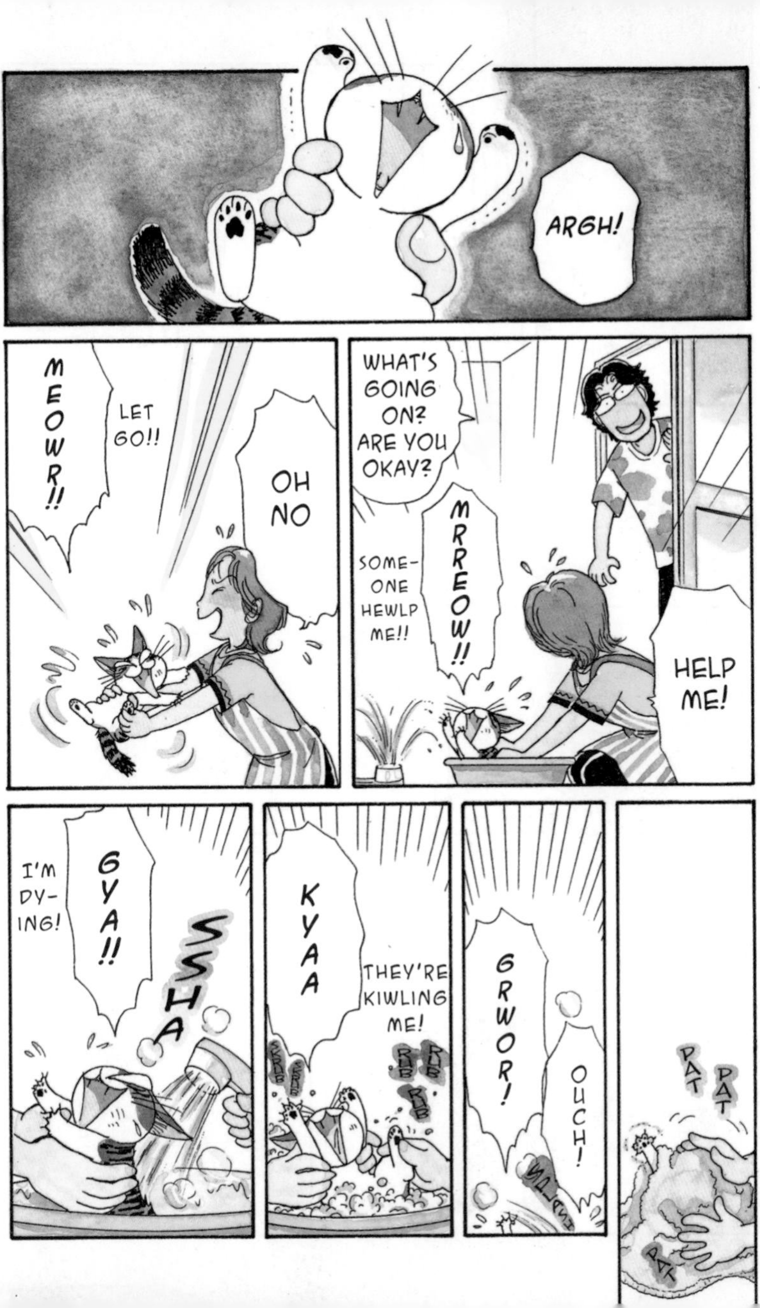
ARGH!
MEOWR!!
LET GO!!
OH NO
WHAT'S GOING ON? ARE YOU OKAY?
MRREOW!!
SOME-ONE HEWLP ME!!
HELP ME!
I'M DY-ING!
GYA!!
SSHA
KYAA
THEY'RE KIWLING ME!
SCRUB SCRUB
RUB RUB RUB
GRWOR!
OUCH!
PAT PAT
PAT

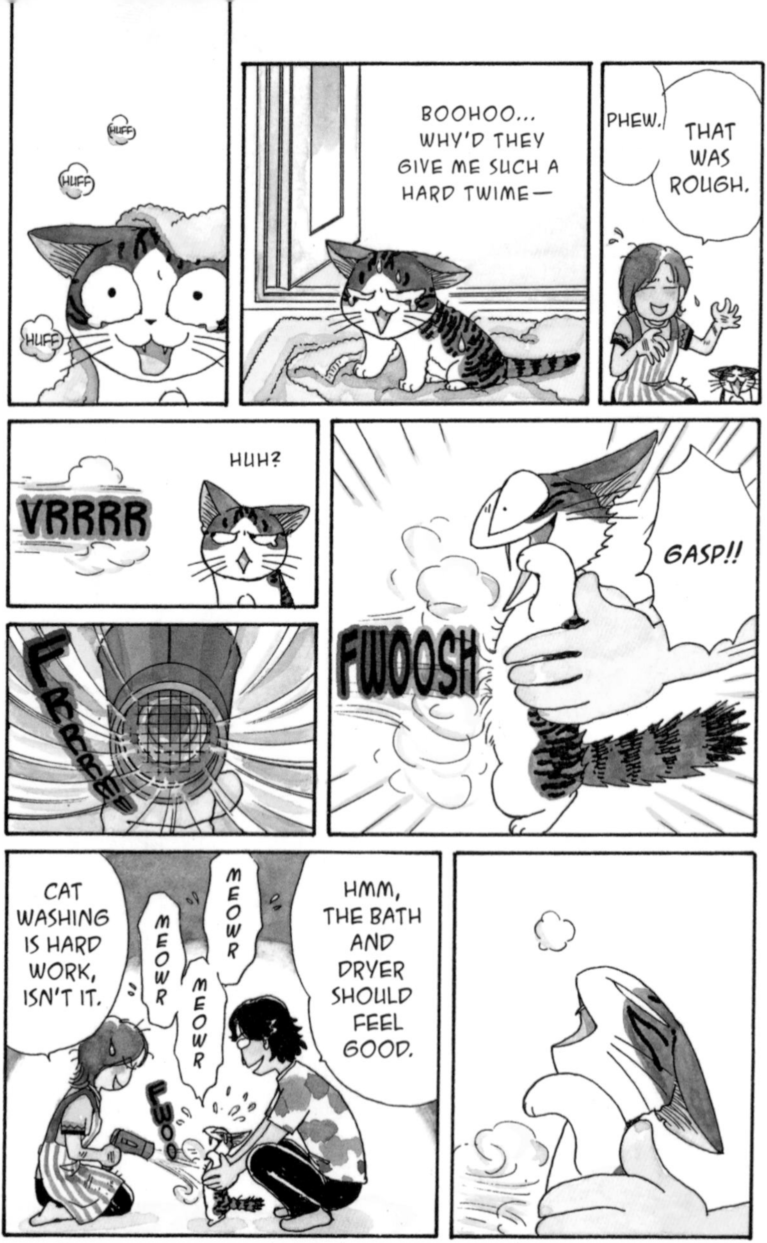
HUFF
HUFF
HUFF
BOOHOO... WHY'D THEY GIVE ME SUCH A HARD TWIME—
PHEW.
THAT WAS ROUGH.
HUH?
VRRRR
FRRRRR
GASP!!
FWOOSH
CAT WASHING IS HARD WORK, ISN'T IT.
MEOWR
MEOWR
MEOWR
FWOO
HMM, THE BATH AND DRYER SHOULD FEEL GOOD.

WOBBL
WOBBL
WOBBL
WOBBL
STUMBLE
FWUMP
I'M GWAD
I DIDN'T DIE.
BUT...

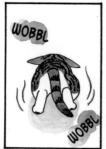

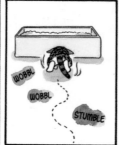

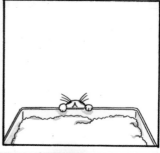

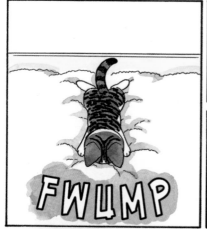

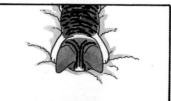

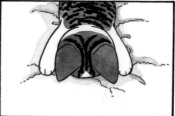

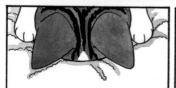

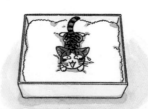

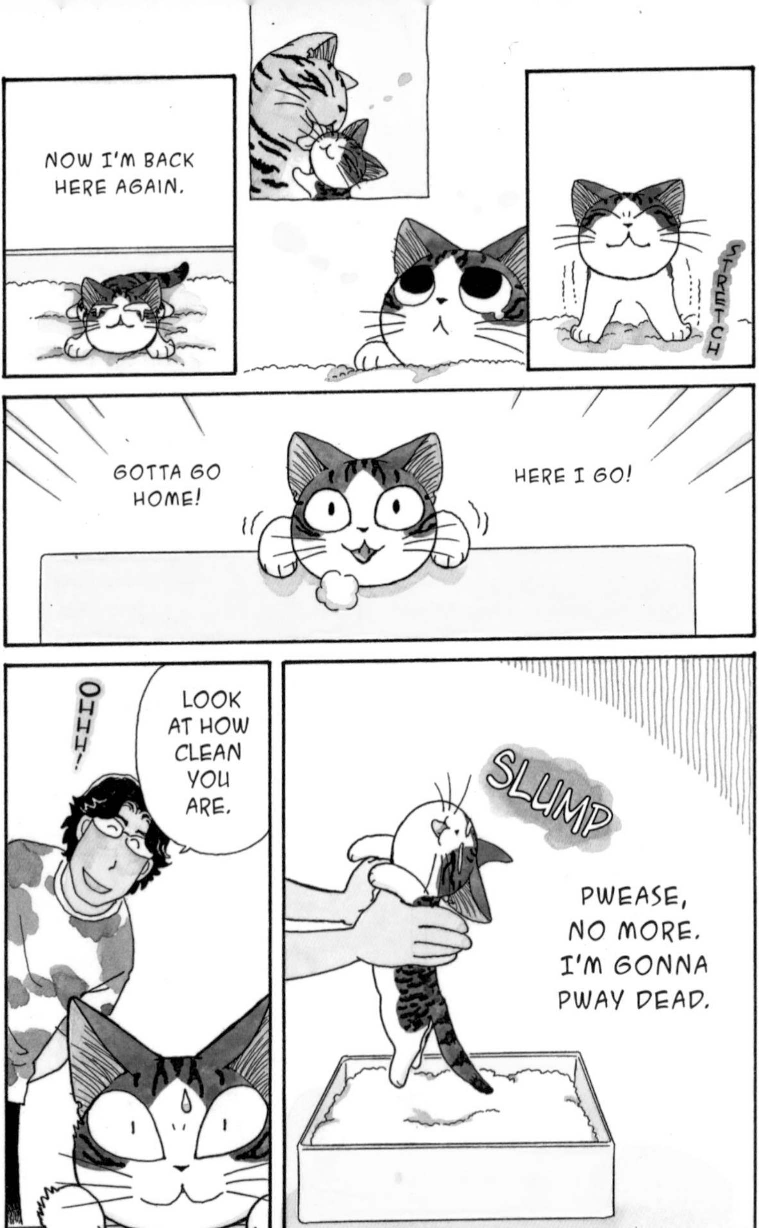

NOW I'M BACK HERE AGAIN.
STRETCH
GOTTA GO HOME!
HERE I GO!
OHHH!
LOOK AT HOW CLEAN YOU ARE.
SLUMP
PWEASE, NO MORE. I'M GONNA PWAY DEAD.

the end

homemade 4: a cat forgets

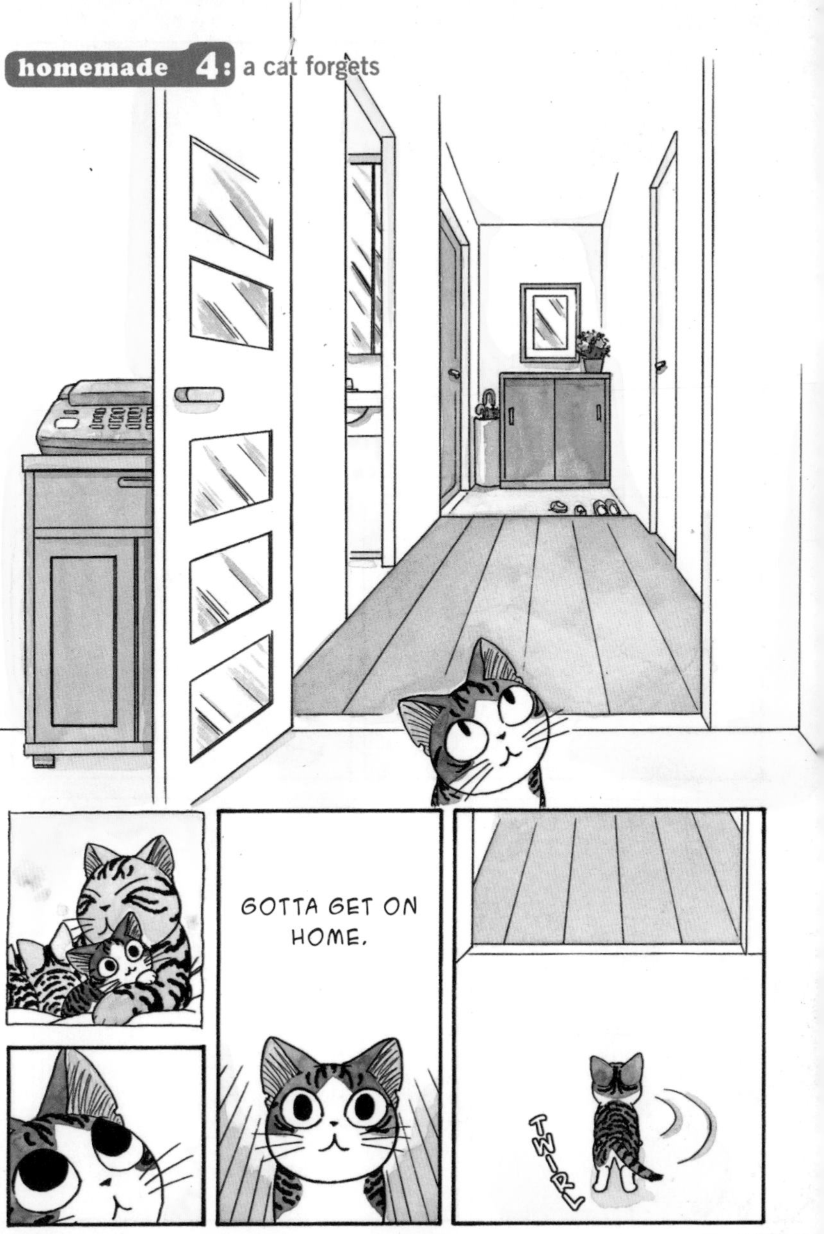
GOTTA GET ON HOME.
TWIRL

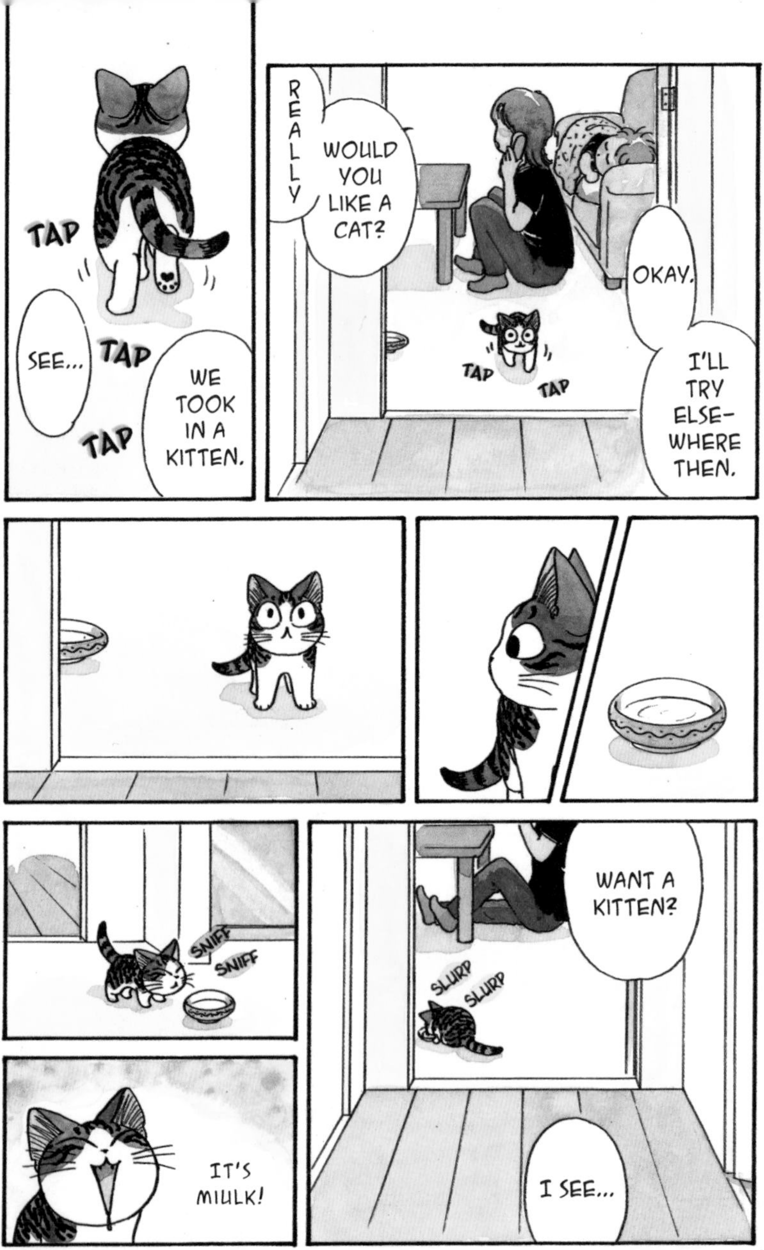
TAP
SEE...
TAP
TAP
WE TOOK IN A KITTEN.
REALLY
WOULD YOU LIKE A CAT?
OKAY.
TAP
TAP
I'LL TRY ELSEWHERE THEN.
SNIFF
SNIFF
IT'S MIULK!
WANT A KITTEN?
SLURP
SLURP
I SEE...

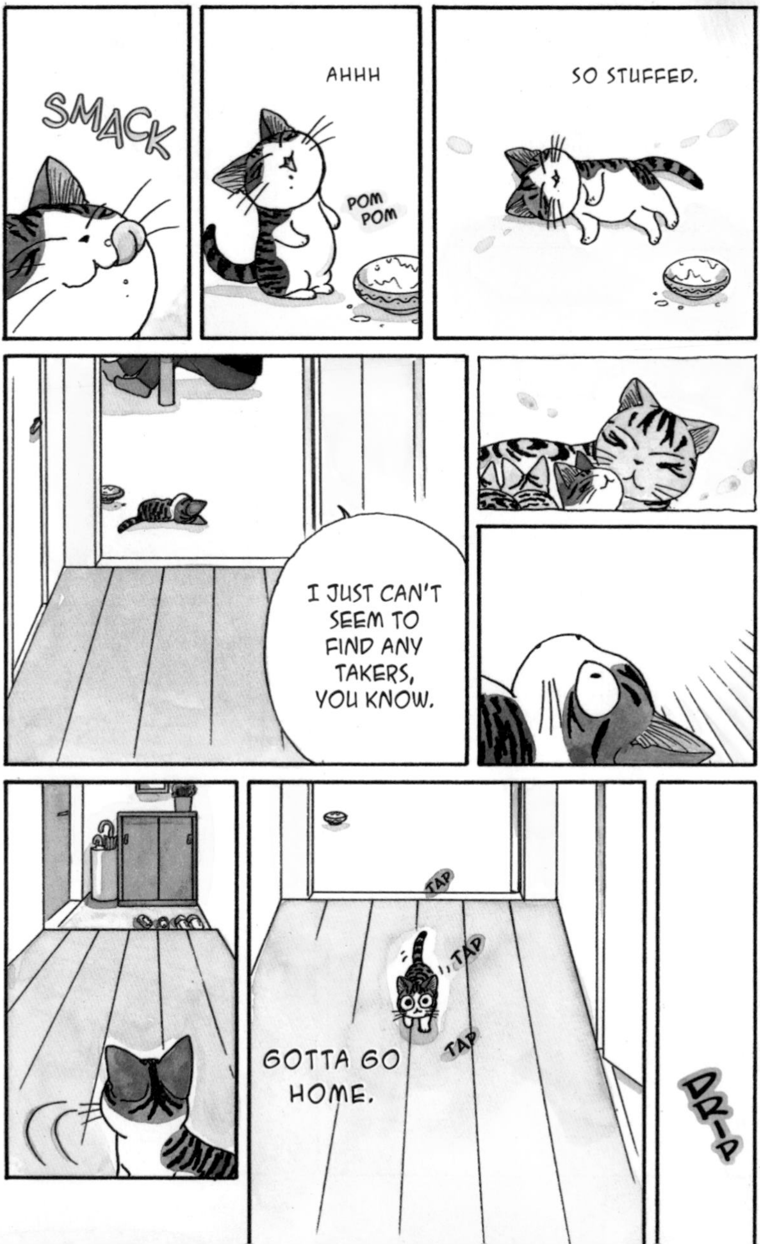
SMACK
AHHH
POM POM
SO STUFFED.
I JUST CAN'T SEEM TO FIND ANY TAKERS, YOU KNOW.
TAP
TAP
TAP
GOTTA GO HOME.
DRIP

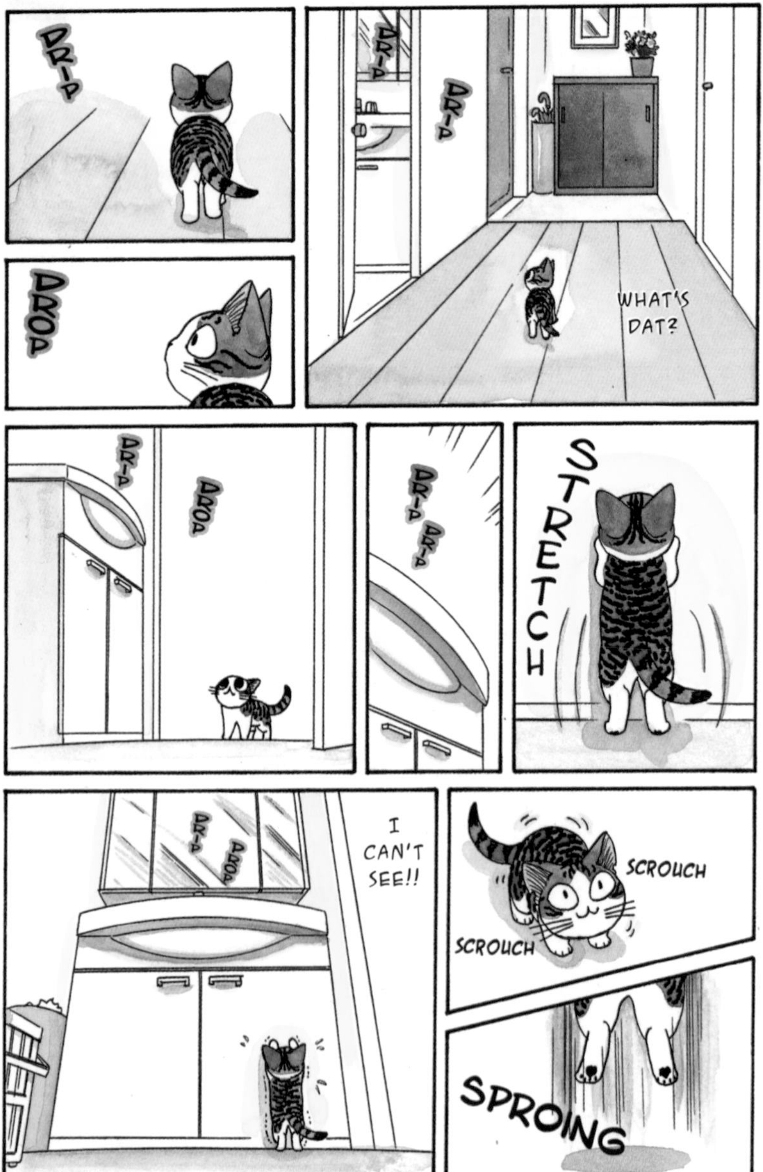
DRIP
DROP
DRIP
DRIP
WHAT'S DAT?
DRIP
DROP
DRIP
DRIP
STRETCH
DRIP
DROP
I CAN'T SEE!!
SCROUCH
SCROUCH
SPROING

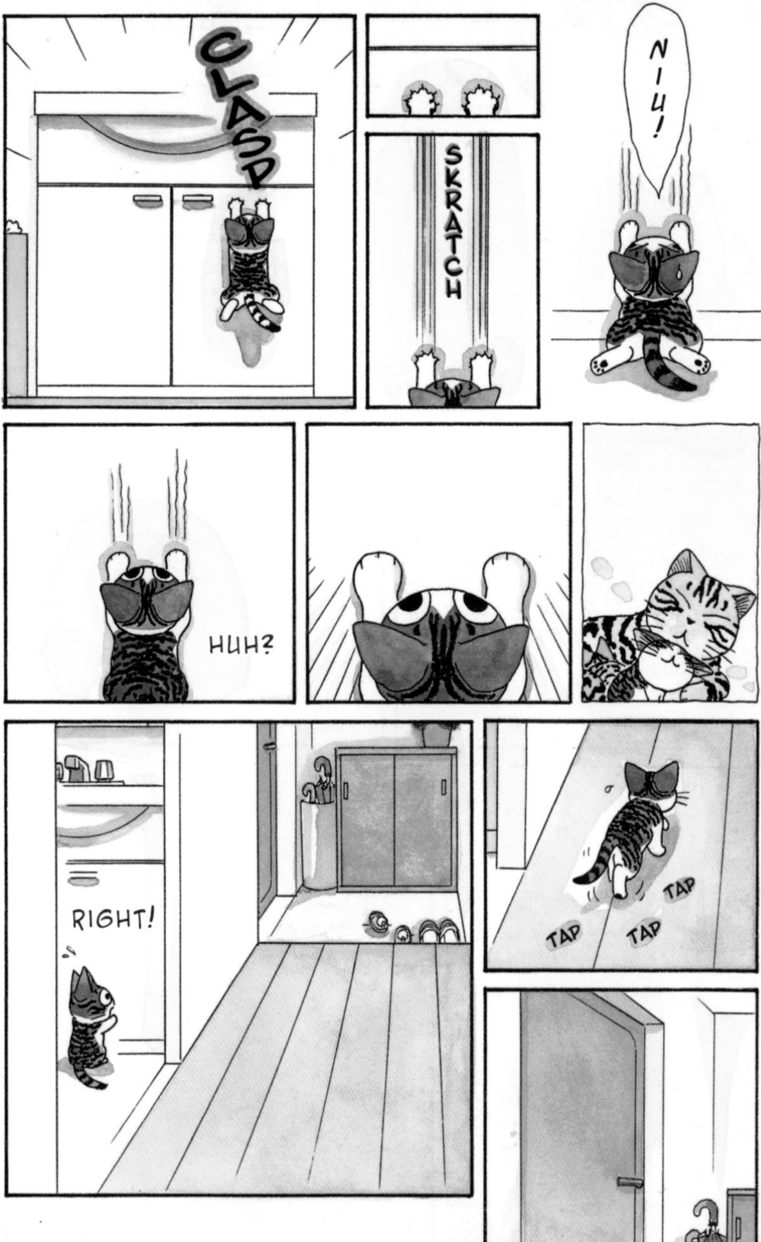
CLASP
SKRATCH
NIU!
HUH?
RIGHT!
TAP
TAP
TAP

I'M GOWING HOME!

HOP

OH?

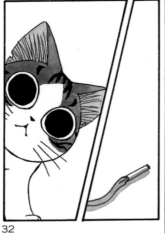

SPROING!

MEOWR

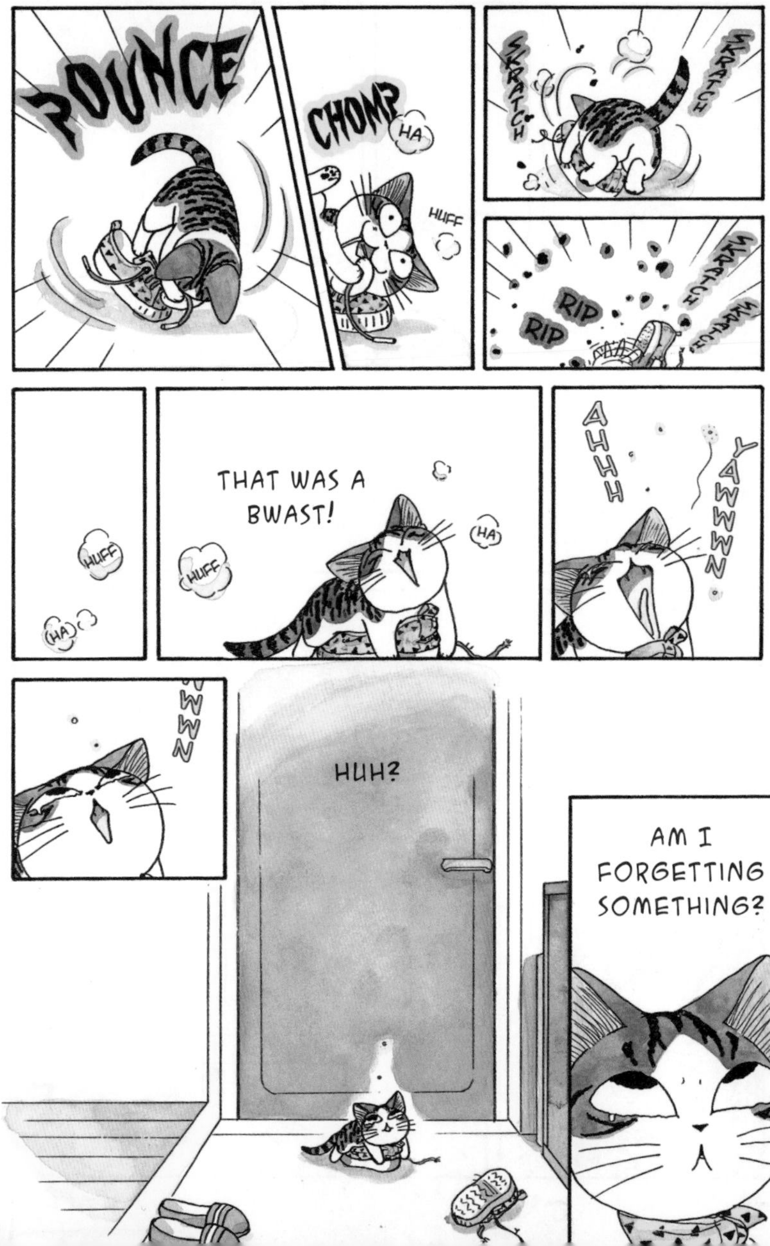
POUNCE
CHOMP
HA
HUFF
SKRATCH
SKRATCH
RIP
RIP
SKRATCH
SKRATCH
HUFF
HA
HUFF
THAT WAS A BWAST!
HA
AHHH
YAWWWN
AWWN
HUH?
AM I FORGETTING SOMETHING?

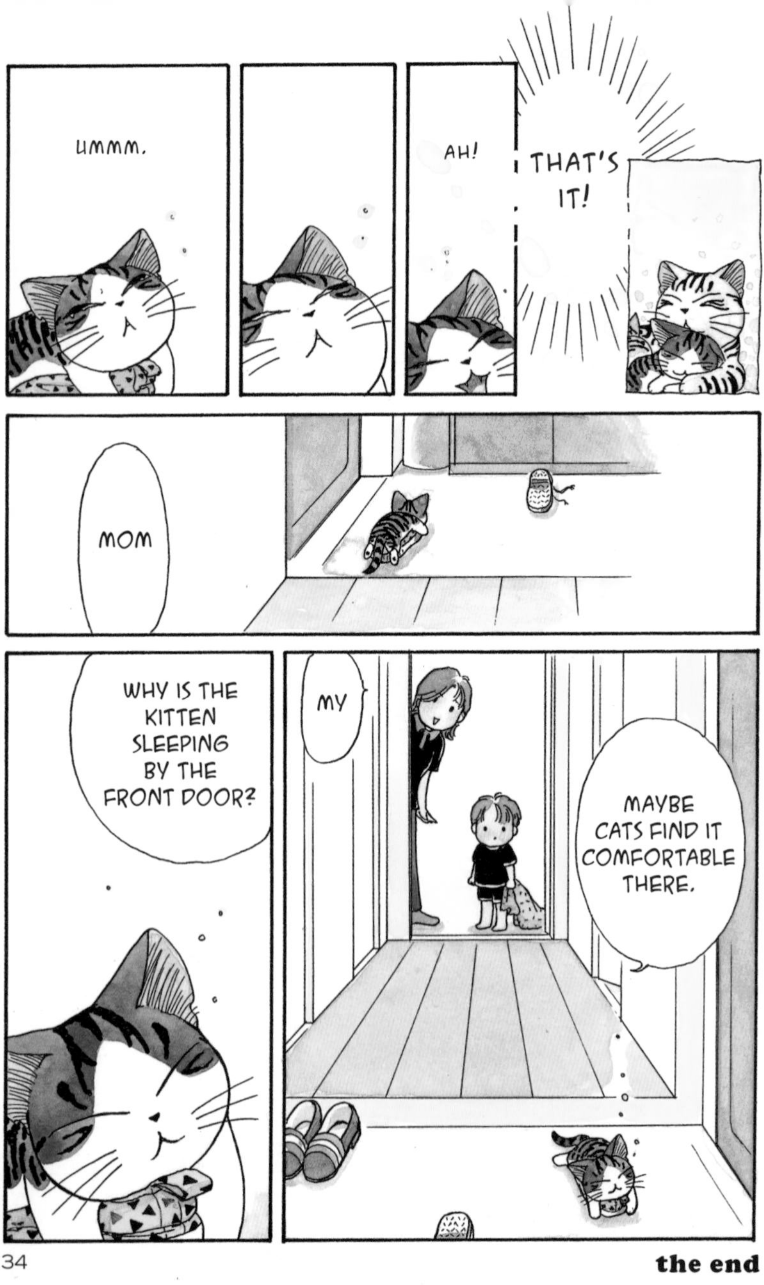
UMMM.
AH!
THAT'S IT!
MOM
WHY IS THE KITTEN SLEEPING BY THE FRONT DOOR?
MY
MAYBE CATS FIND IT COMFORTABLE THERE.

the end

homemade 5: a cat begins

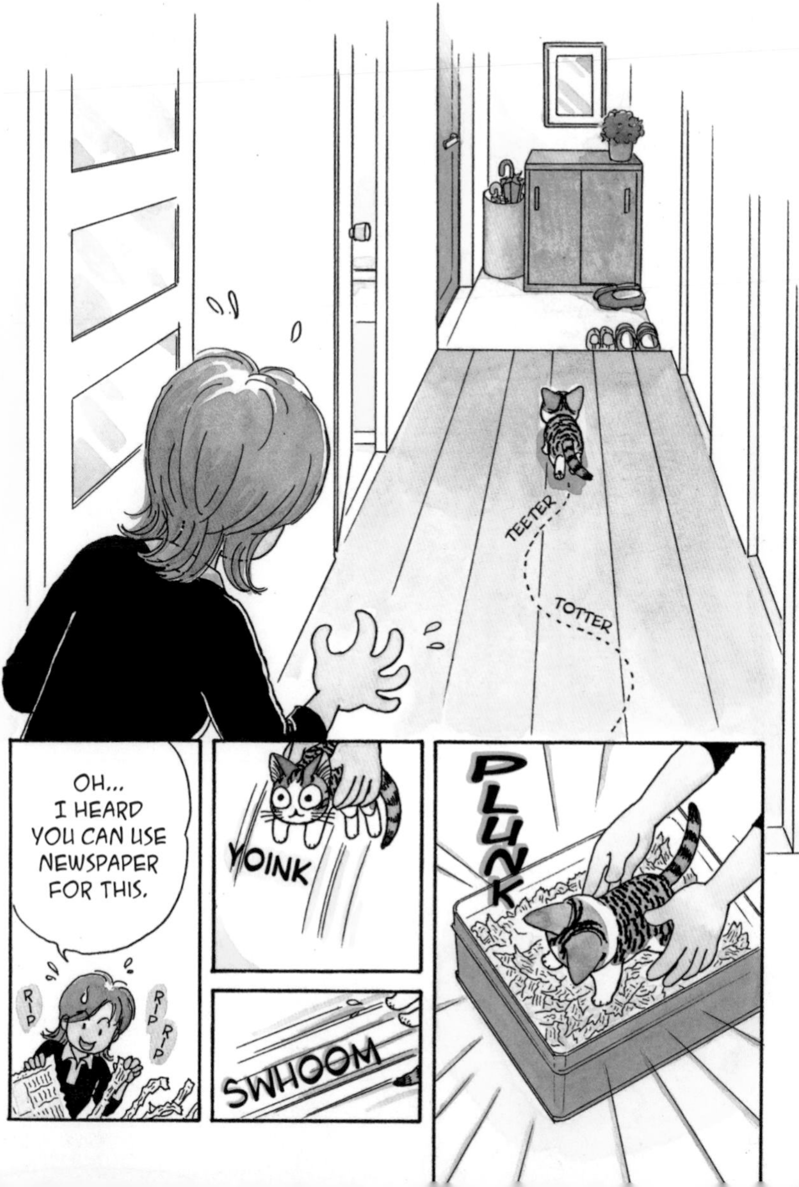

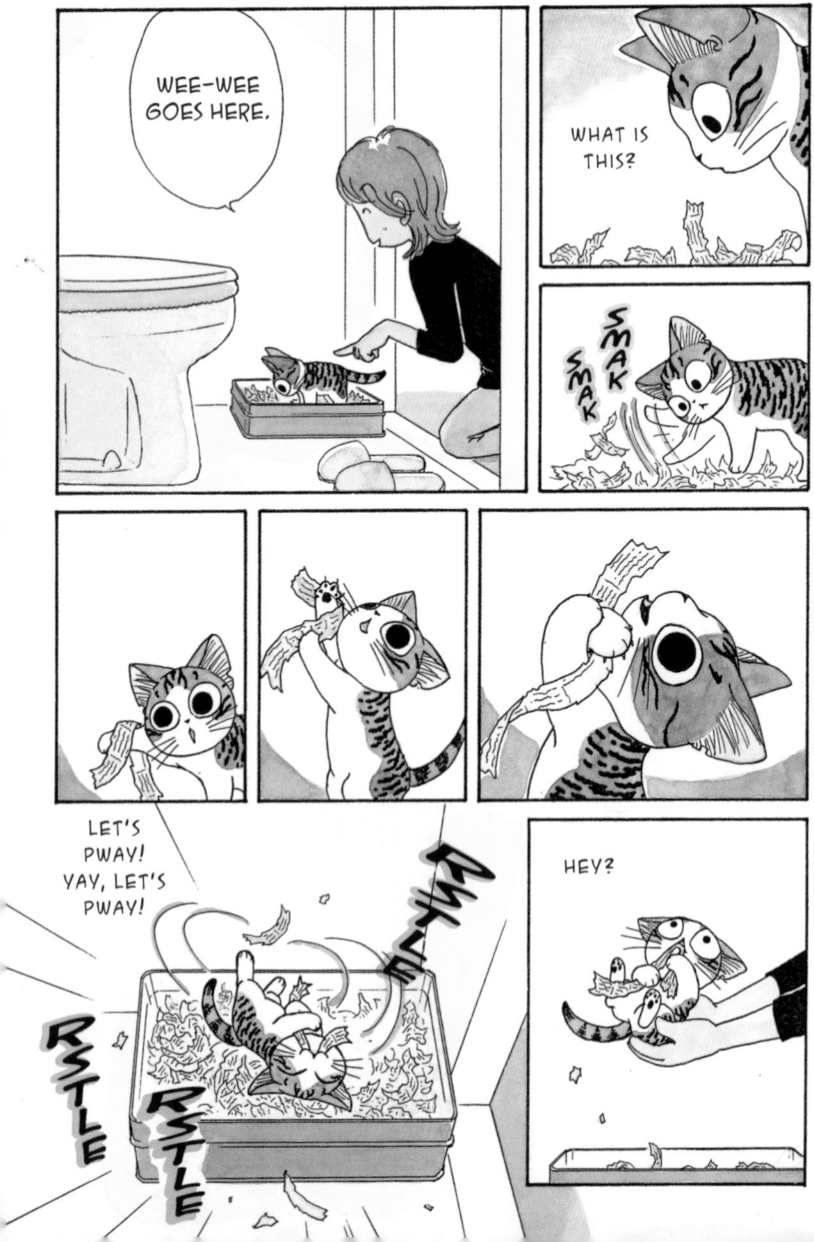
WEE-WEE GOES HERE.
WHAT IS THIS?
SMAK SMAK
LET'S PWAY! YAY, LET'S PWAY!
RSTLE
RSTLE
RSTLE
HEY?

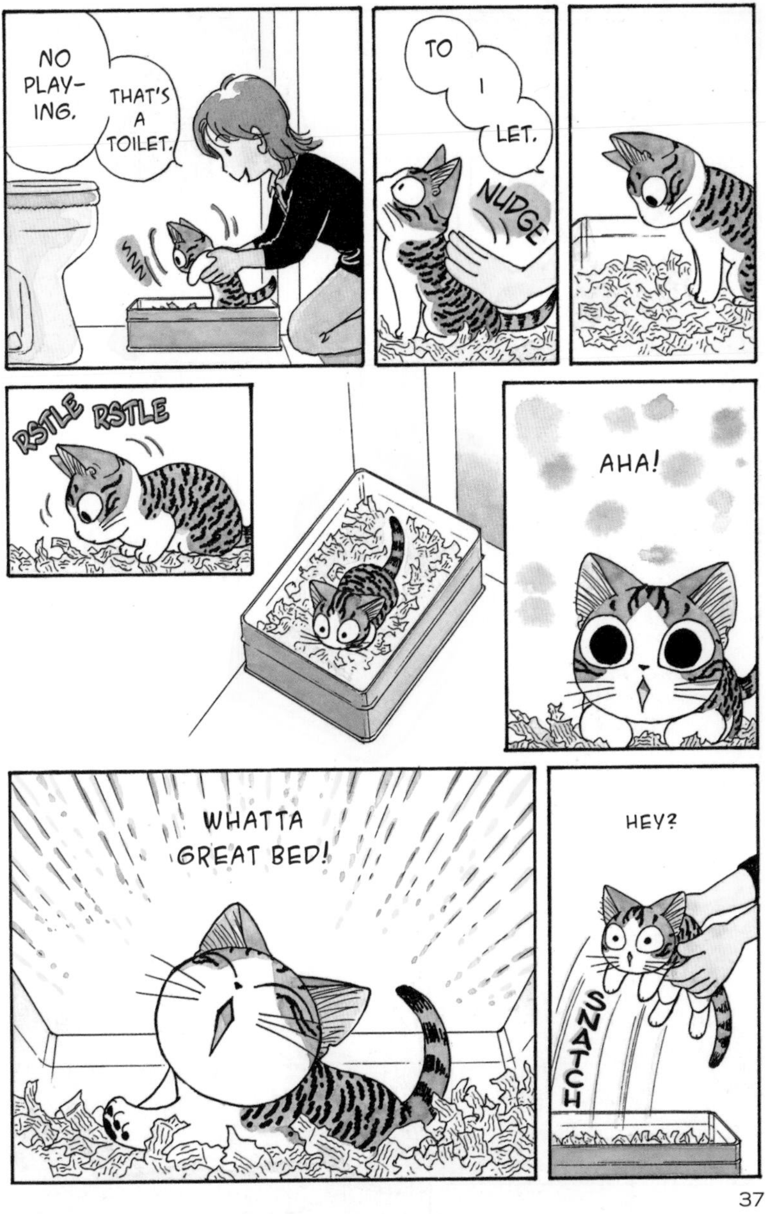
NO PLAYING.
THAT'S A TOILET.
TO I LET.
NUDGE
RSTLE RSTLE
AHA!
WHATTA GREAT BED!
HEY?
SNATCH

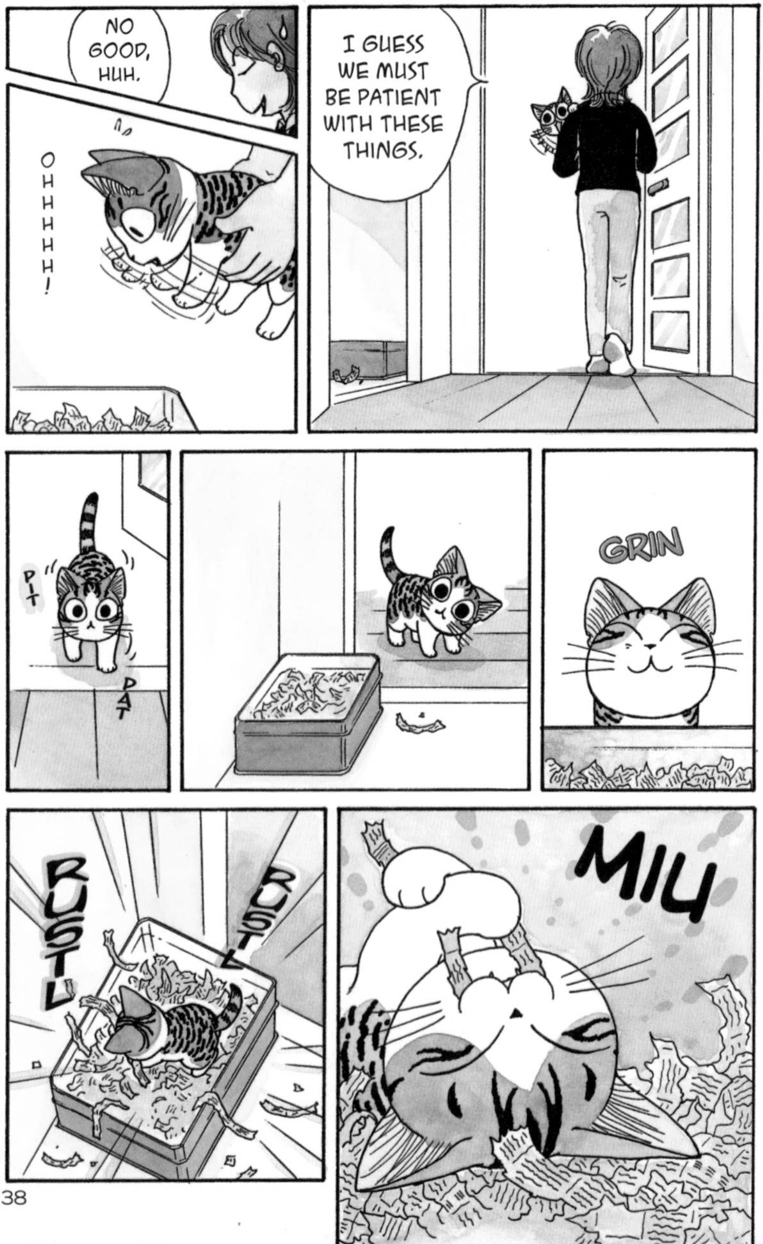
NO GOOD, HUH.
OHHHHHH!
I GUESS WE MUST BE PATIENT WITH THESE THINGS.
PIT
PAT
GRIN
RUSTL
RUSTL
MIU

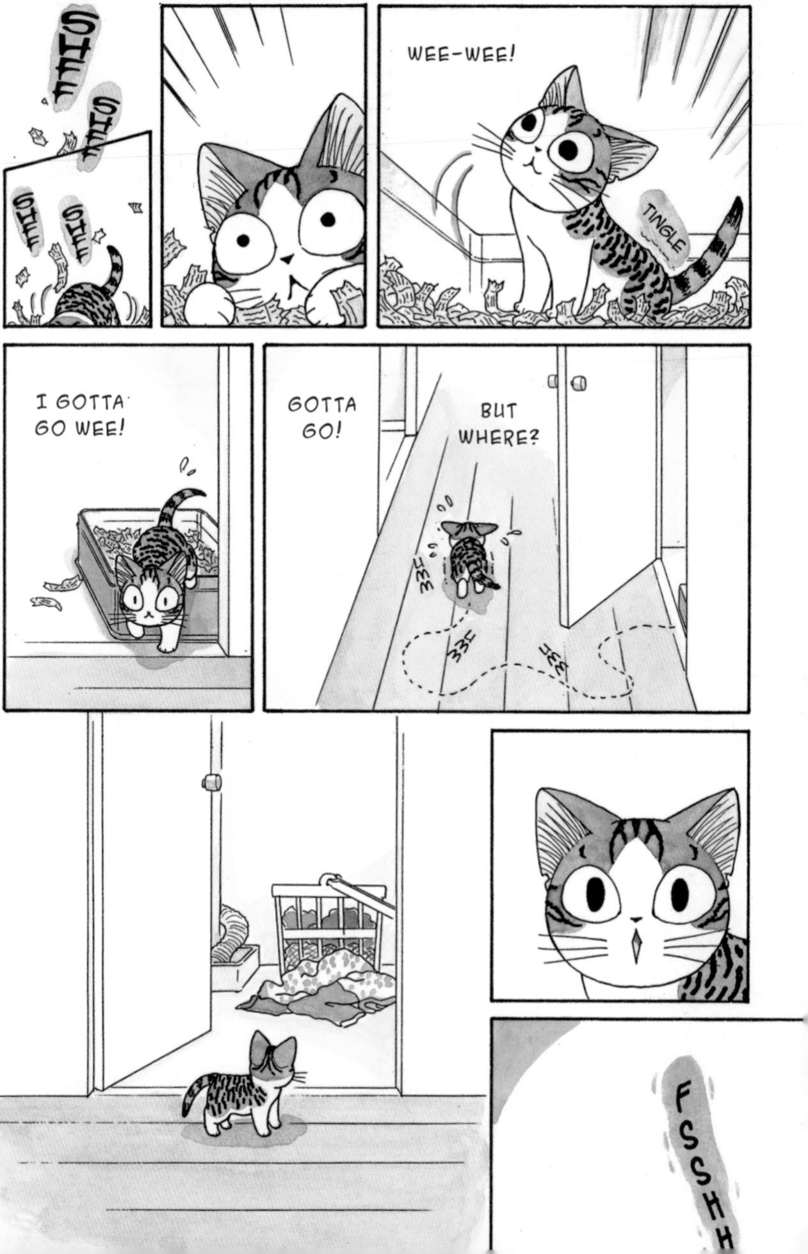
SHEFF
SHEFF
SHEFF
SHEFF
WEE-WEE!
TINGLE
I GOTTA GO WEE!
GOTTA GO!
BUT WHERE?
FSSHH

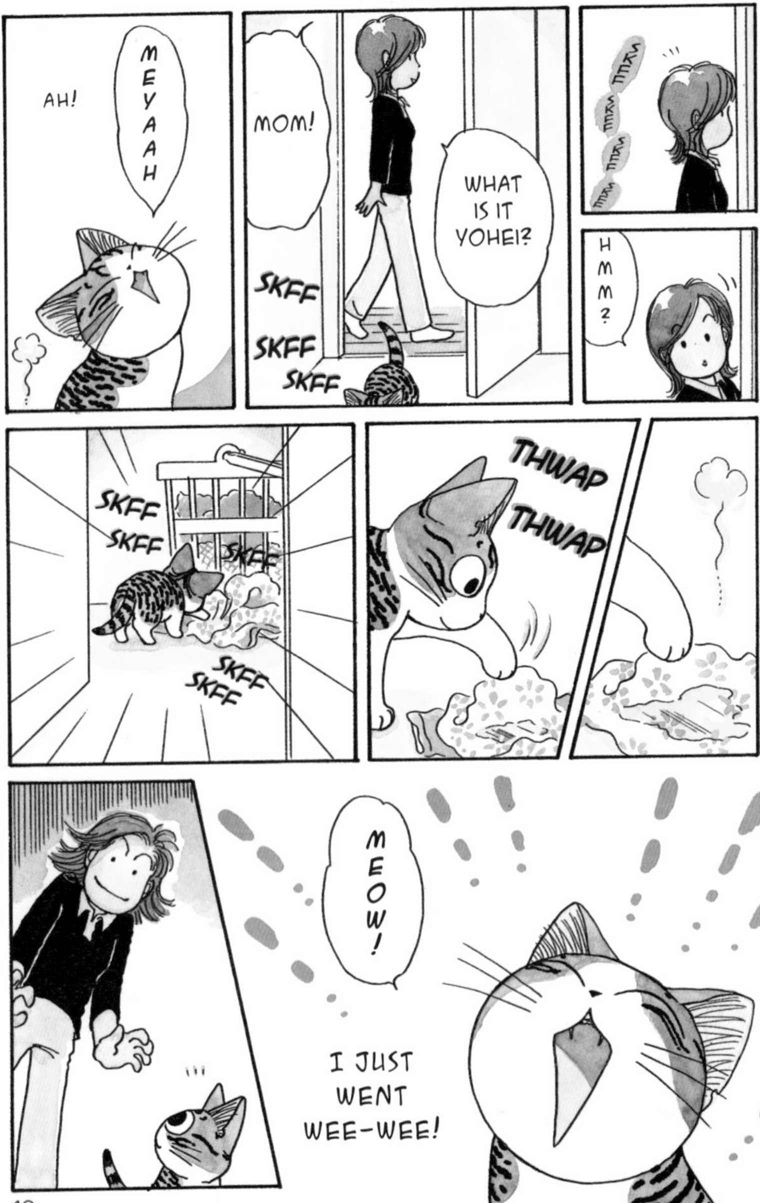
AH!
MEYAAH
MOM!
WHAT IS IT YOHEI?
SKFF
SKFF
SKFF
SKFF SKFF SKFF SKFF
HMMM?
SKFF
SKFF
SKFF
SKFF
SKFF
THWAP
THWAP
MEOW!
I JUST WENT WEE-WEE!

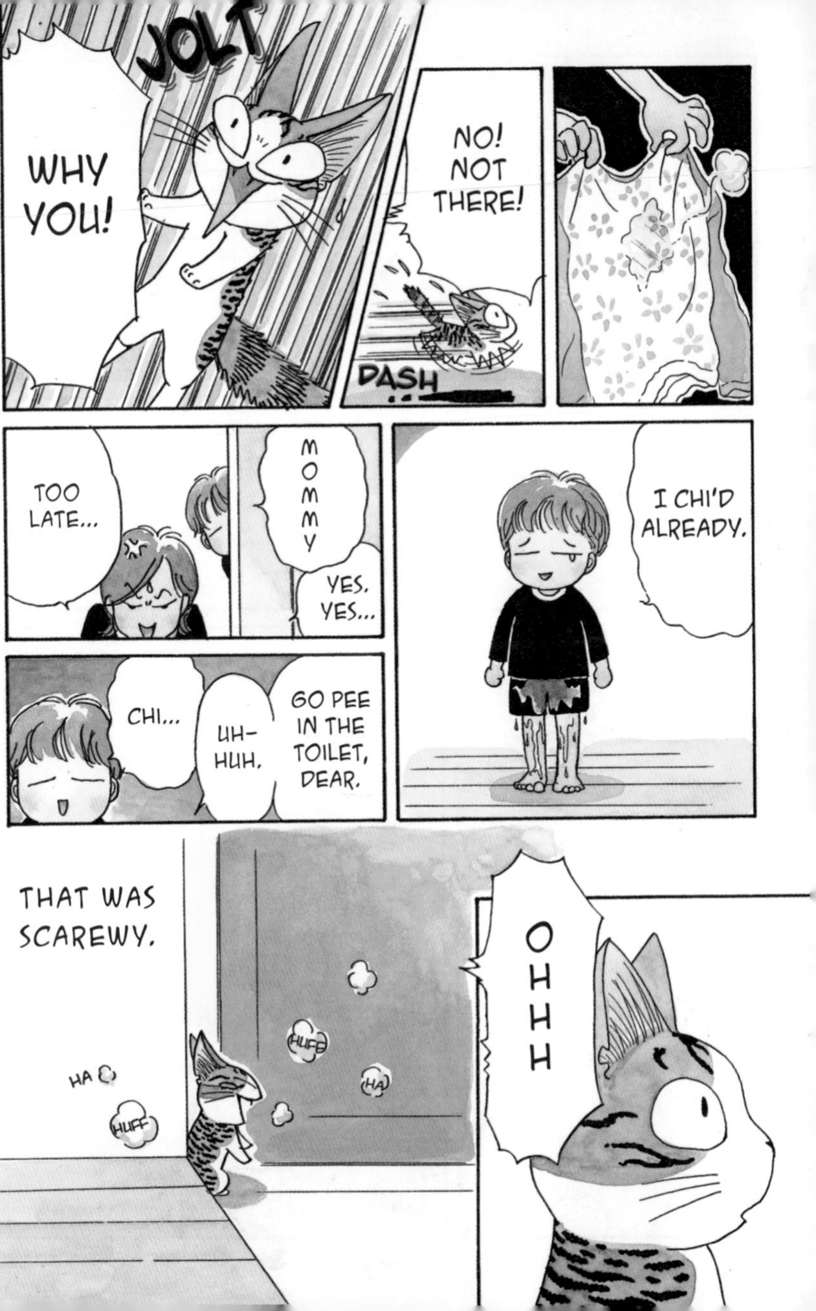
JOLT
WHY YOU!
NO! NOT THERE!
DASH
TOO LATE...
MOMMY
YES. YES...
I CHI'D ALREADY.
CHI...
UH-HUH.
GO PEE IN THE TOILET, DEAR.
THAT WAS SCAREWY.
HA
HUFF
HUFF
HA
OHHH

THAT'S NO GOOD.

PEAK

THMP THMP

YOU HAVE TO GO TO THE TOILET BEFORE YOU WEE-WEE.

?

SNIFF SNIFF

SNIFF

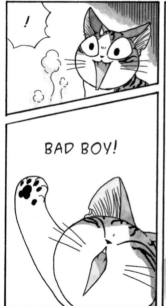

!

BAD BOY!

DON'T FORGET TO COVER UP YOUR WEE-WEE WITH SAND OR DIRT.

SKFF SKFF

SKFF SKFF

the end

homemade 6: a cat is disappointed

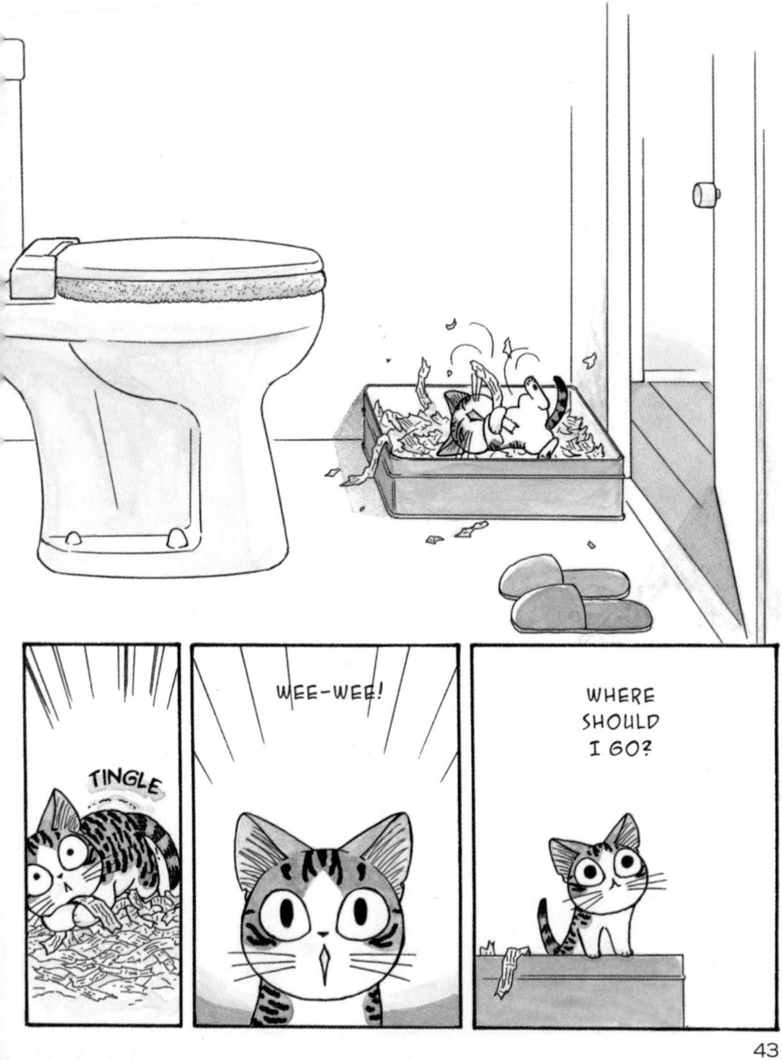
TINGLE
WEE-WEE!
WHERE SHOULD I GO?

WANDER

WANDER

THIS LOOKS LIKE A GOOD SPOT.

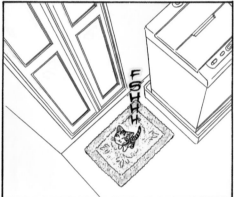

FSHHH

AH!

SKEE SKEE SKEE

TUMP TUMP

ARGH!

44

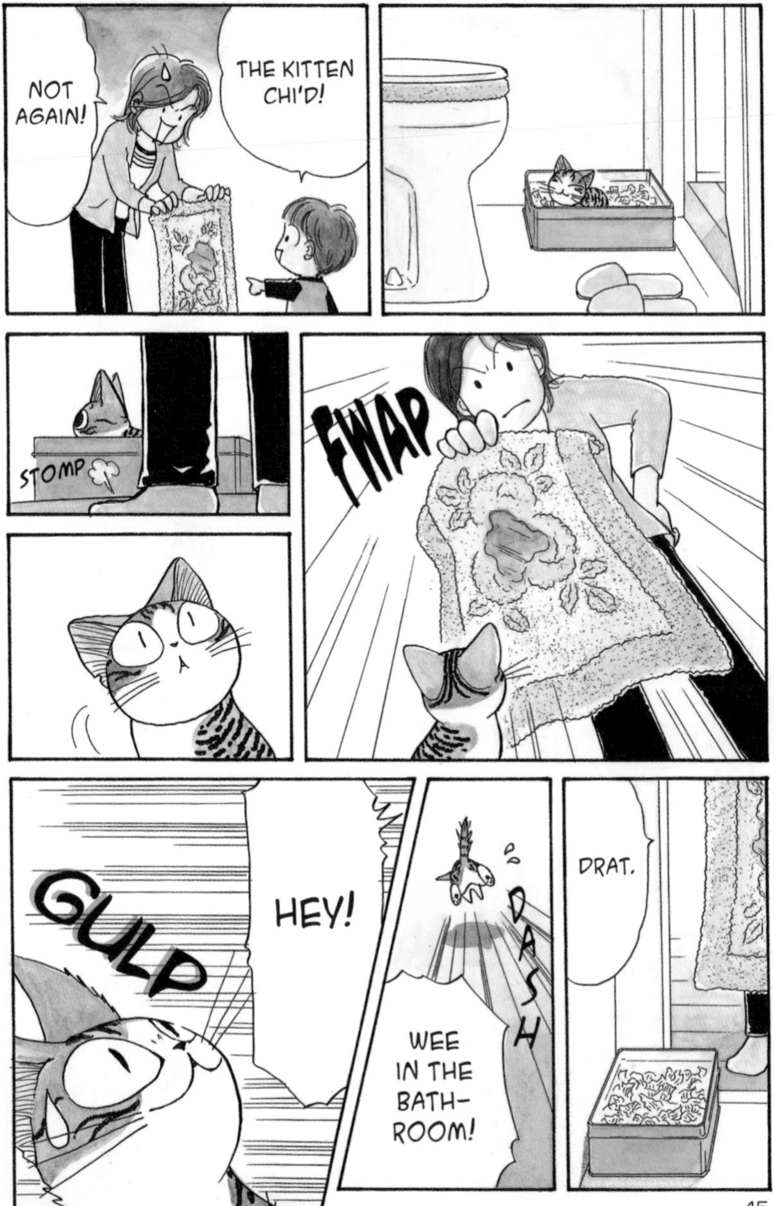
NOT AGAIN!
THE KITTEN CHI'D!
STOMP
FWAP
GULP
HEY!
DASH
WEE IN THE BATH-ROOM!
DRAT.

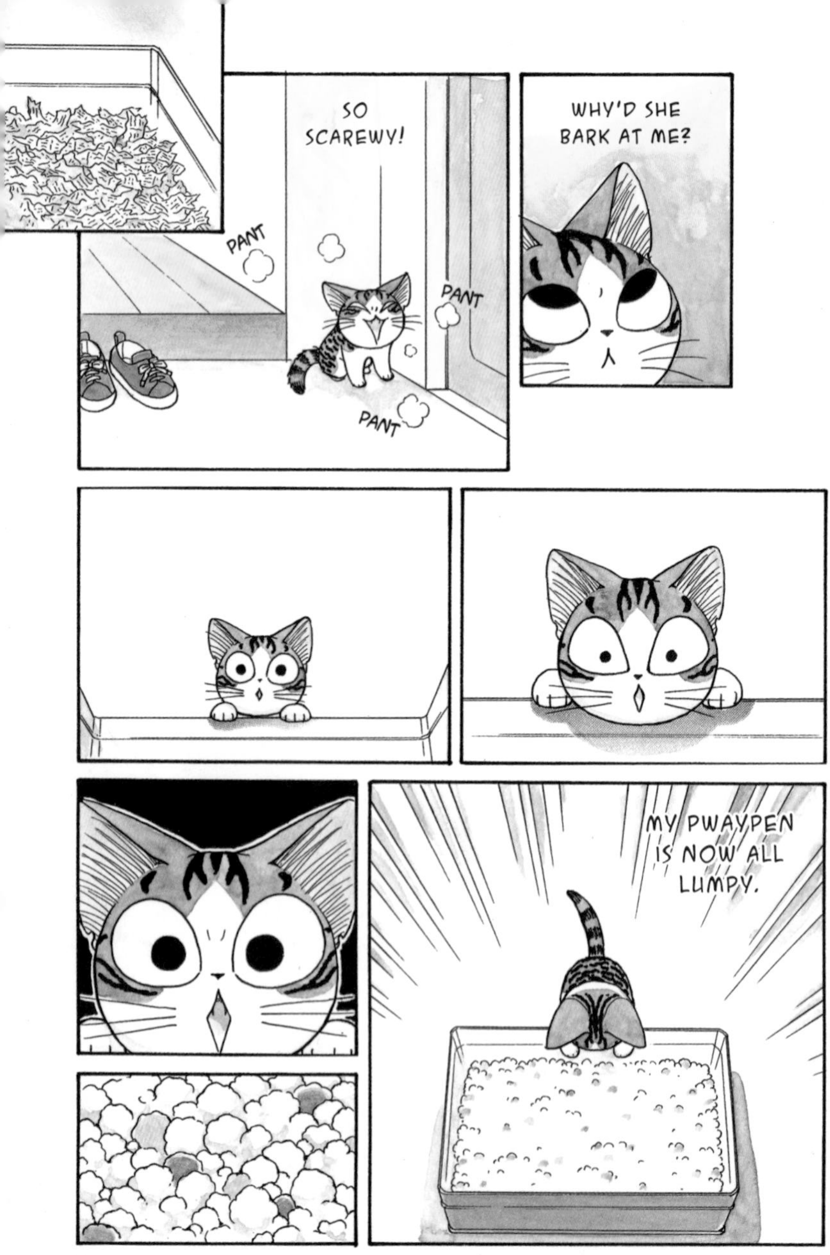
PANT
SO SCAREWY!
PANT
PANT
WHY'D SHE BARK AT ME?
MY PWAYPEN IS NOW ALL LUMPY.

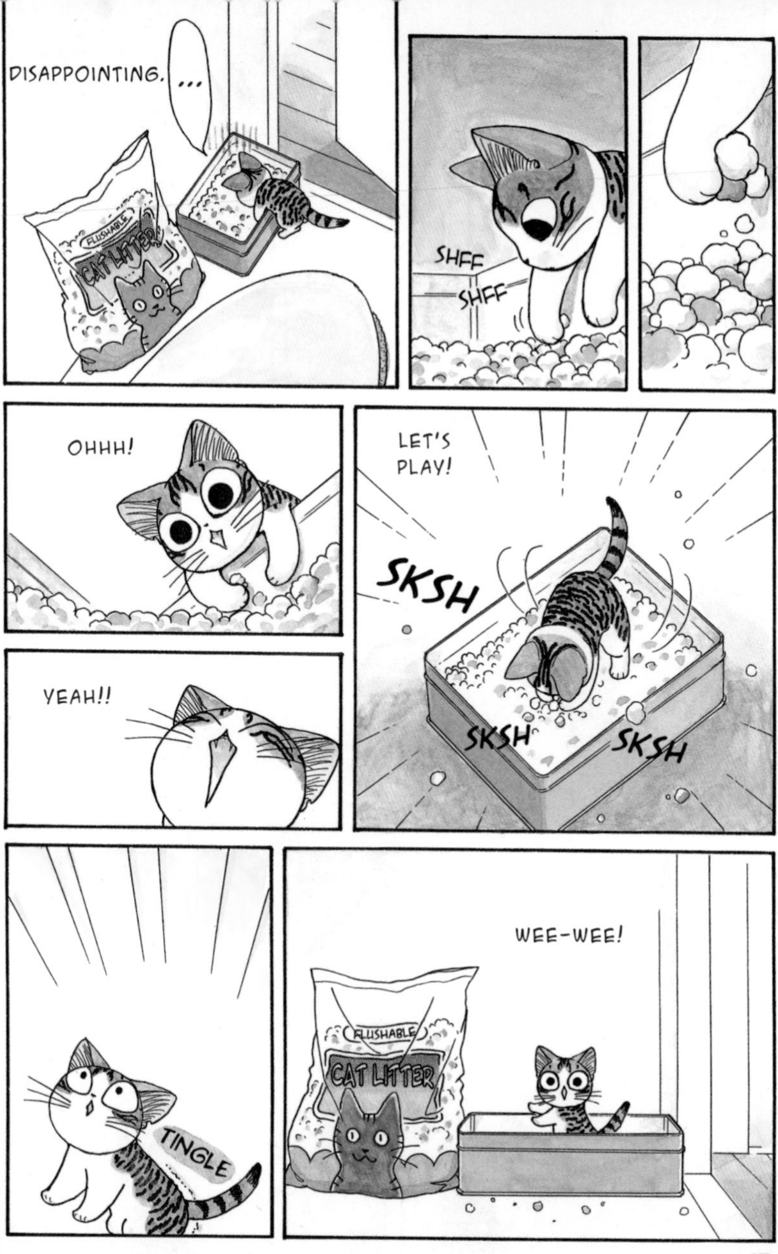
DISAPPOINTING.
...
FLUSHABLE
CAT LITTER
SHFF
SHFF
OHHH!
YEAH!!
LET'S PLAY!
SKSH
SKSH
SKSH
TINGLE
WEE-WEE!
FLUSHABLE
CAT LITTER

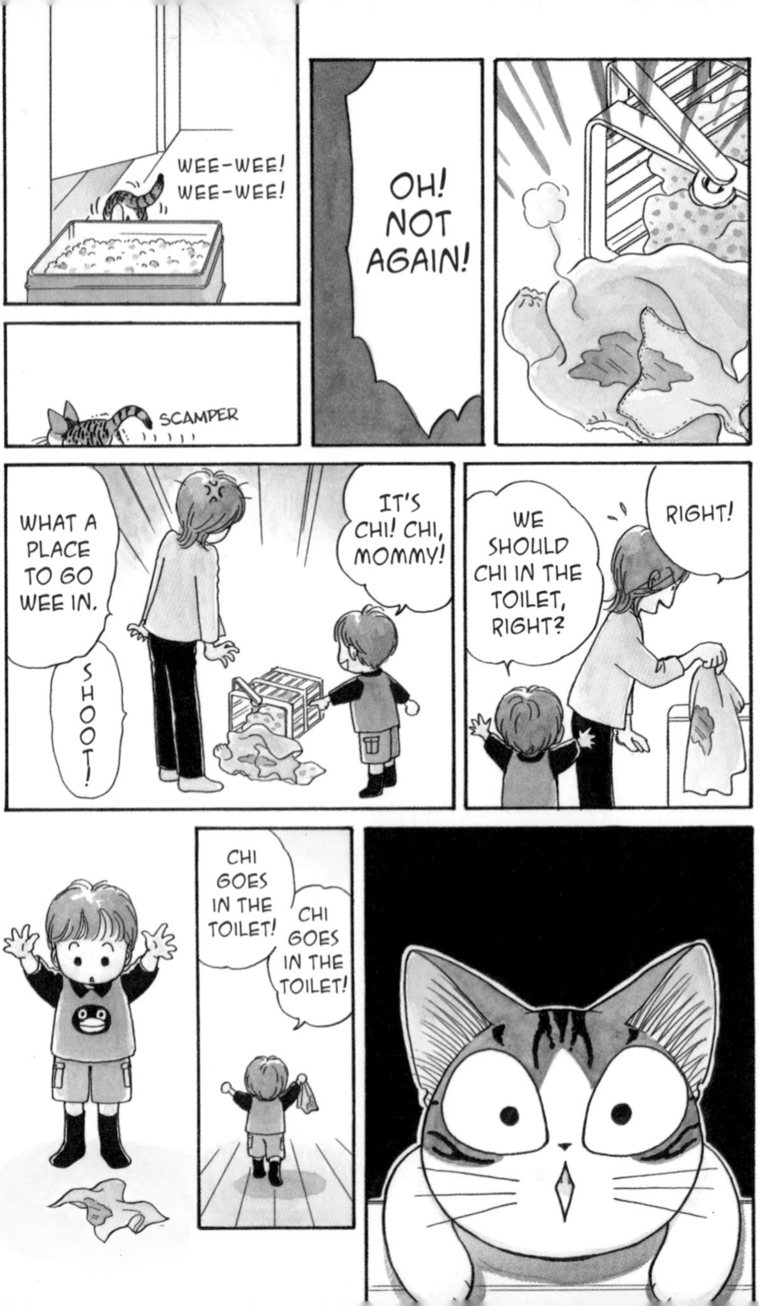
WEE-WEE! WEE-WEE!
SCAMPER
OH! NOT AGAIN!
WHAT A PLACE TO GO WEE IN.
IT'S CHI! CHI, MOMMY!
SHOOT!
WE SHOULD CHI IN THE TOILET, RIGHT?
RIGHT!
CHI GOES IN THE TOILET!
CHI GOES IN THE TOILET!

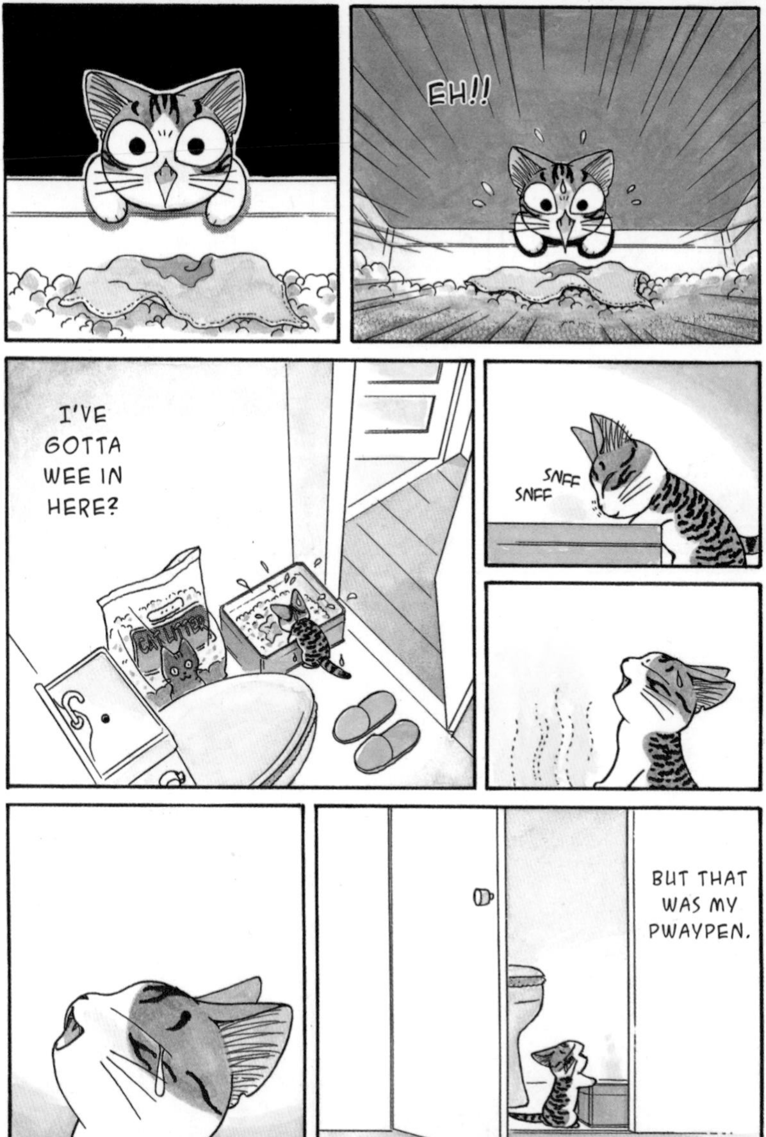
EH!!
I'VE GOTTA WEE IN HERE?
CAT LITTER
SNFF
SNFF
BUT THAT WAS MY PWAYPEN.

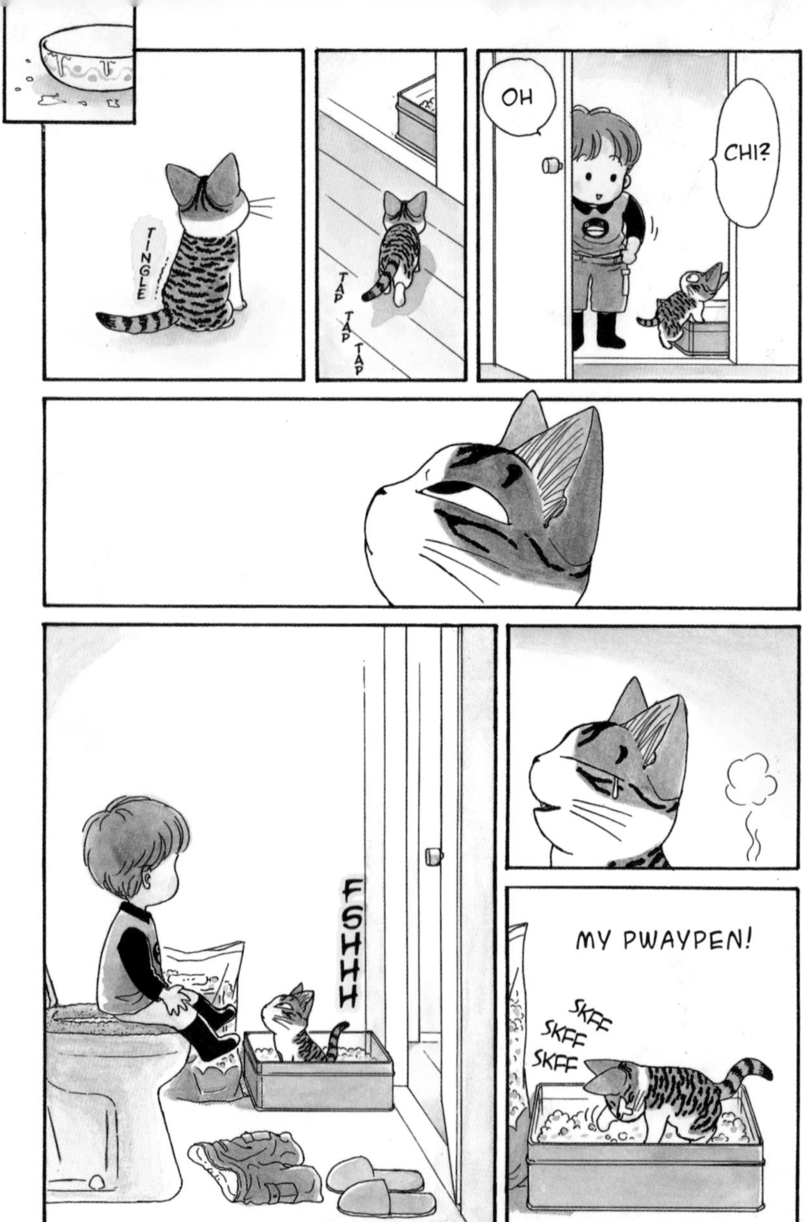
TINGLE
TAP TAP TAP TAP
OH
CHI?
FSHHH
MY PWAYPEN!
SKFF SKFF SKFF

the end

homemade 7: a cat understands

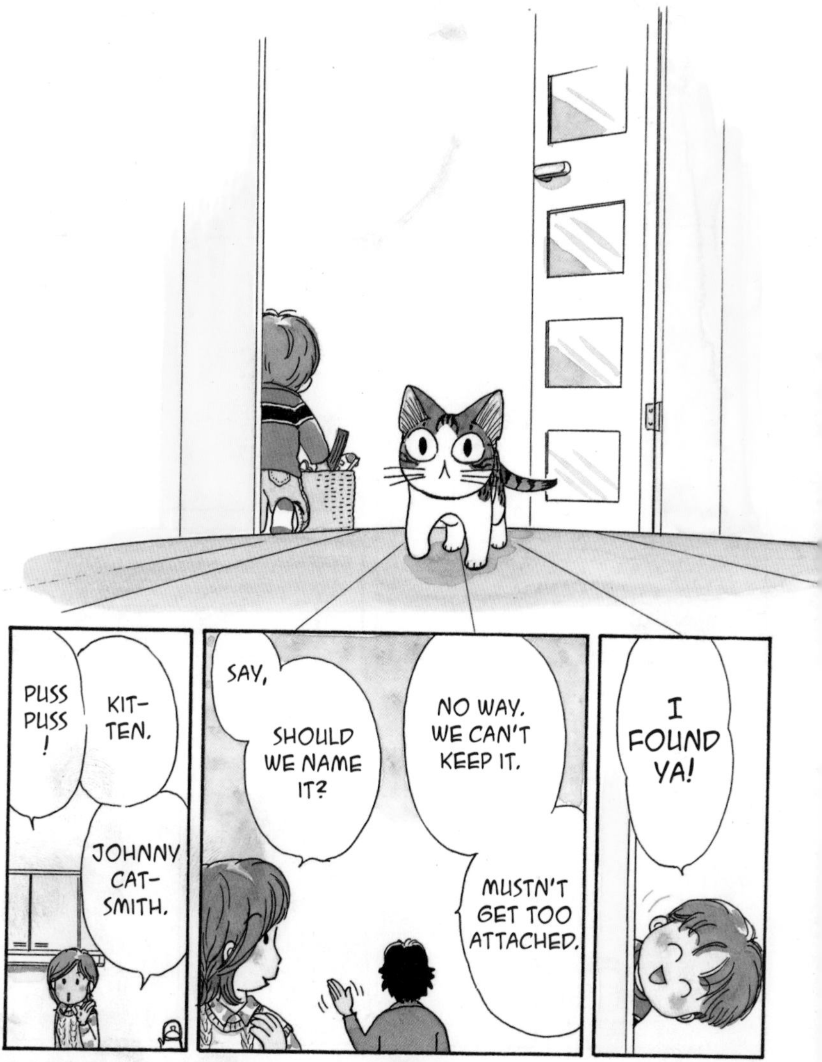
PUSS PUSS !
KIT-TEN.
JOHNNY CAT-SMITH.
SAY,
SHOULD WE NAME IT?
NO WAY. WE CAN'T KEEP IT.
MUSTN'T GET TOO ATTACHED.
I FOUND YA!

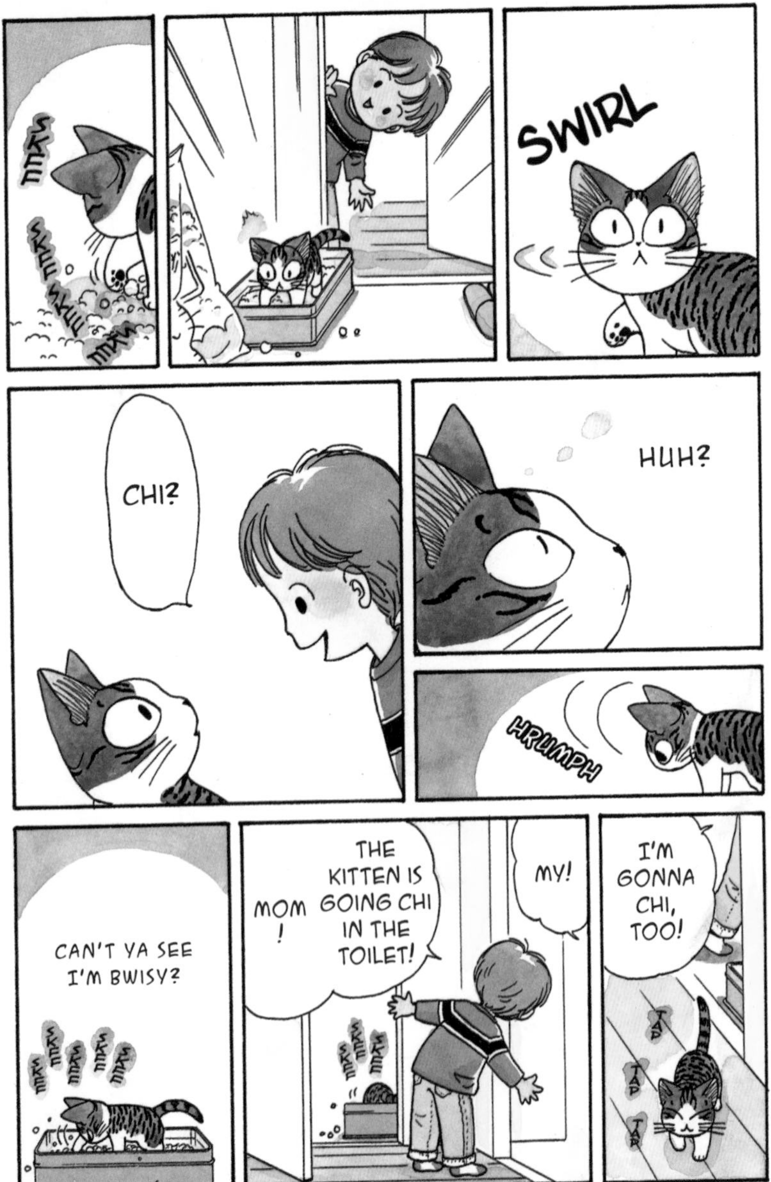
SKEE
SKEE SKEE SKEE
SWIRL
CHI?
HUH?
HRUMPH
CAN'T YA SEE I'M BWISY?
SKEE SKEE SKEE SKEE
MOM!
THE KITTEN IS GOING CHI IN THE TOILET!
SKEE SKEE SKEE
MY!
I'M GONNA CHI, TOO!
TAP TAP TAP

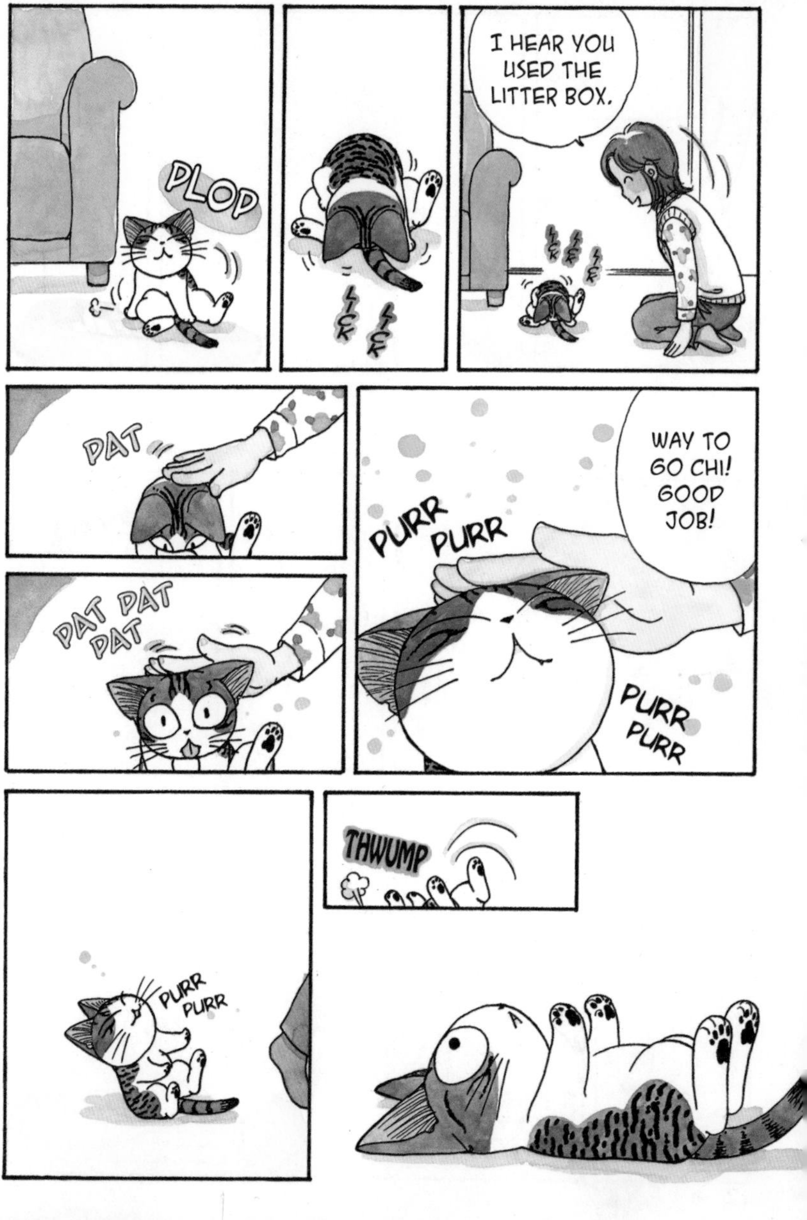

PLOP
LICK LICK
I HEAR YOU USED THE LITTER BOX.
LICK LICK LICK
PAT
PAT PAT PAT
WAY TO GO CHI! GOOD JOB!
PURR PURR
PURR PURR
PURR PURR
THWUMP

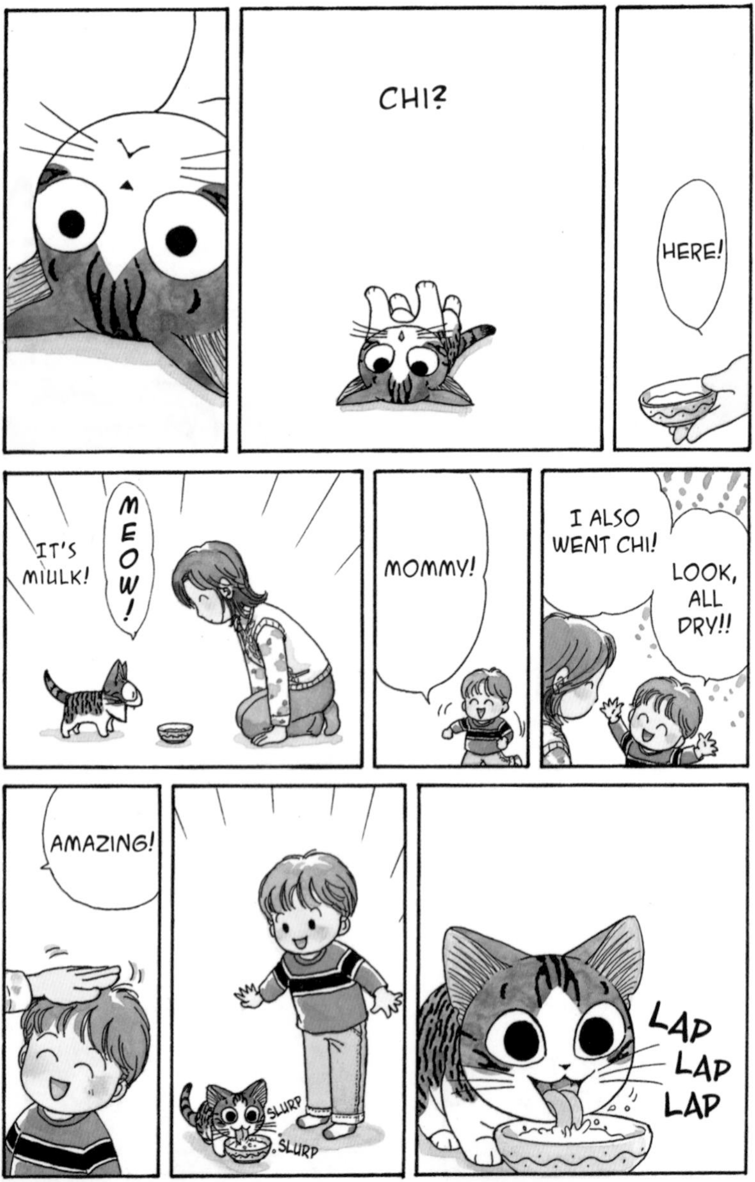
CHI?
HERE!
IT'S MIULK!
MEOW!
MOMMY!
I ALSO WENT CHI!
LOOK, ALL DRY!!
AMAZING!
SLURP
SLURP
LAP
LAP
LAP

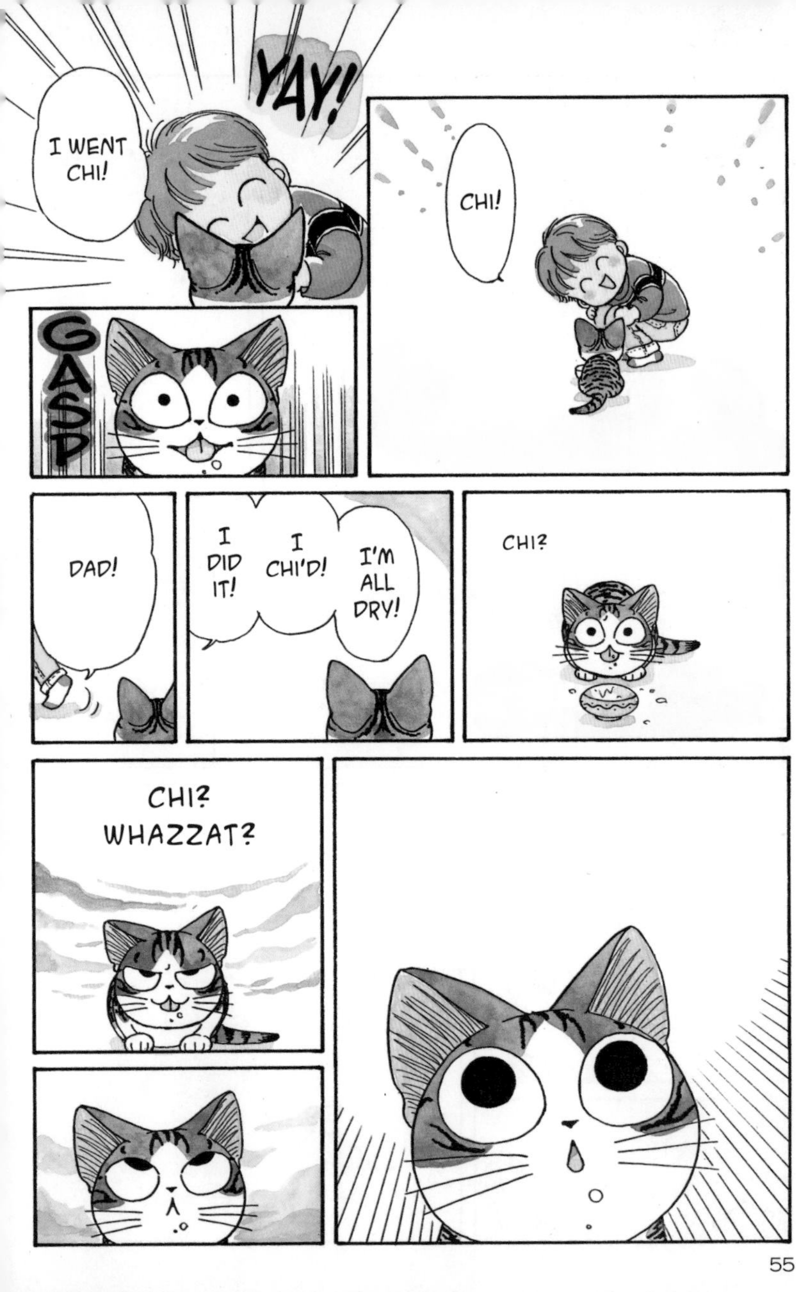

I WENT CHI!
YAY!
GASP
CHI!
DAD!
I DID IT!
I CHI'D!
I'M ALL DRY!
CHI?
CHI? WHAZZAT?

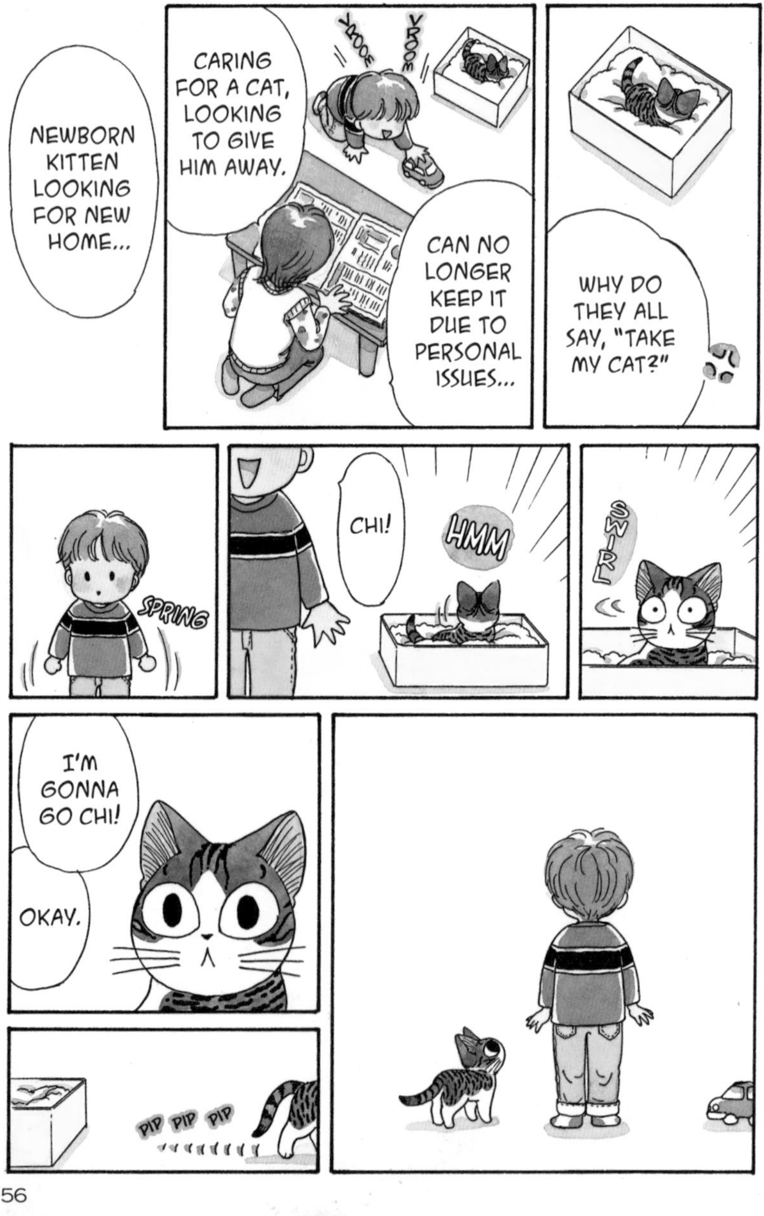
NEWBORN KITTEN LOOKING FOR NEW HOME...
CARING FOR A CAT, LOOKING TO GIVE HIM AWAY.
VROOM
VROOM
CAN NO LONGER KEEP IT DUE TO PERSONAL ISSUES...
WHY DO THEY ALL SAY, "TAKE MY CAT?"
SPRING
CHI!
HMM
SWIRL
I'M GONNA GO CHI!
OKAY.
PIP PIP PIP

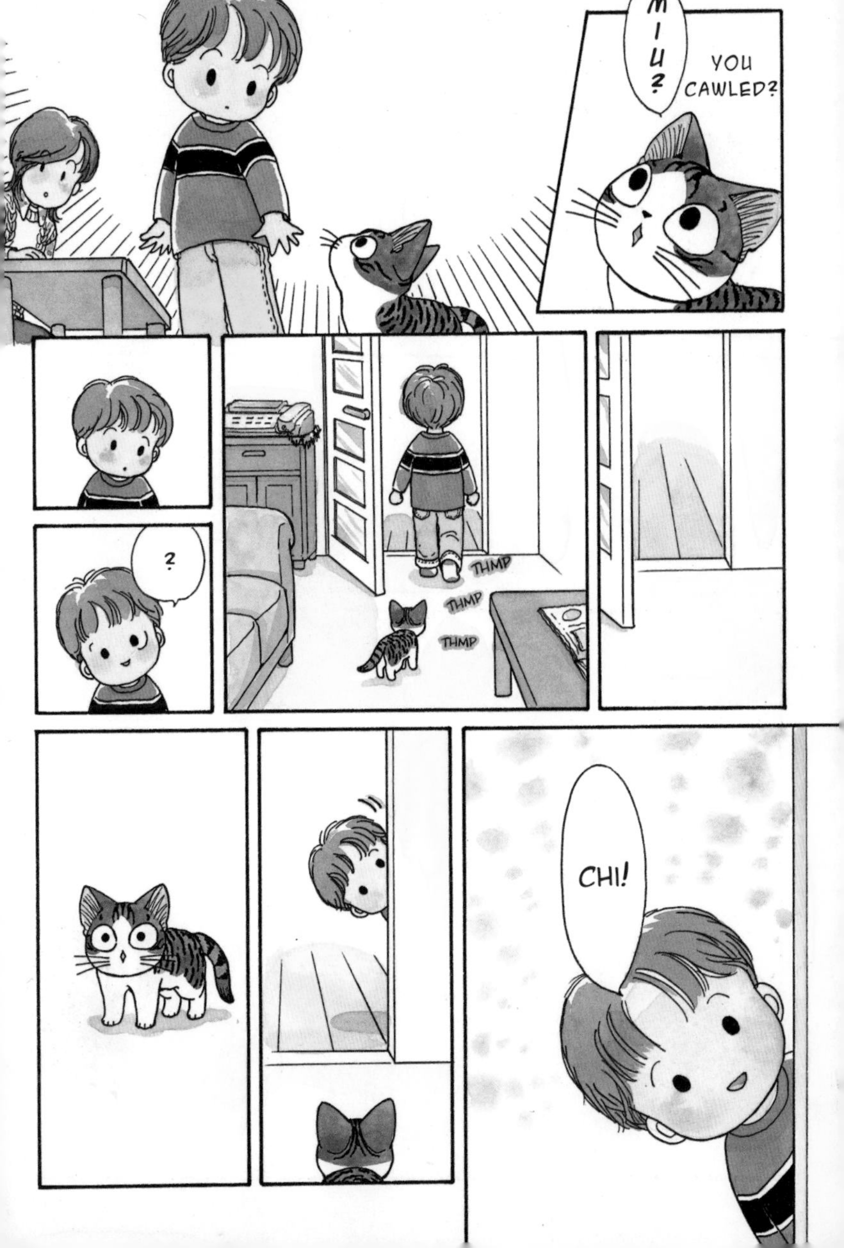
MIU?
YOU CAWLED?
?
THMP
THMP
THMP
CHI!

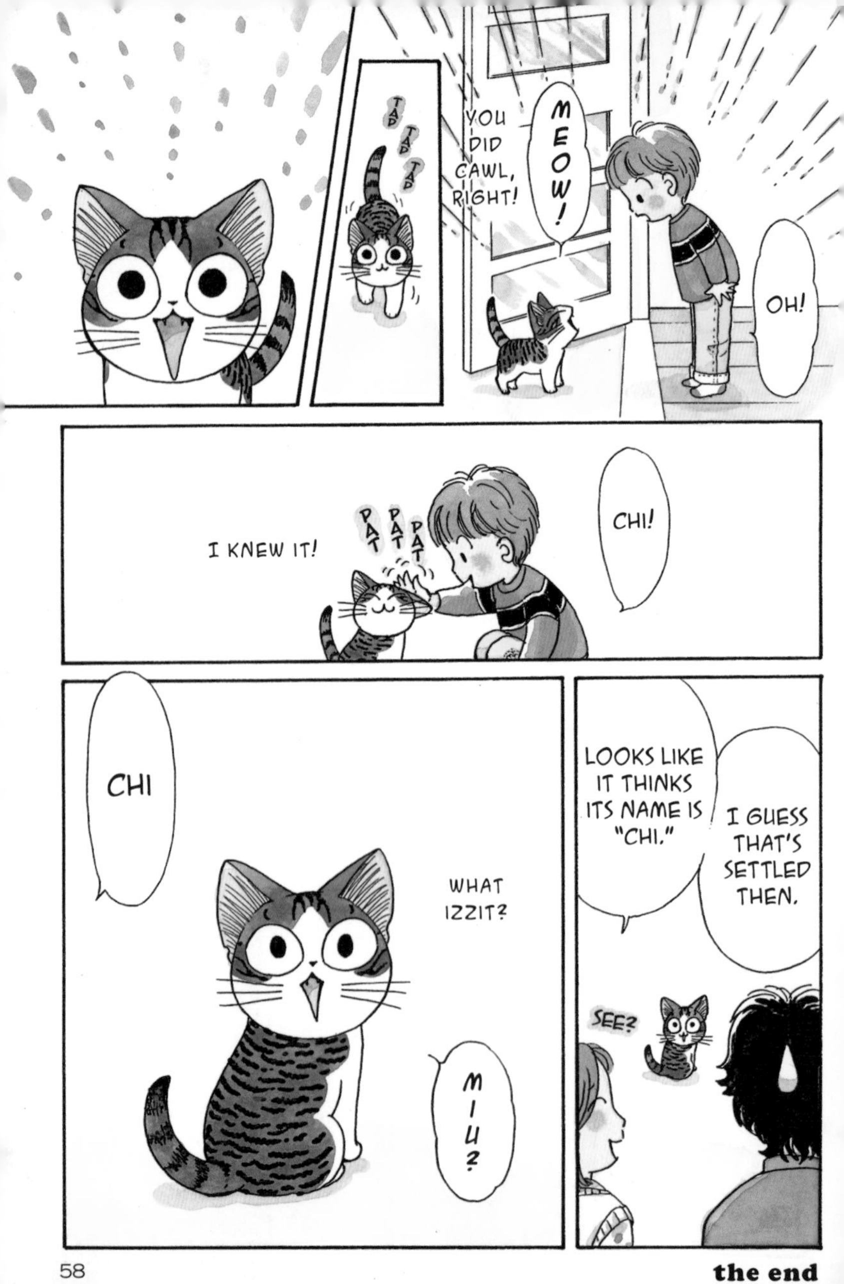
TAP TAP TAP
YOU DID CAWL, RIGHT!
MEOW!
OH!
I KNEW IT!
PAT PAT PAT
CHI!
CHI
WHAT IZZIT?
MIU?
LOOKS LIKE IT THINKS ITS NAME IS "CHI."
I GUESS THAT'S SETTLED THEN.
SEE?

the end

homemade 8: a cat remembers

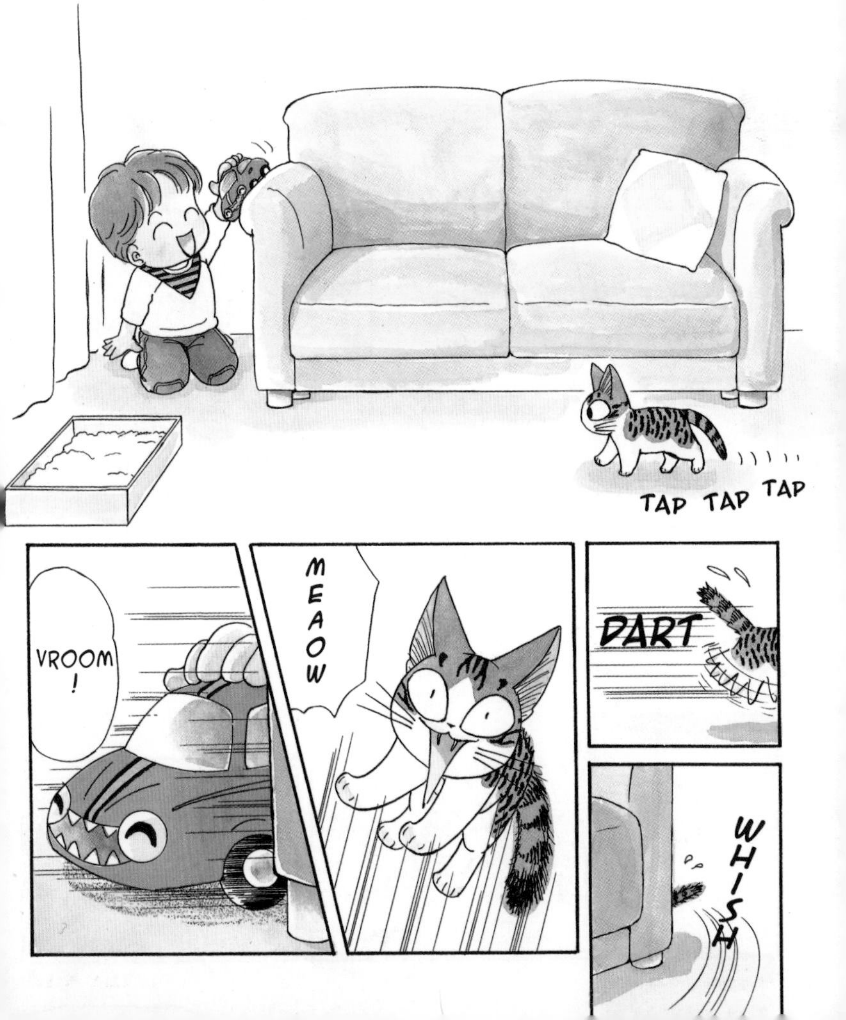
TAP TAP TAP
VROOM!
MEAOW
DART
WHISH

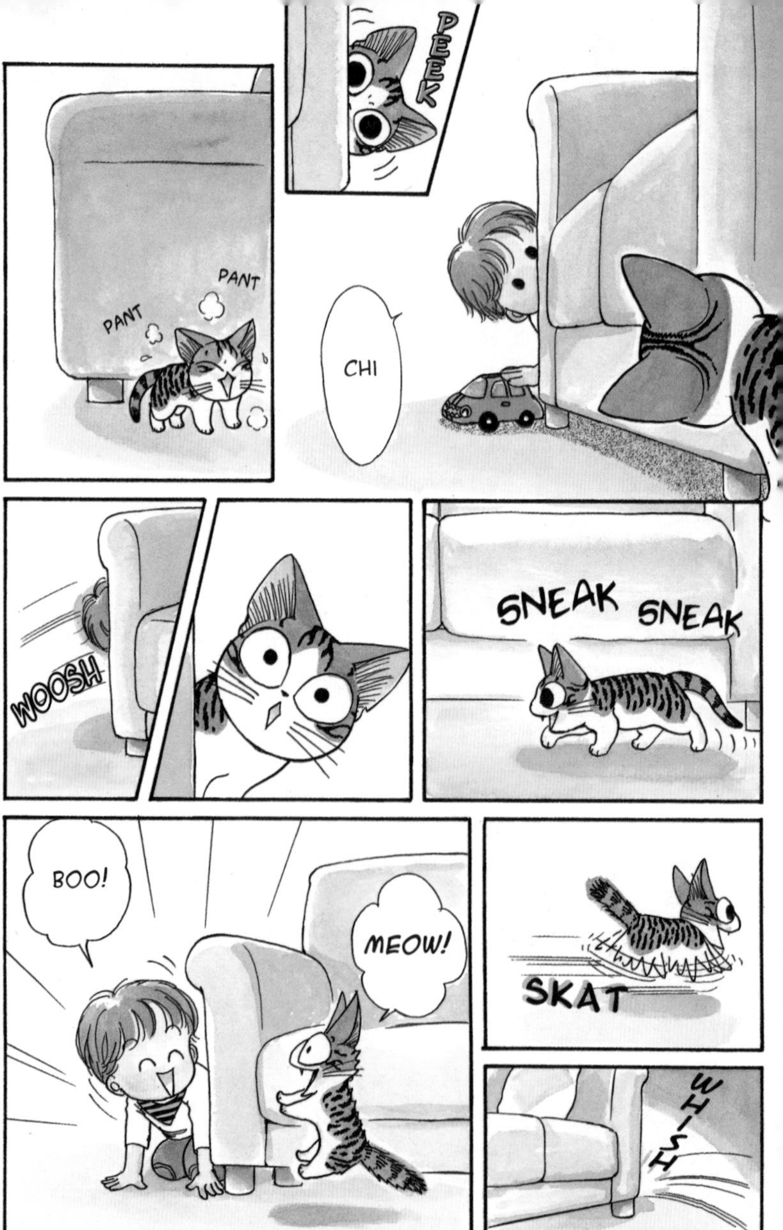
PANT
PANT
PEEK
CHI
WOOSH
SNEAK SNEAK
BOO!
MEOW!
SKAT
WHISH

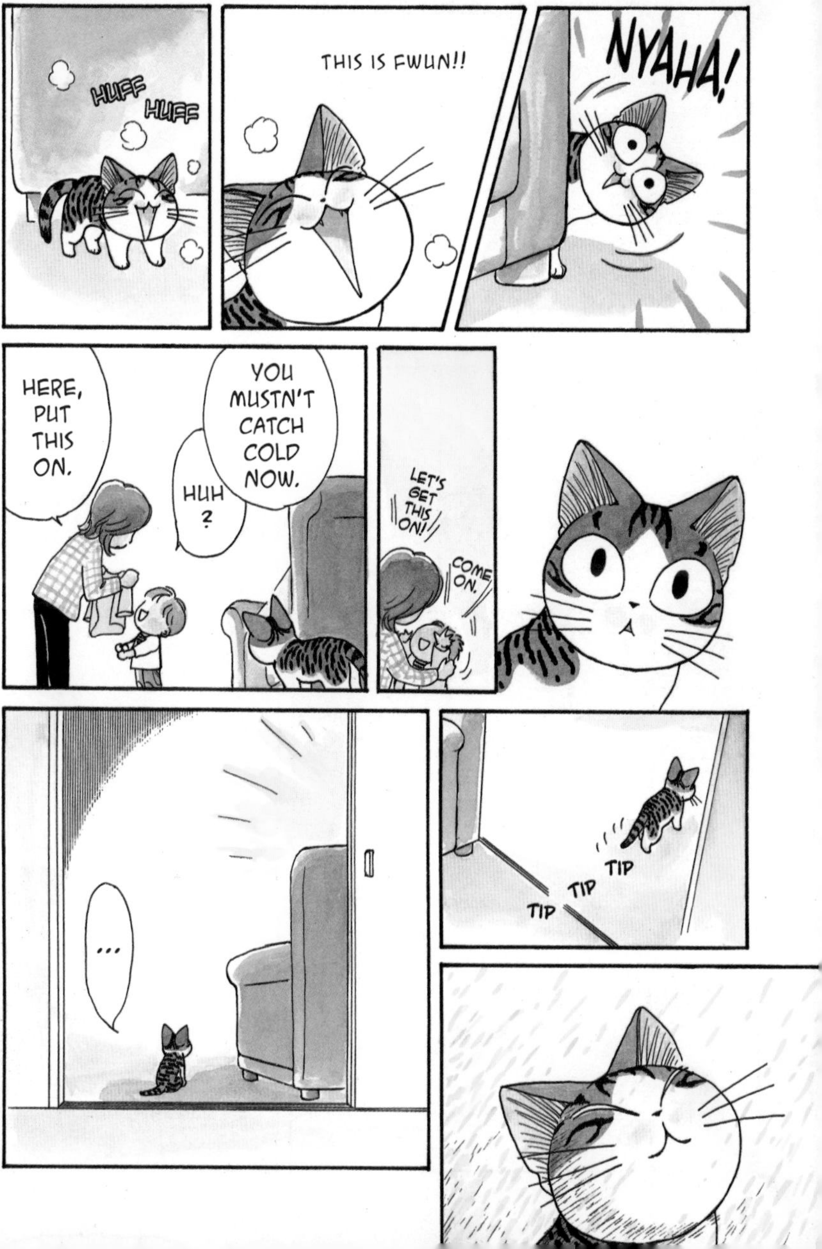
HUFF
HUFF
THIS IS FWUN!!
NYAHA!
HERE, PUT THIS ON.
HUH?
YOU MUSTN'T CATCH COLD NOW.
LET'S GET THIS ON!
COME ON.
...
TIP
TIP
TIP

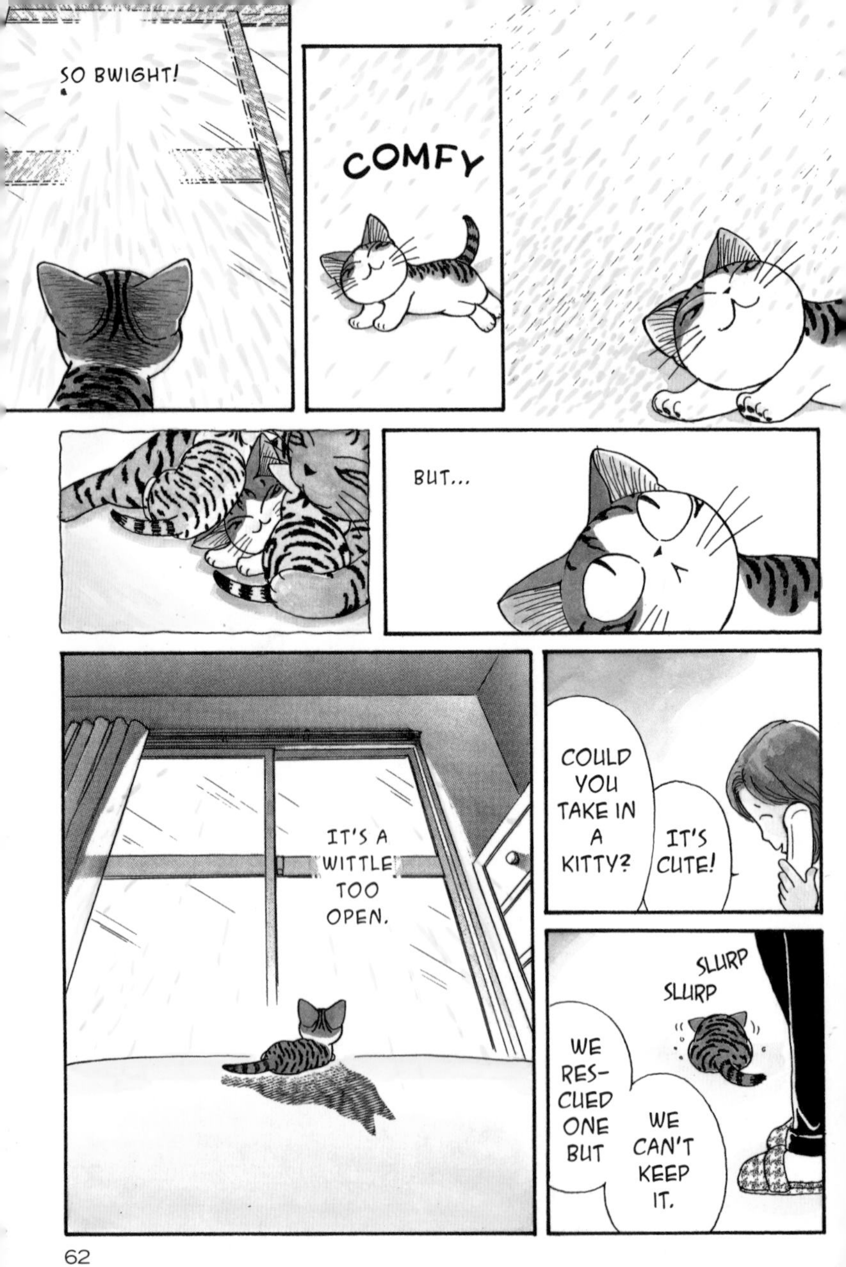
SO BWIGHT!
COMFY
BUT...
IT'S A WITTLE TOO OPEN.
COULD YOU TAKE IN A KITTY?
IT'S CUTE!
SLURP
SLURP
WE RES-CUED ONE BUT
WE CAN'T KEEP IT.

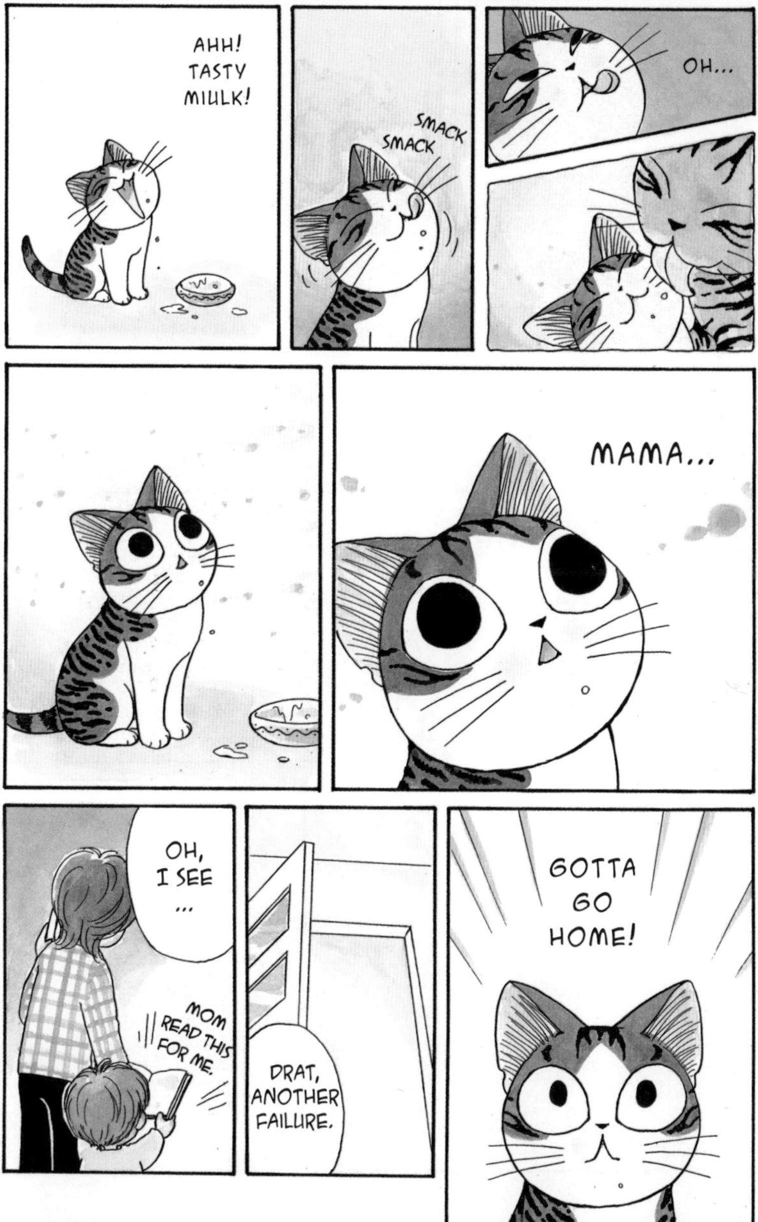
AHH! TASTY MIULK!
SMACK SMACK
OH...
MAMA...
OH, I SEE ...
MOM READ THIS FOR ME.
DRAT, ANOTHER FAILURE.
GOTTA GO HOME!

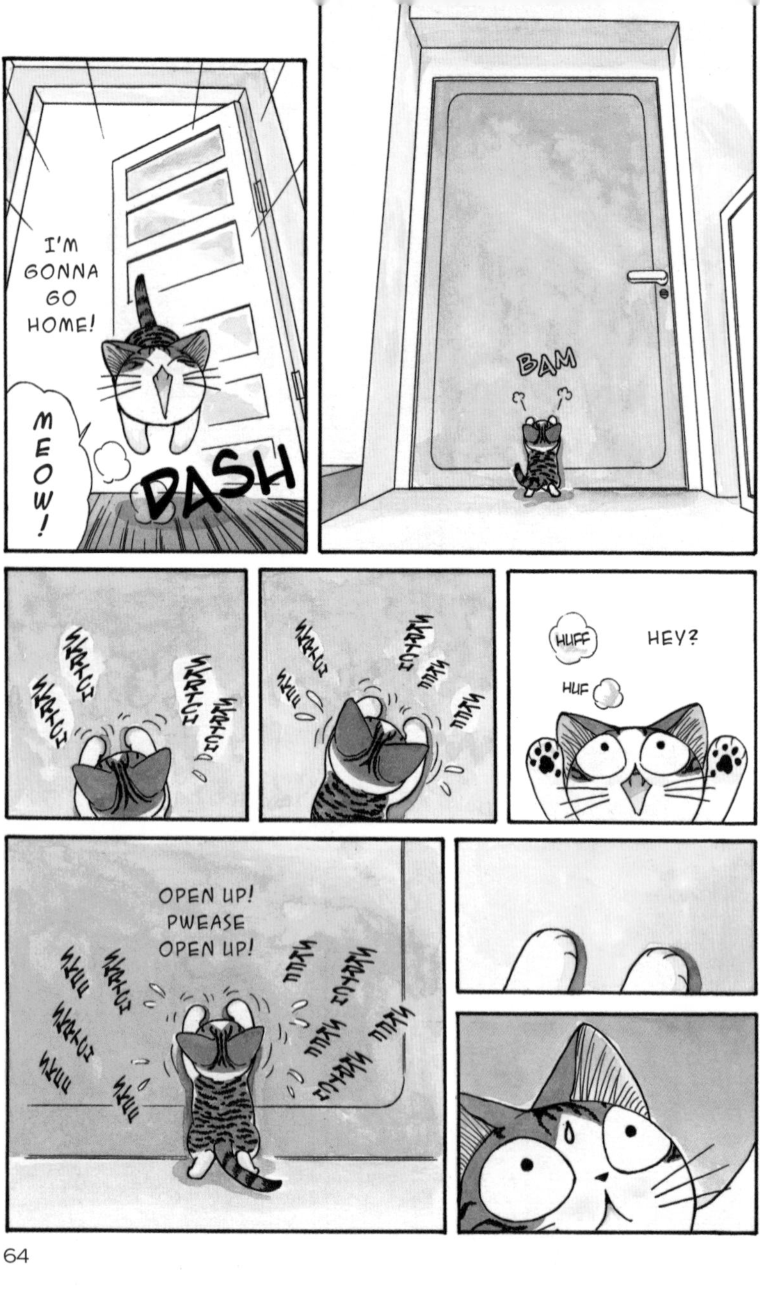
I'M GONNA GO HOME!
MEOW!
DASH
BAM
SKRITCH
SKRITCH
SKRITCH
SKRITCH
HUFF
HEY?
HUF
OPEN UP! PWEASE OPEN UP!

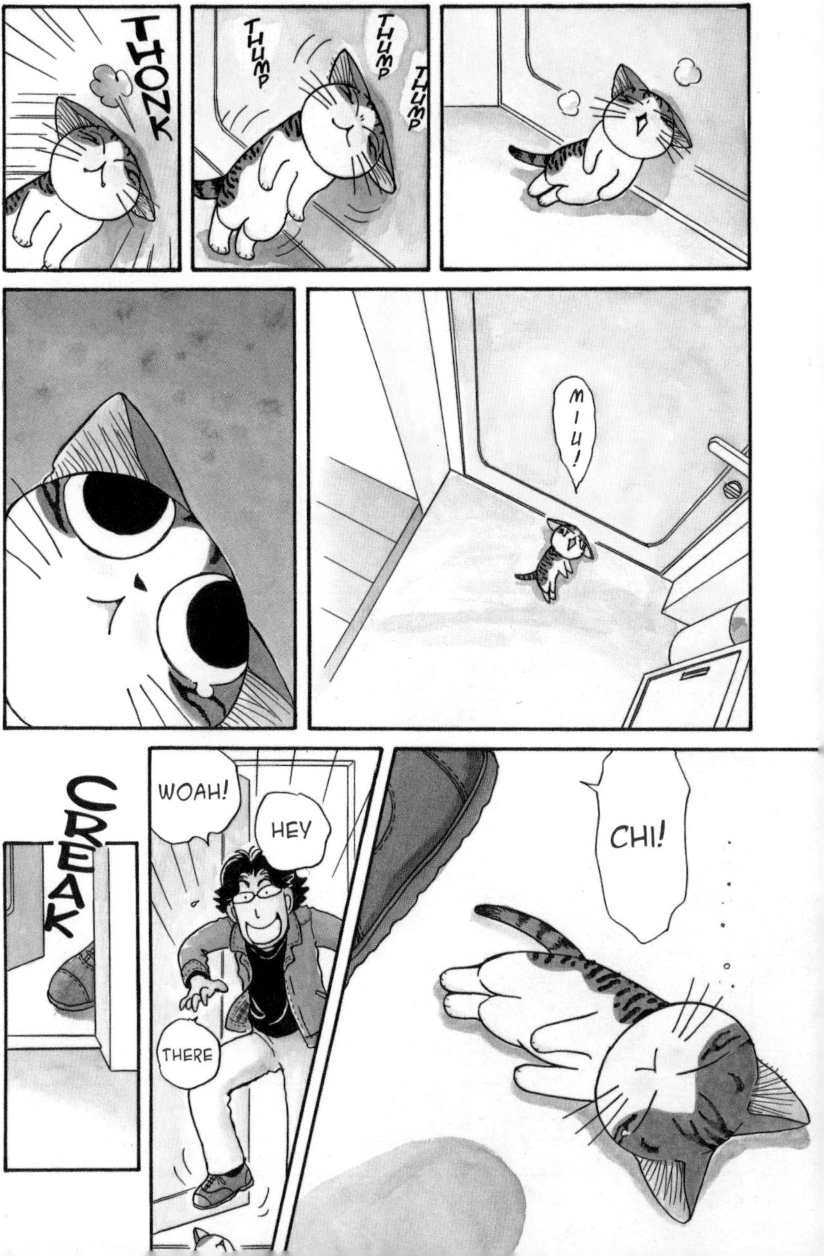
THONK
THUMP
THUMP
THUMP
MIU!
CREAK
WOAH!
HEY
THERE
CHI!

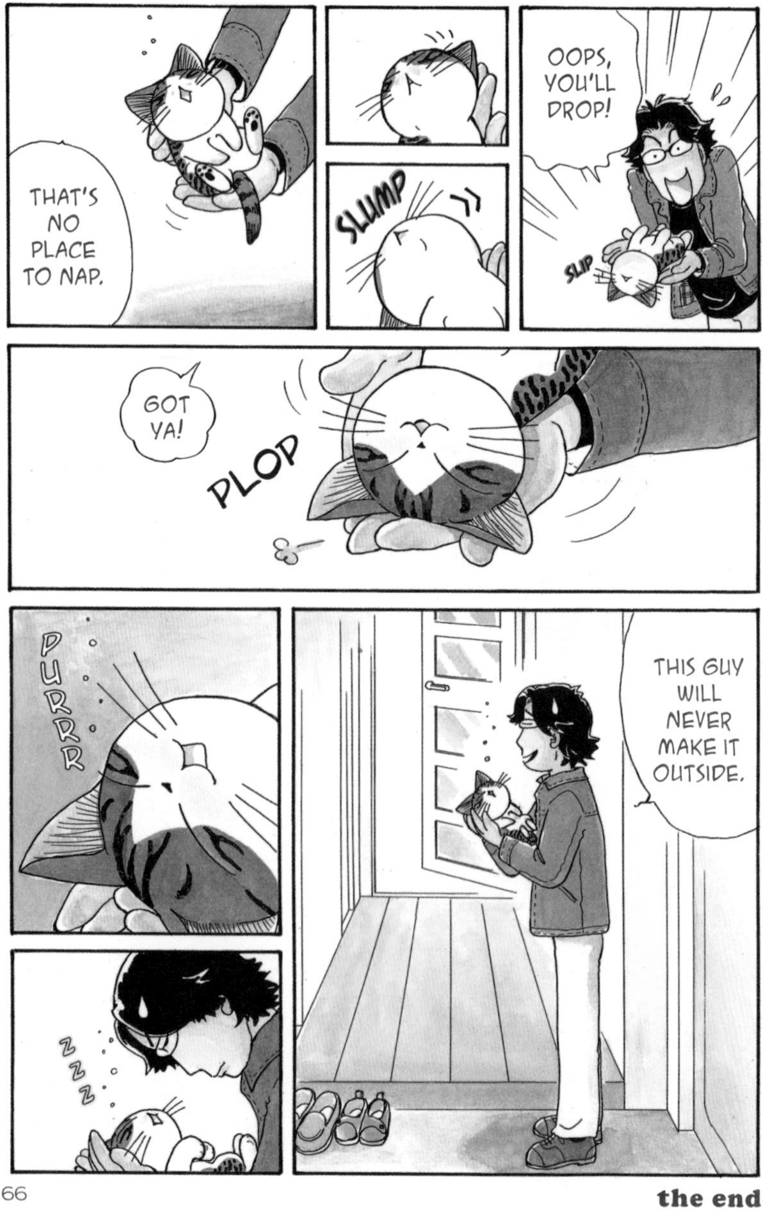
THAT'S NO PLACE TO NAP.
SLUMP
OOPS, YOU'LL DROP!
SLIP
GOT YA!
PLOP
PURRR
ZZZ
THIS GUY WILL NEVER MAKE IT OUTSIDE.

the end

homemade 9: a cat dreams

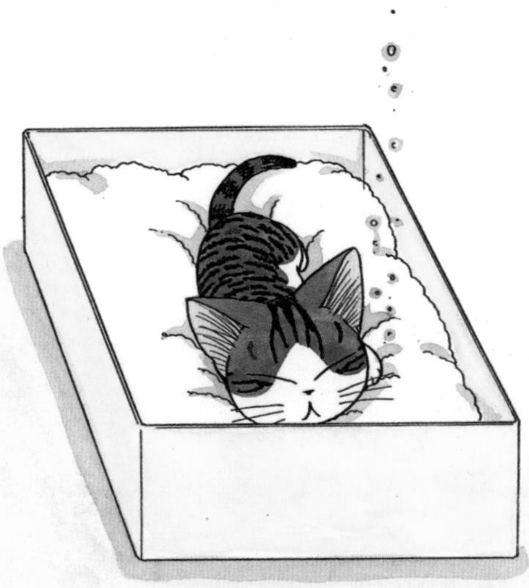

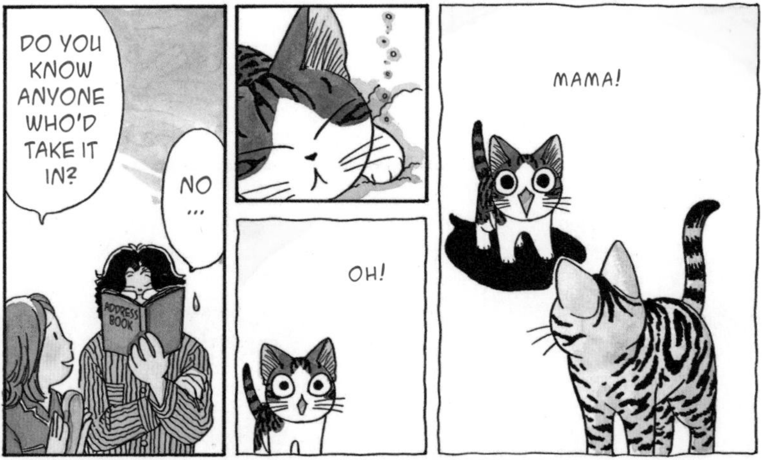
DO YOU KNOW ANYONE WHO'D TAKE IT IN?
ADDRESS BOOK
NO ...
OH!
MAMA!

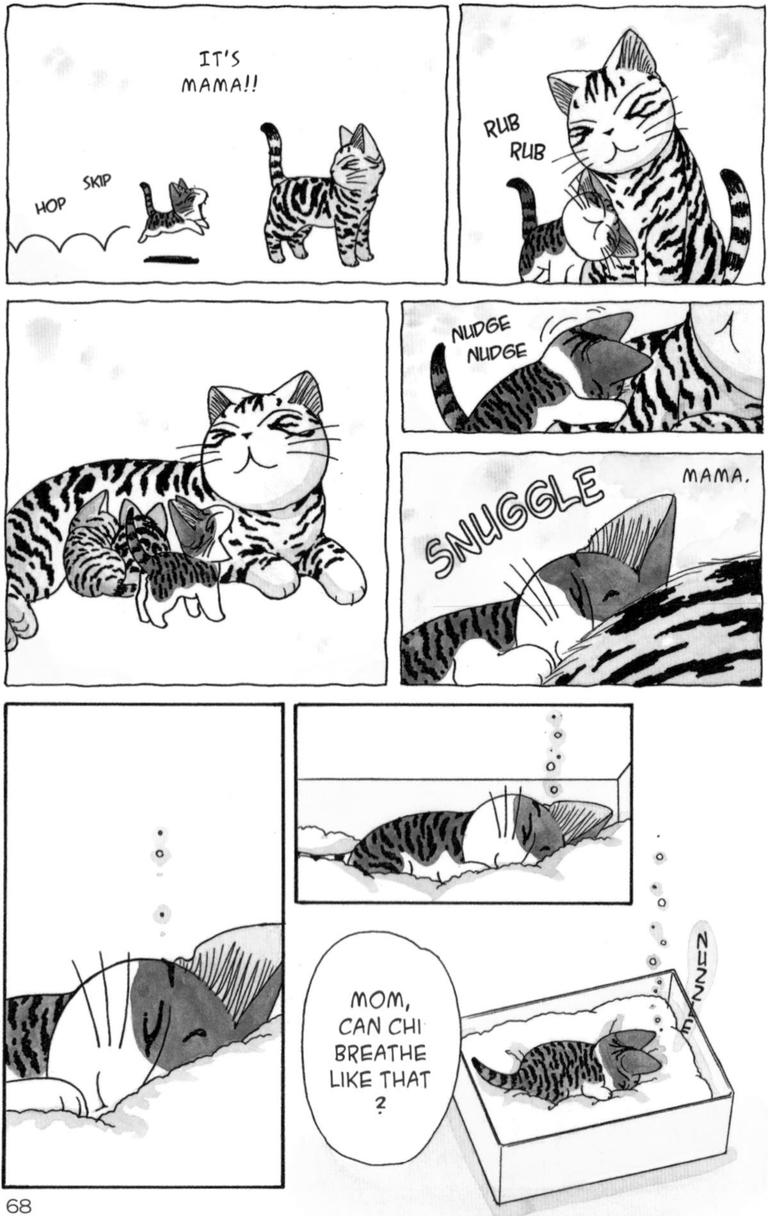
IT'S MAMA!!
HOP
SKIP
RUB RUB
NUDGE NUDGE
SNUGGLE
MAMA.
MOM, CAN CHI BREATHE LIKE THAT?
NUZZLE

WELL, IT'S SOUND ASLEEP.

AND BABIES SLEEP A LOT.

WE'RE SURE IN A BIND. WE NEED TO FIND IT A HOME.

BED-TIME, YOHEI!

GOOD NIGHT DAD.

NIGHT!

CAN I SLEEP WITH YOU MOM?

SURE, CAN'T SLEEP BY YOUR-SELF YET?

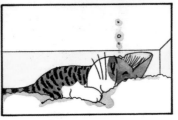

TWITCH TWITCH

69

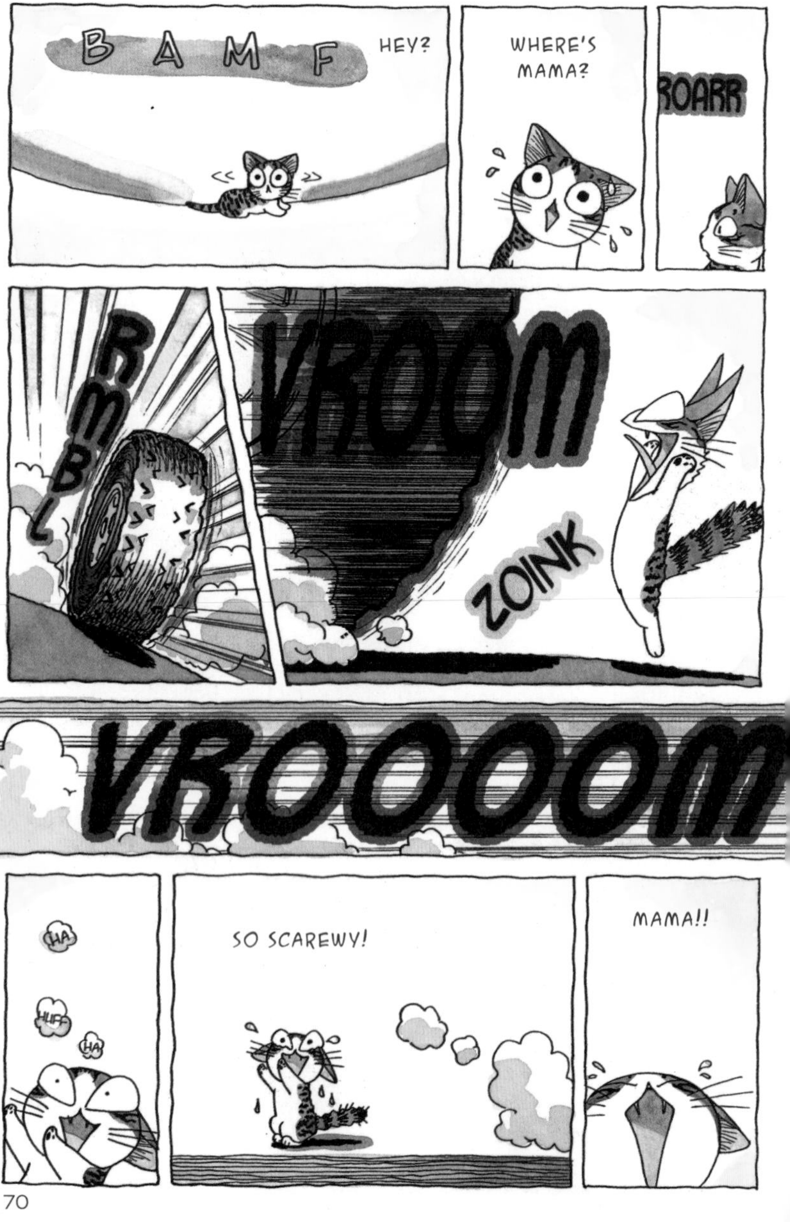
BAMF
HEY?
WHERE'S MAMA?
ROARR
RMBL
VROOM
ZOINK
VROOOOM
HA
HUFF
HA
SO SCAREWY!
MAMA!!

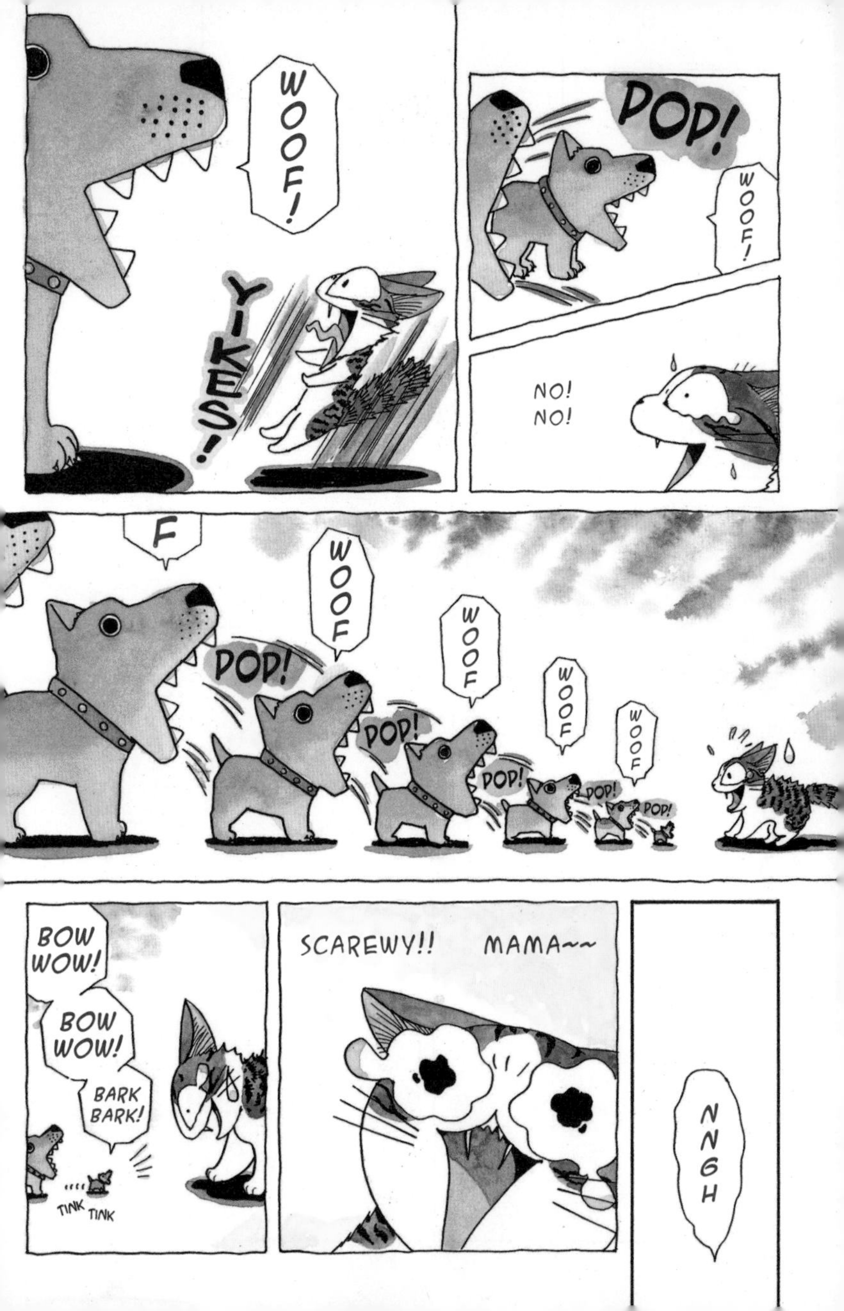
WOOF!
YIKES!
POP!
WOOF!
NO! NO!
F
WOOF
POP!
WOOF
POP!
WOOF
POP!
WOOF
POP!
POP!
BOW WOW!
BOW WOW!
BARK BARK!
TINK TINK
SCAREWY!!
MAMA~~
NNGH

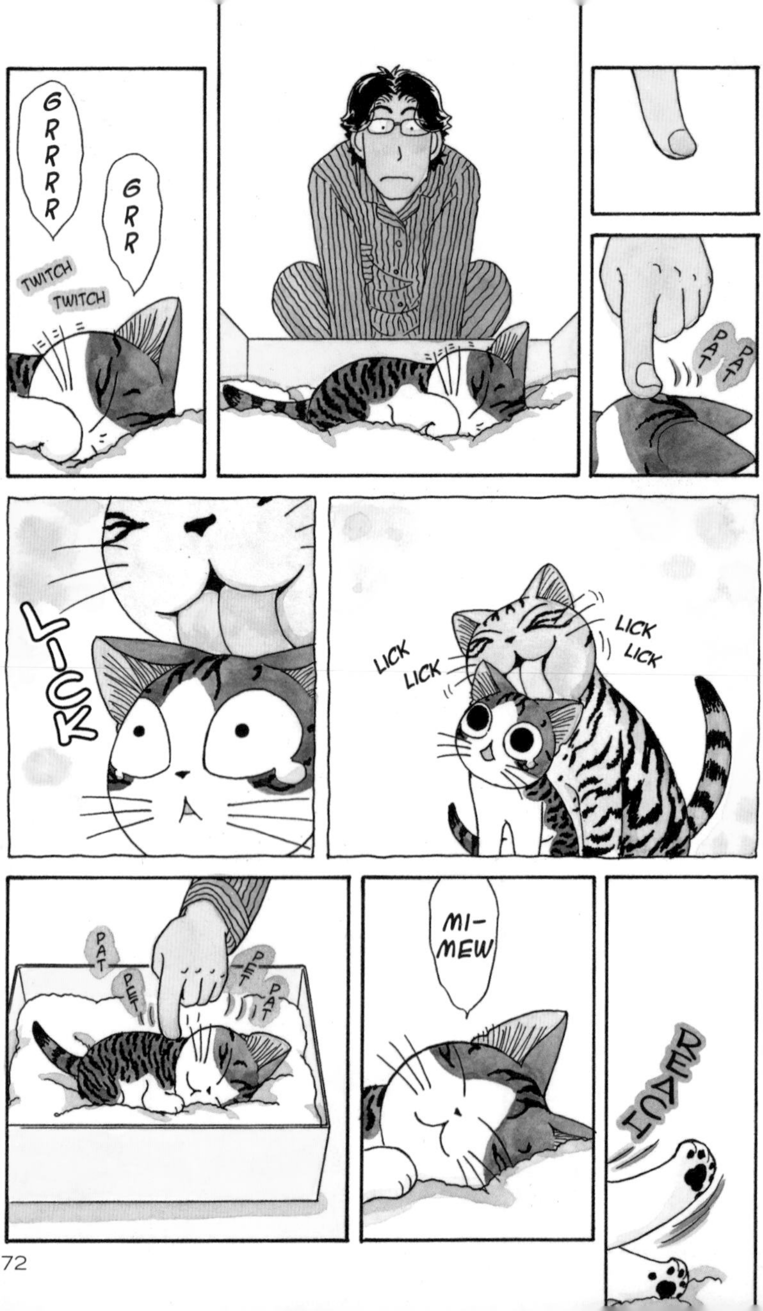
GRRRR
GRR
TWITCH
TWITCH
PAT PAT
LICK
LICK
LICK
LICK
LICK
PAT
PET
PET
PAT
MI-MEW
REACH

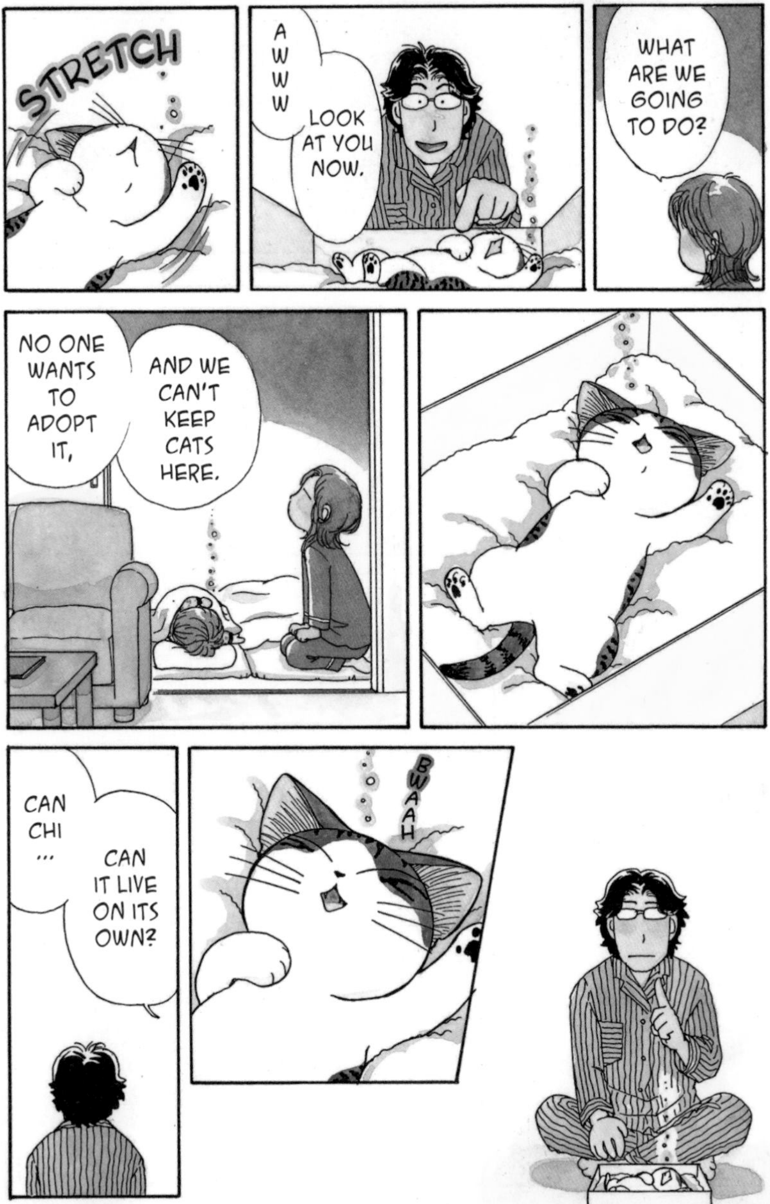
STRETCH
AWWW
LOOK AT YOU NOW.
WHAT ARE WE GOING TO DO?
NO ONE WANTS TO ADOPT IT,
AND WE CAN'T KEEP CATS HERE.
CAN CHI ...
CAN IT LIVE ON ITS OWN?
BWAAH

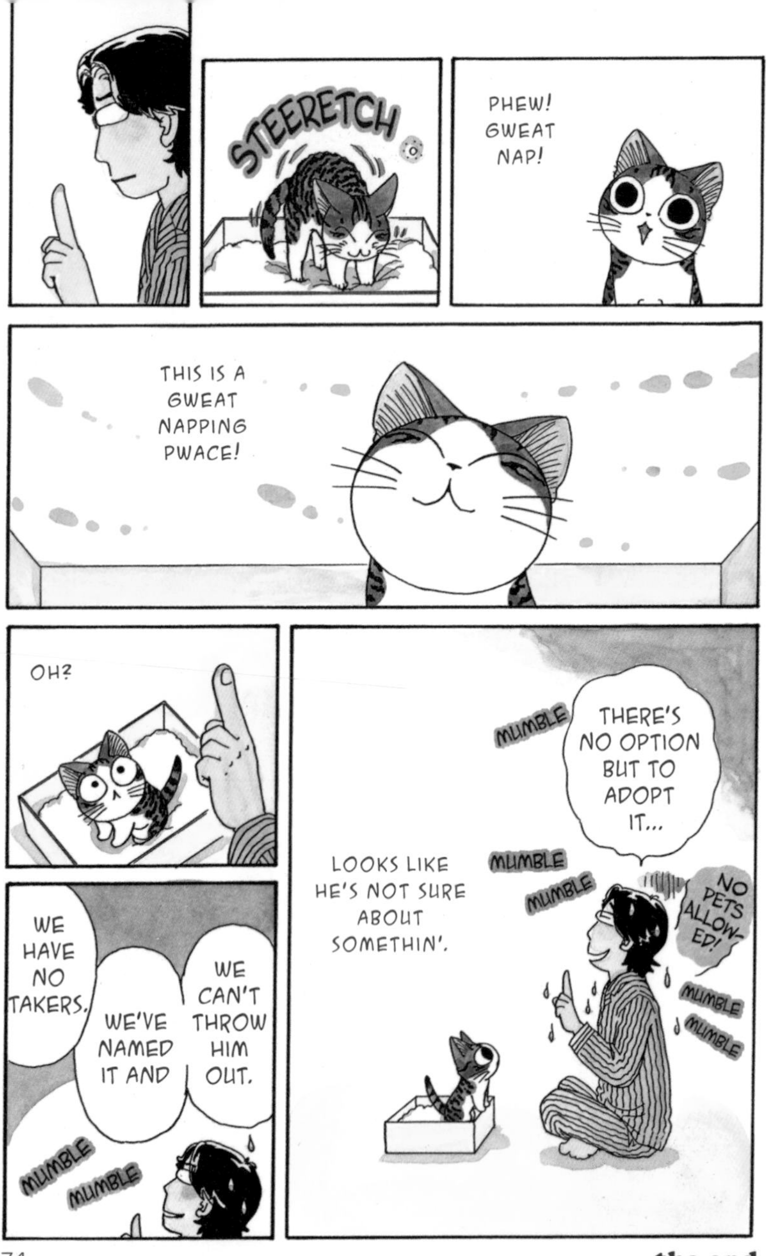
STEERETCH
PHEW! GWEAT NAP!
THIS IS A GWEAT NAPPING PWACE!
OH?
WE HAVE NO TAKERS.
WE'VE NAMED IT AND
WE CAN'T THROW HIM OUT.
MUMBLE
MUMBLE
LOOKS LIKE HE'S NOT SURE ABOUT SOMETHIN'.
MUMBLE
THERE'S NO OPTION BUT TO ADOPT IT...
MUMBLE
MUMBLE
NO PETS ALLOWED!
MUMBLE
MUMBLE

the end

homemade 10: a cat is fired up

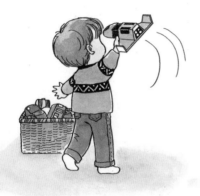

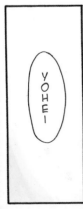

YOHEI
YOHEI
YOHEI.

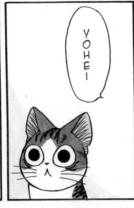

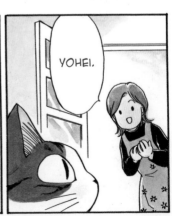

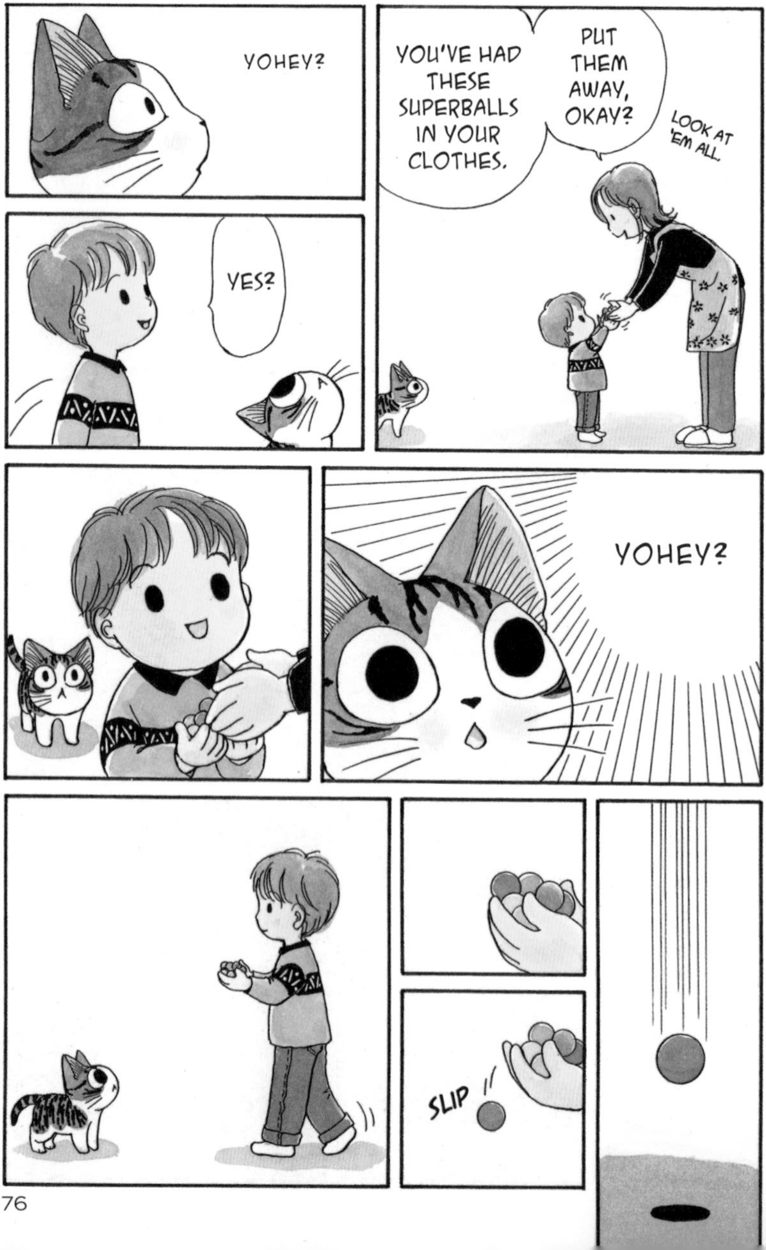
YOHEY?
YOU'VE HAD THESE SUPERBALLS IN YOUR CLOTHES.
PUT THEM AWAY, OKAY?
LOOK AT 'EM ALL.
YES?
YOHEY?
SLIP

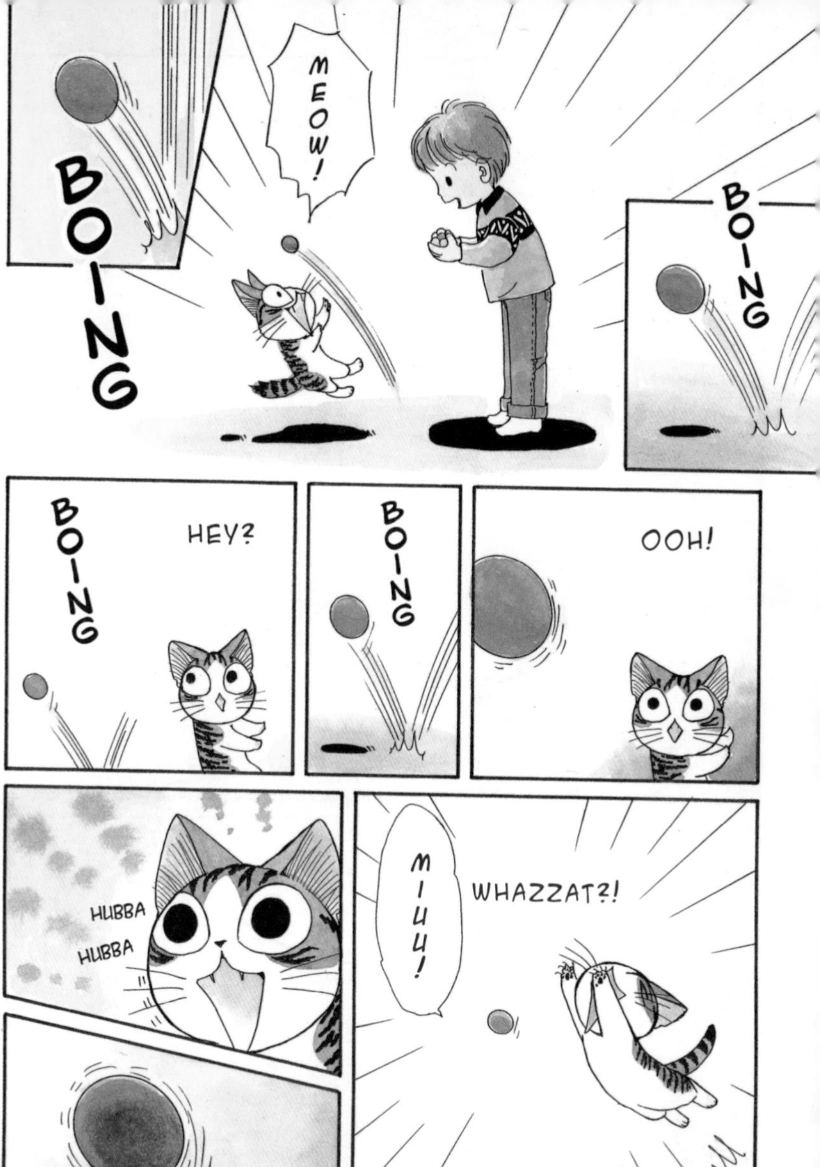
BOING
MEOW!
BOING
BOING
HEY?
BOING
OOH!
HUBBA
HUBBA
MIUU!
WHAZZAT?!

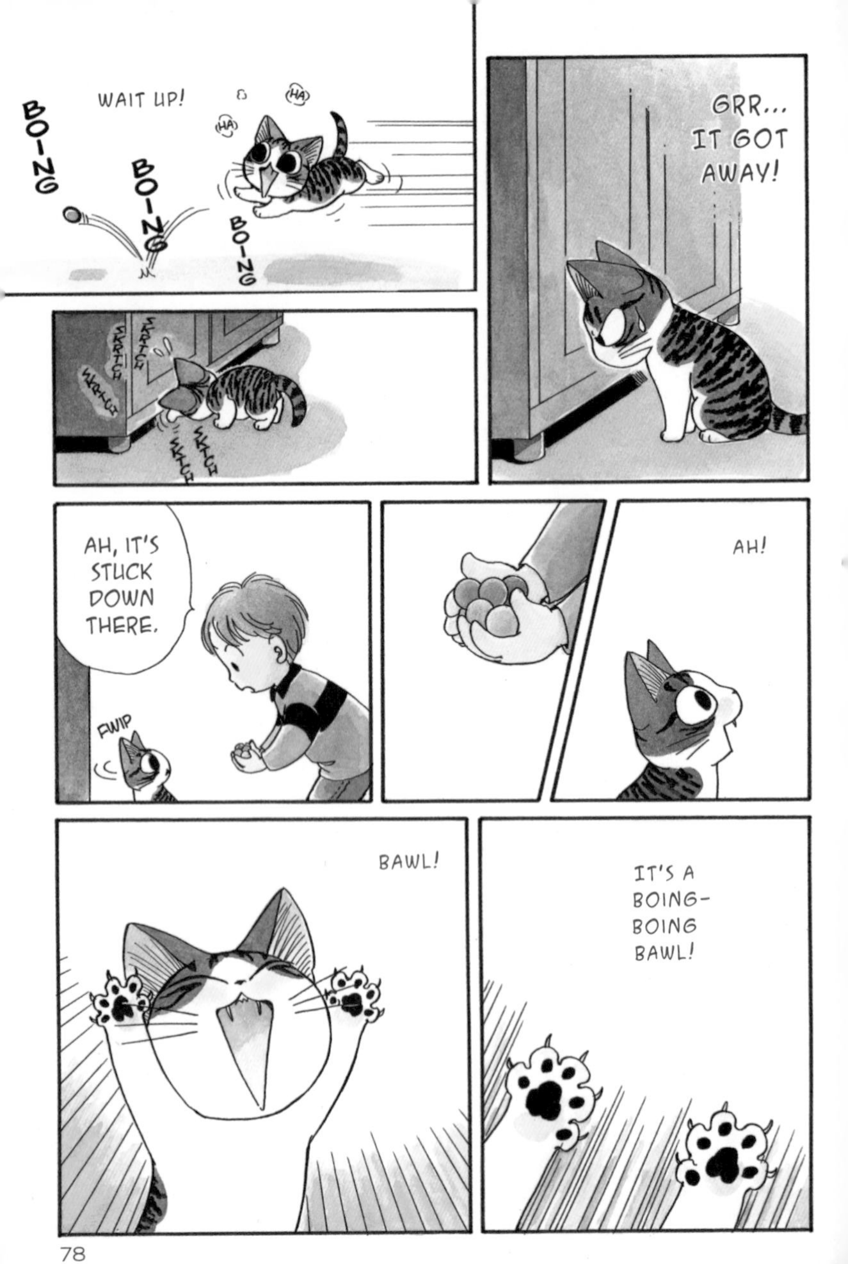

BOING
WAIT UP!
BOING
HA
HA
BOING
GRR... IT GOT AWAY!
SKRITCH
SKRITCH
SKRITCH
SKRITCH
SKRITCH
AH, IT'S STUCK DOWN THERE.
FWIP
AH!
BAWL!
IT'S A BOING-BOING BAWL!

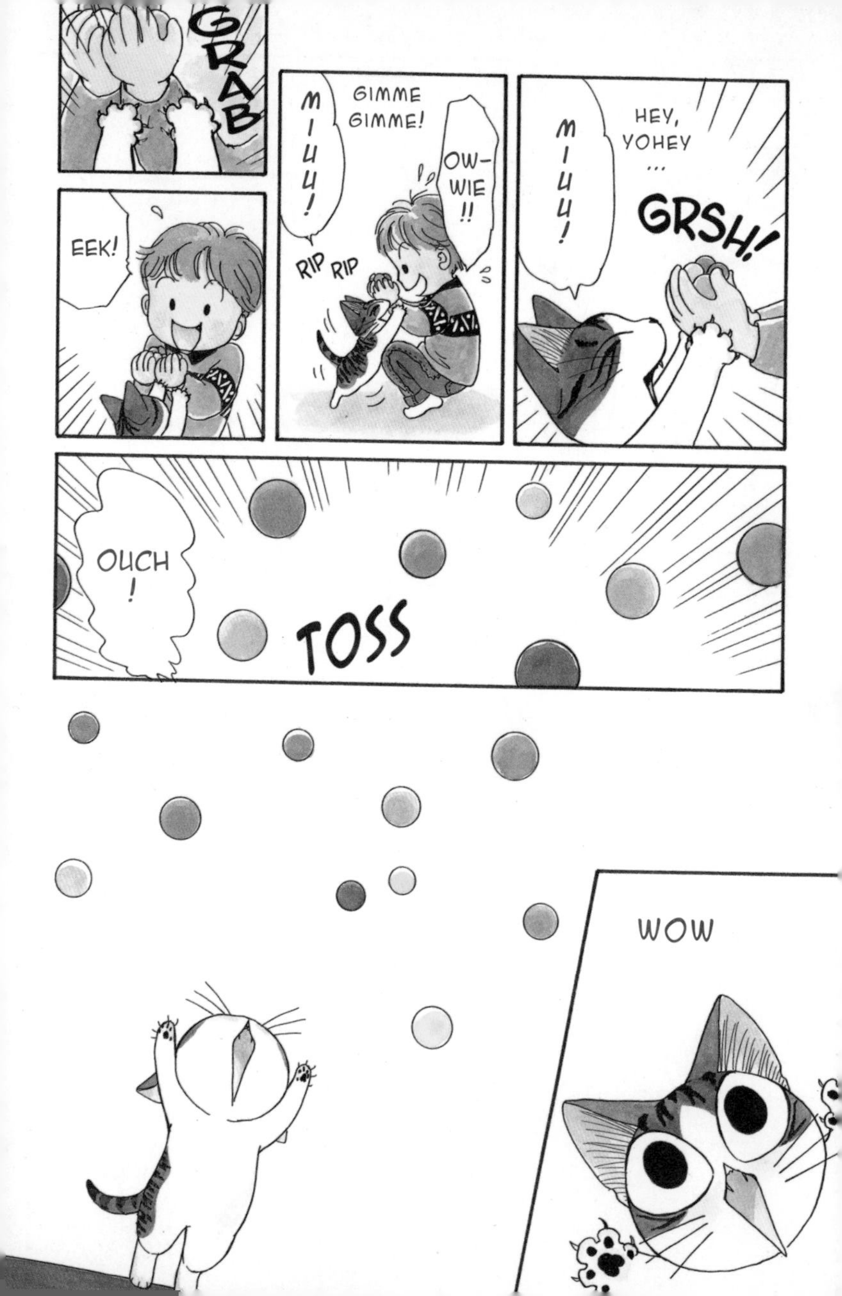
GRAB
EEK!
MIUU!
GIMME GIMME!
OW-WIE!!
RIP RIP
MIUU!
HEY, YOHEY ...
GRSH!
OUCH!
TOSS
WOW

BOING
BOING
BOING
BOING
UGYAA!!
MEOW!
WHOA!
BOING
BOING
BOING
BOING
BOING
BOING
BOING
BOING
YOHEY'S AMAZING!!
MEOW!
POUNCE
HUFF
HUFF
HA
HUFF
BOING
BOING
BOING
BOING
BOING

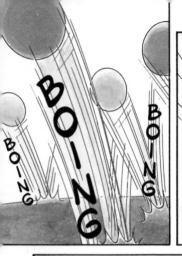

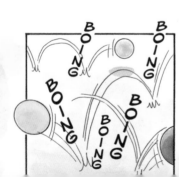

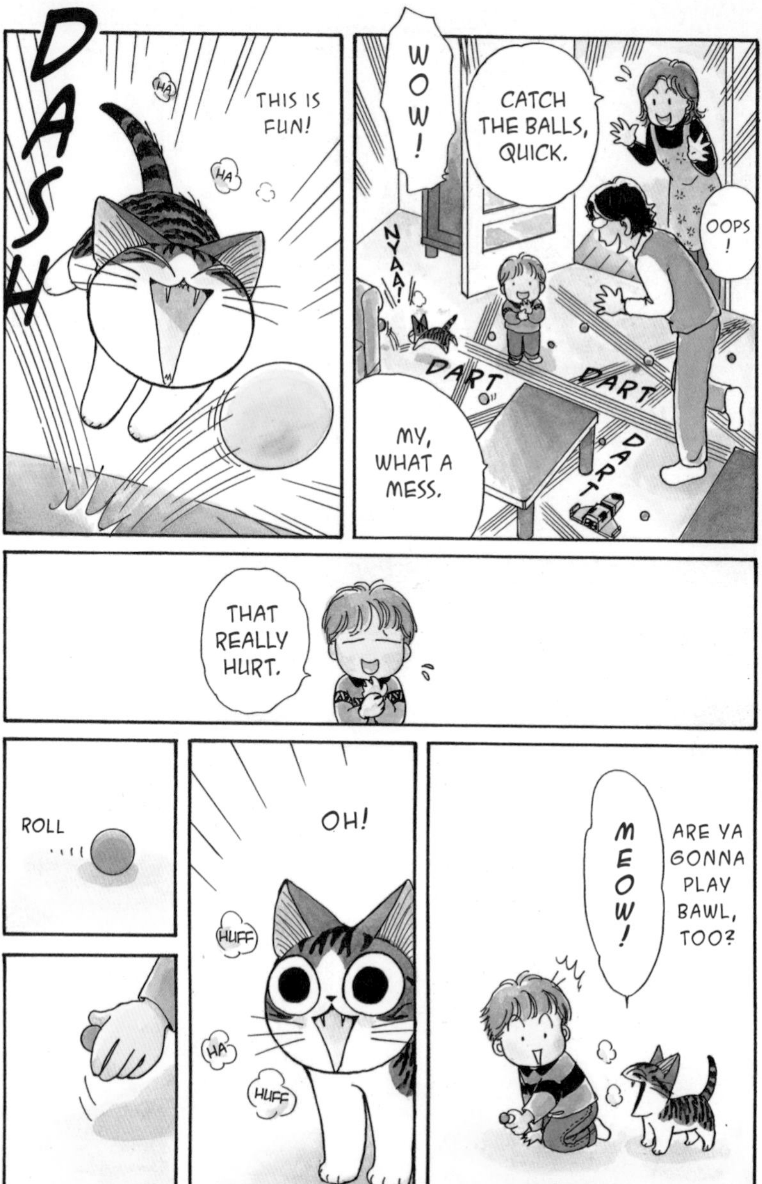
DASH
HA
THIS IS FUN!
HA
WOW!
CATCH THE BALLS, QUICK.
OOPS!
NYAA!
DART
DART
DART
MY, WHAT A MESS.
THAT REALLY HURT.
ROLL
OH!
HUFF
HA
HUFF
MEOW!
ARE YA GONNA PLAY BAWL, TOO?

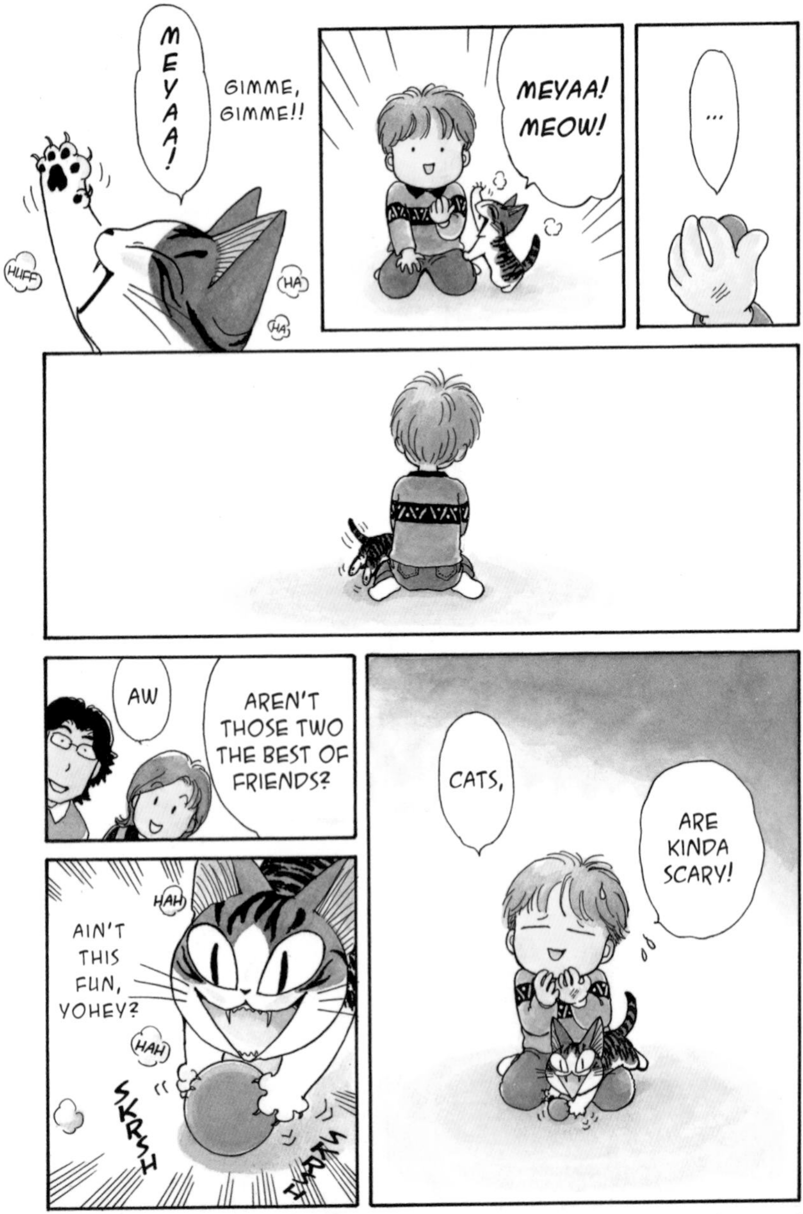
MEYAA!
GIMME, GIMME!!
HUFF
HA
HA
MEYAA! MEOW!
...
AW
AREN'T THOSE TWO THE BEST OF FRIENDS?
HAH
AIN'T THIS FUN, YOHEY?
HAH
SKRSH
CATS,
ARE KINDA SCARY!

the end

homemade 11: a cat plays

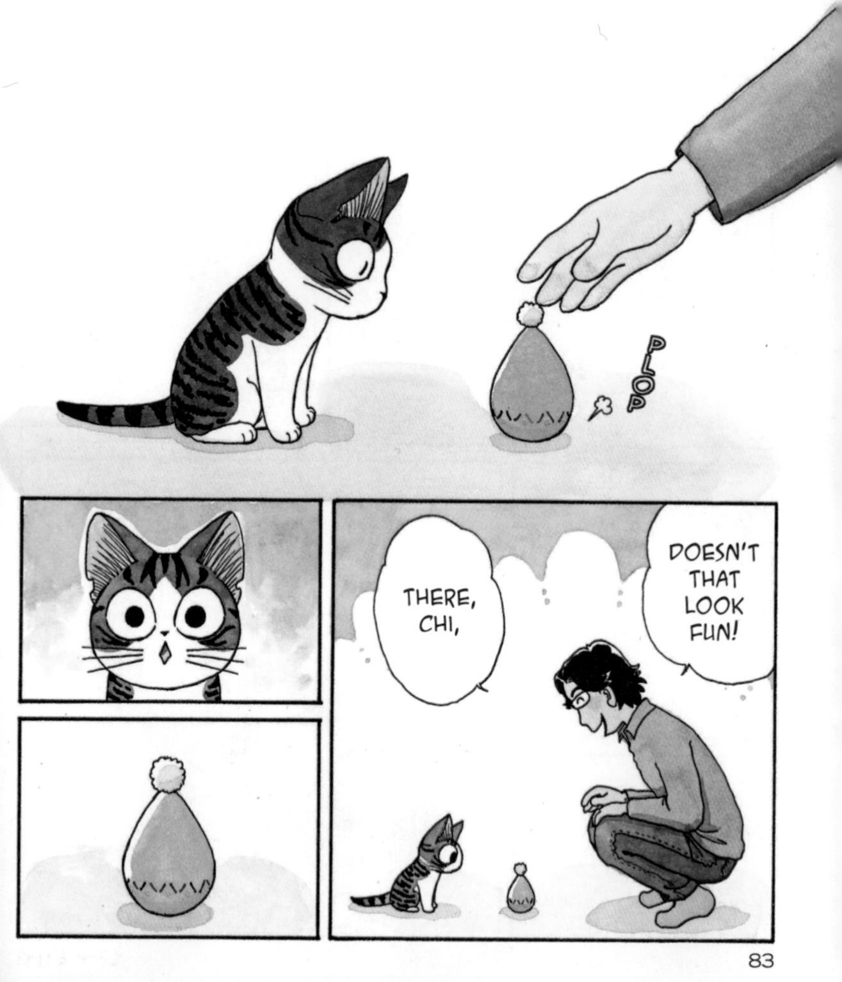

PLOP
THERE, CHI,
DOESN'T THAT LOOK FUN!

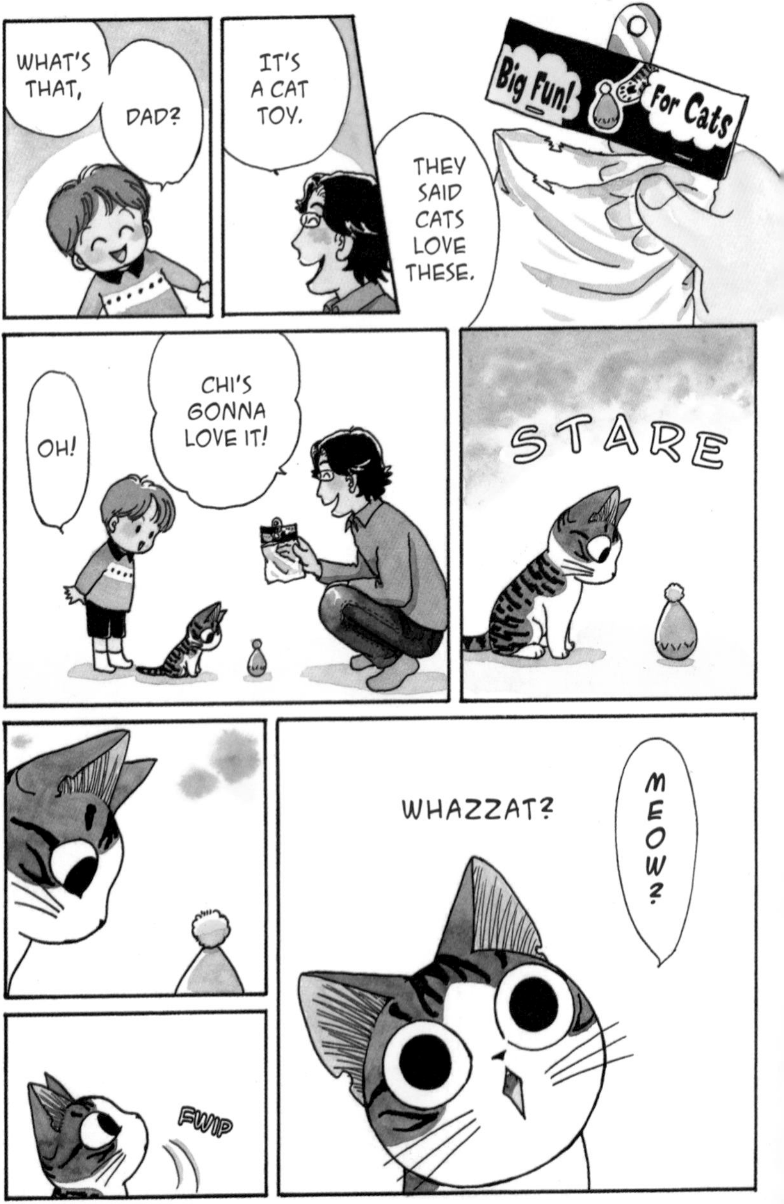
WHAT'S THAT,
DAD?
IT'S A CAT TOY.
THEY SAID CATS LOVE THESE.
Big Fun!
For Cats
OH!
CHI'S GONNA LOVE IT!
STARE
FWIP
WHAZZAT?
MEOW?

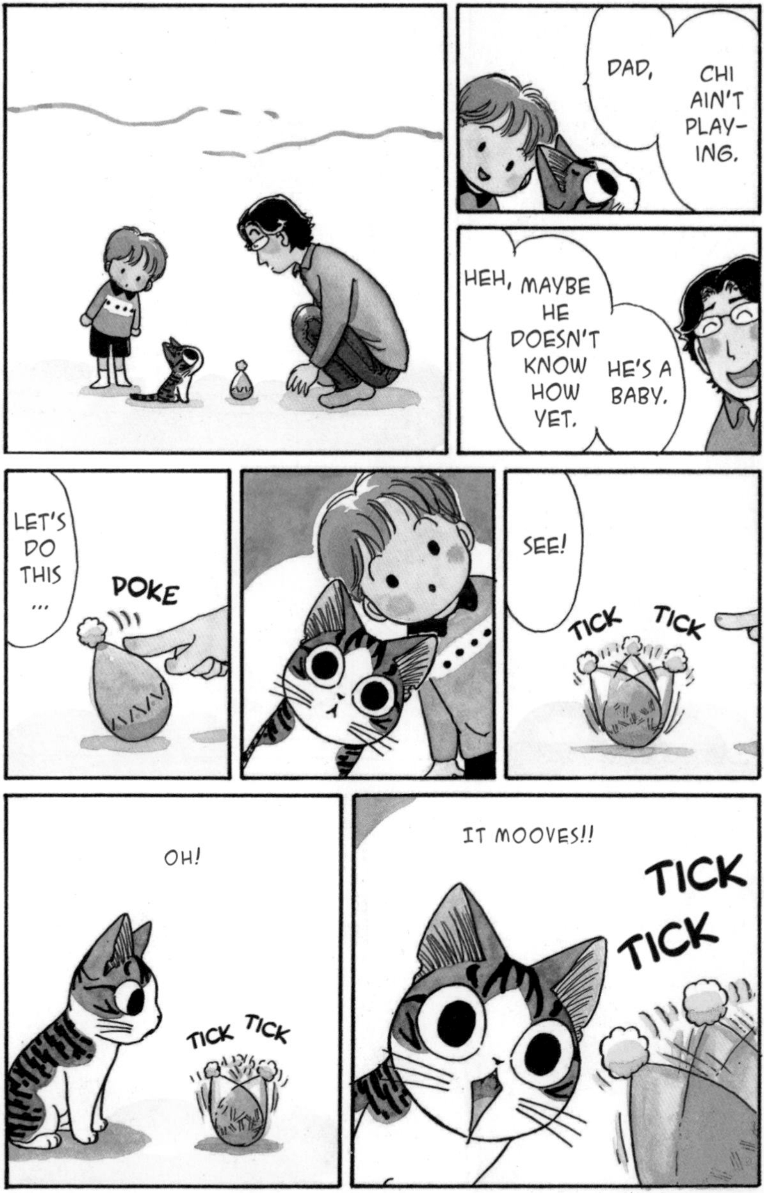
DAD, CHI AIN'T PLAYING.
HEH, MAYBE HE DOESN'T KNOW HOW YET.
HE'S A BABY.
LET'S DO THIS ...
POKE
SEE!
TICK TICK
OH!
TICK TICK
IT MOOVES!!
TICK TICK

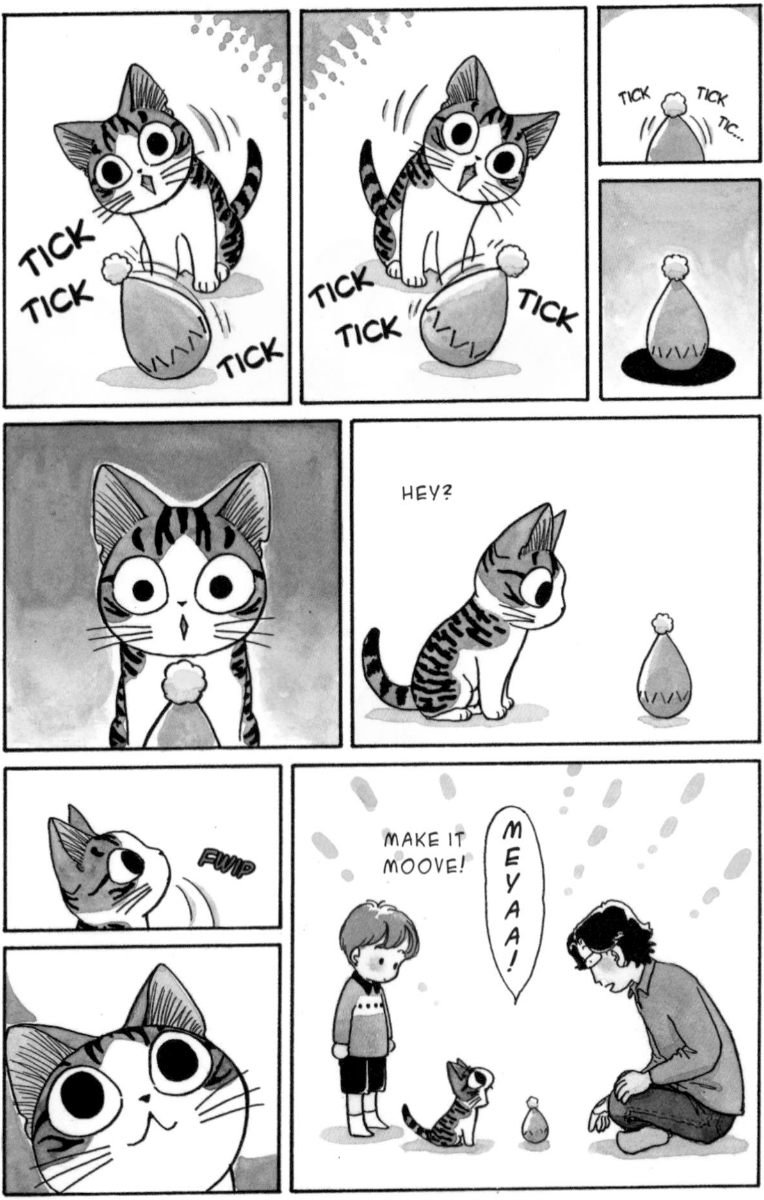

TICK
TICK
TICK
TICK
TICK
TICK
TICK
TICK
TIC...
HEY?
FWIP
MAKE IT MOOVE!
MEYAA!

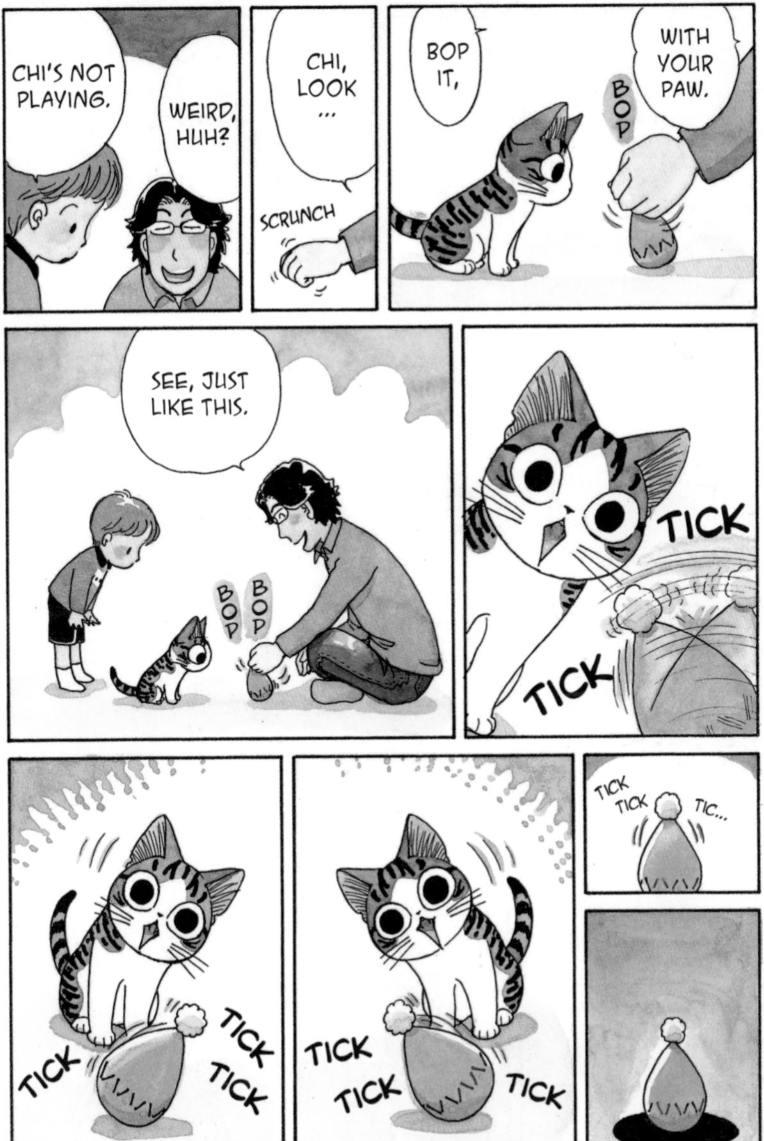
CHI'S NOT PLAYING.
WEIRD, HUH?
CHI, LOOK ...
SCRUNCH
BOP IT,
WITH YOUR PAW.
BOP
SEE, JUST LIKE THIS.
BOP
BOP
TICK
TICK
TICK
TICK
TICK
TICK
TICK
TICK
TICK
TICK
TIC...

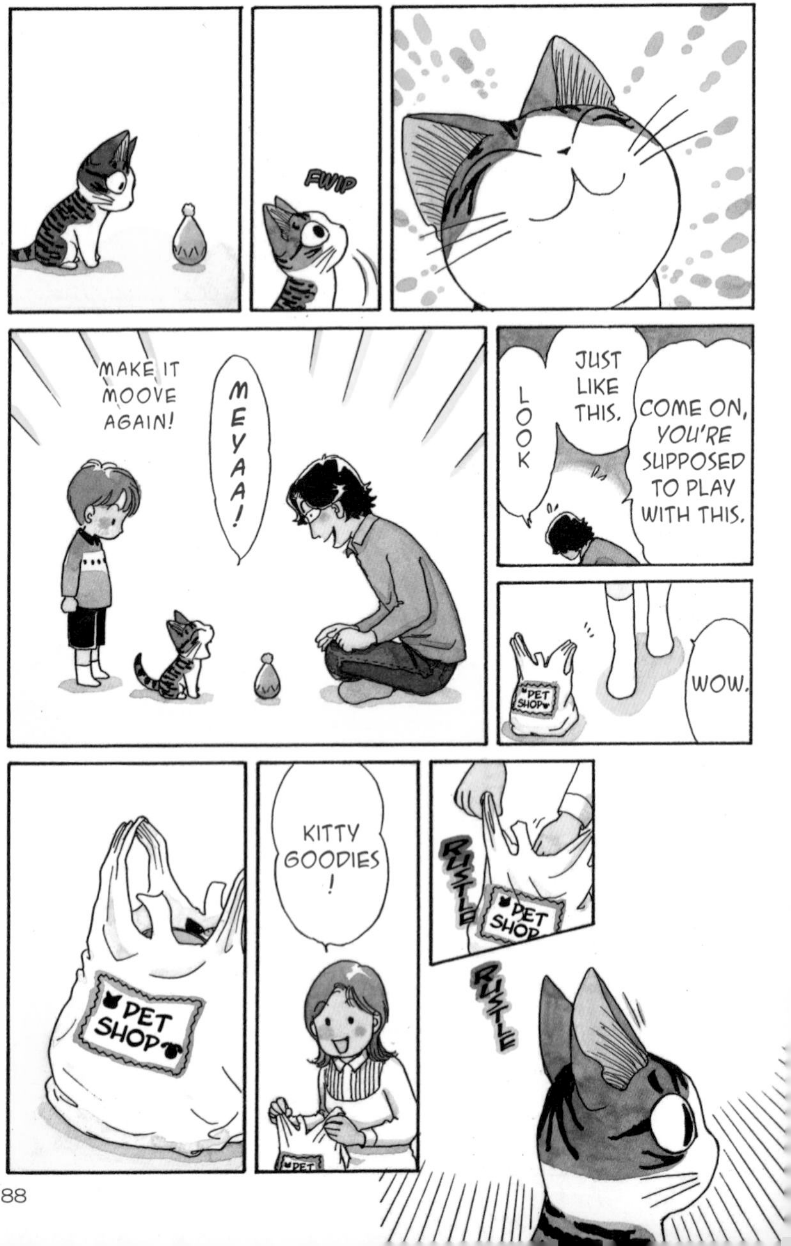
FWIP
MAKE IT MOOVE AGAIN!
MEYAA!
LOOK
JUST LIKE THIS.
COME ON, YOU'RE SUPPOSED TO PLAY WITH THIS.
PET SHOP
WOW.
PET SHOP
KITTY GOODIES!
RUSTLE
PET SHOP
RUSTLE

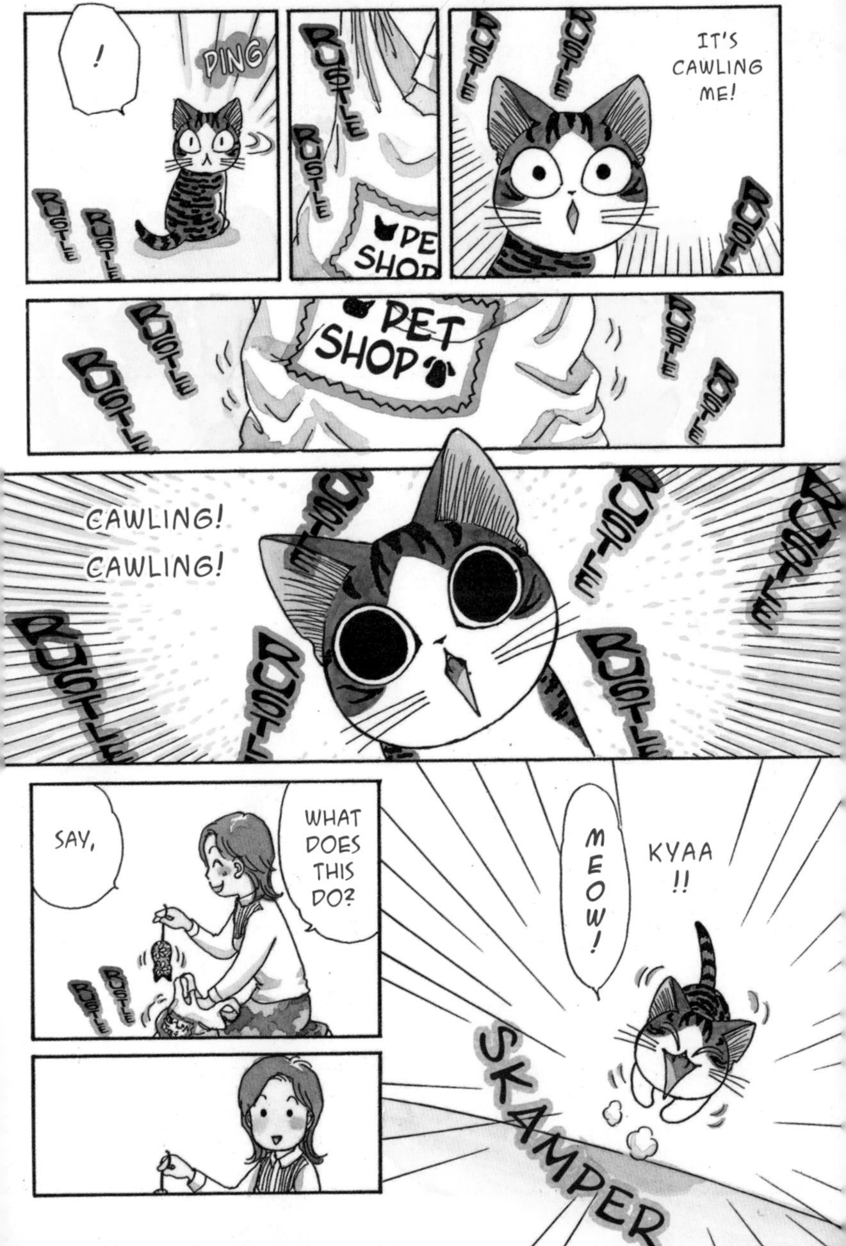
!
PING
RUSTLE
RUSTLE
RUSTLE
RUSTLE
PET SHOP
RUSTLE
RUSTLE
IT'S CAWLING ME!
RUSTLE
RUSTLE
RUSTLE
PET SHOP
RUSTLE
RUSTLE
CAWLING!
CAWLING!
RUSTLE
RUSTLE
RUSTLE
RUSTLE
RUSTLE
RUSTLE
SAY,
WHAT DOES THIS DO?
RUSTLE
RUSTLE
MEOW!
KYAA !!
SKAMPER

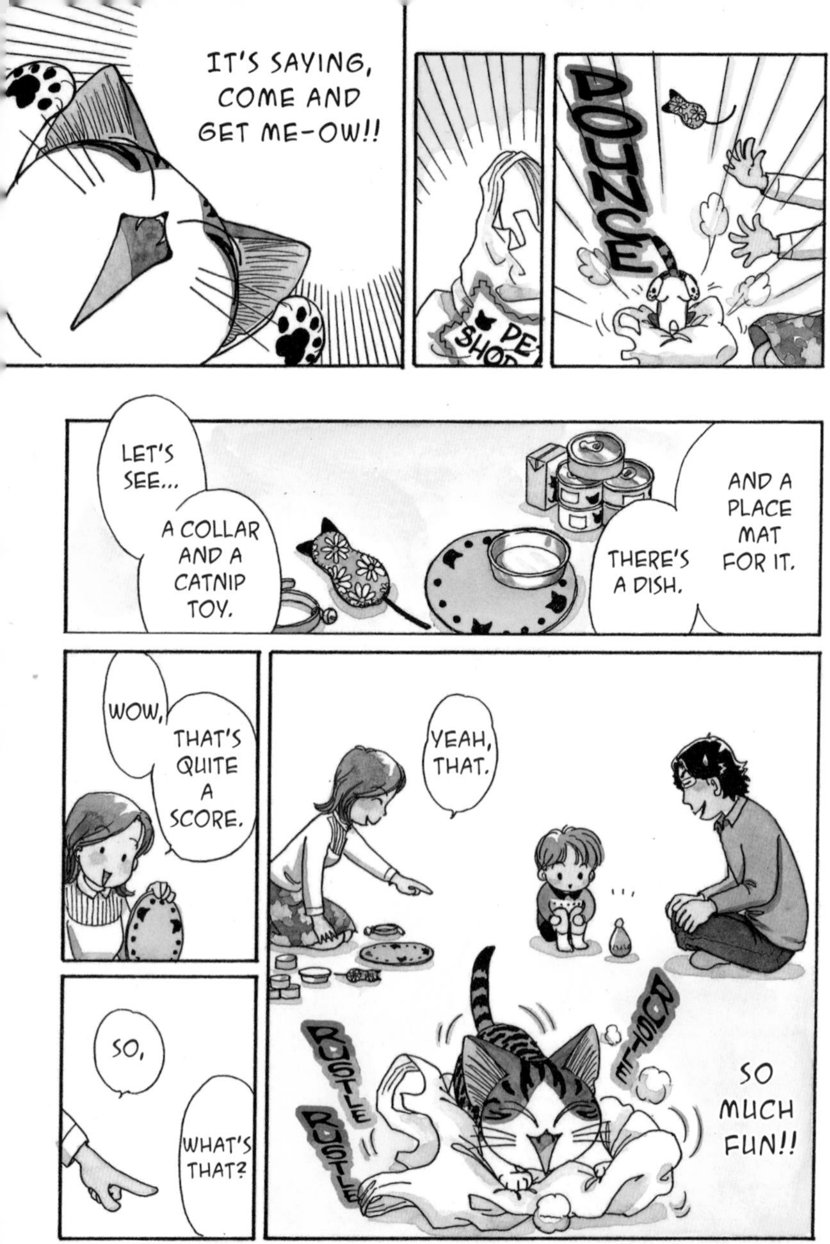

IT'S SAYING, COME AND GET ME-OW!!
PE SHOP
POUNCE
LET'S SEE...
A COLLAR AND A CATNIP TOY.
THERE'S A DISH.
AND A PLACE MAT FOR IT.
WOW,
THAT'S QUITE A SCORE.
SO,
WHAT'S THAT?
YEAH, THAT.
RUSTLE
RUSTLE
CRINKLE
SO MUCH FUN!!

the end

homemade 12: a cat is lost... again

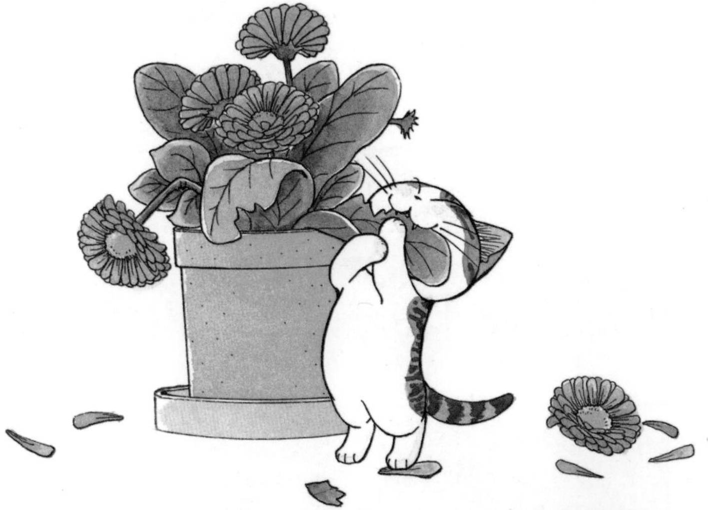

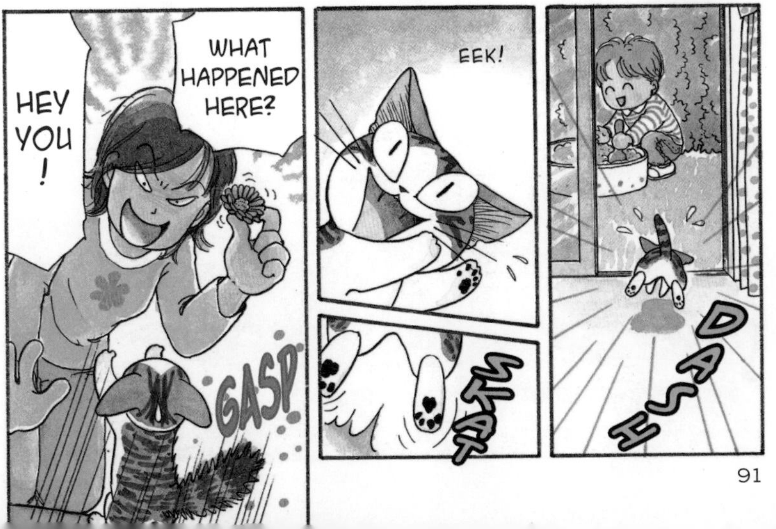
HEY YOU!
WHAT HAPPENED HERE?
GASP
EEK!
SKAT
DASH

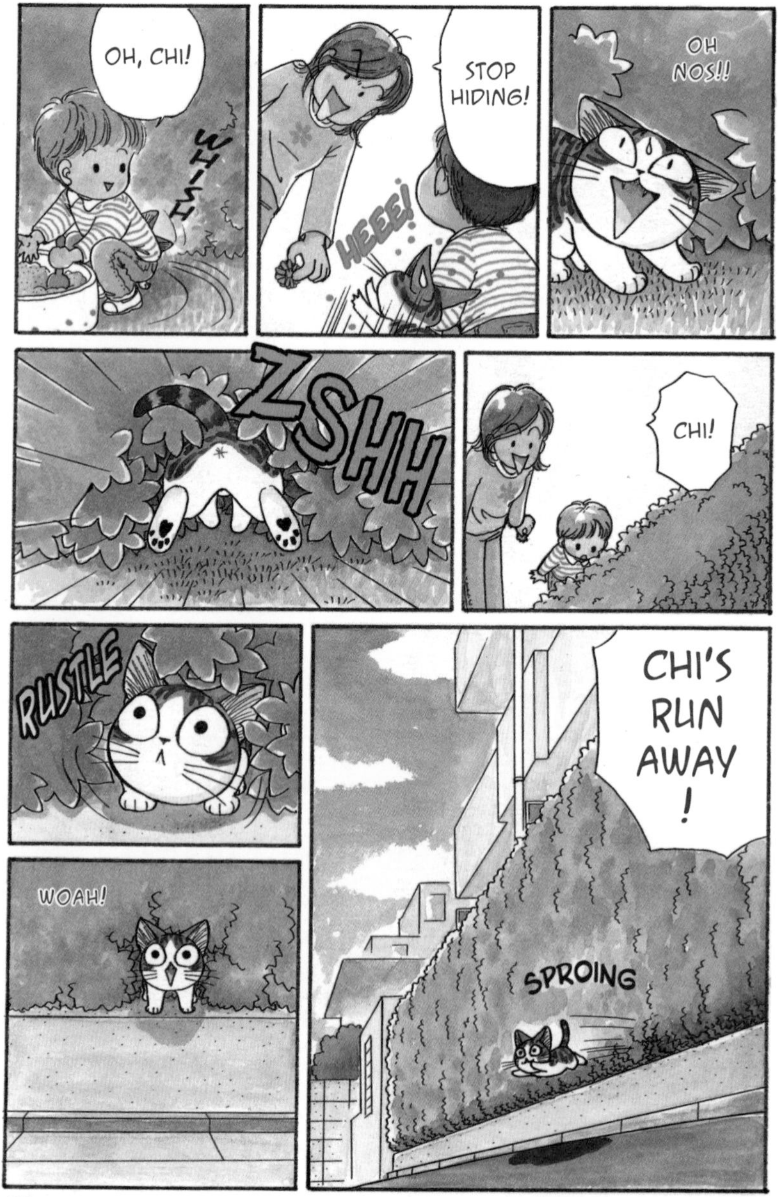
OH, CHI!
WHISH
STOP HIDING!
HEEE!
OH NOS!!
ZSHH
CHI!
RUSTLE
CHI'S RUN AWAY!
WOAH!
SPROING

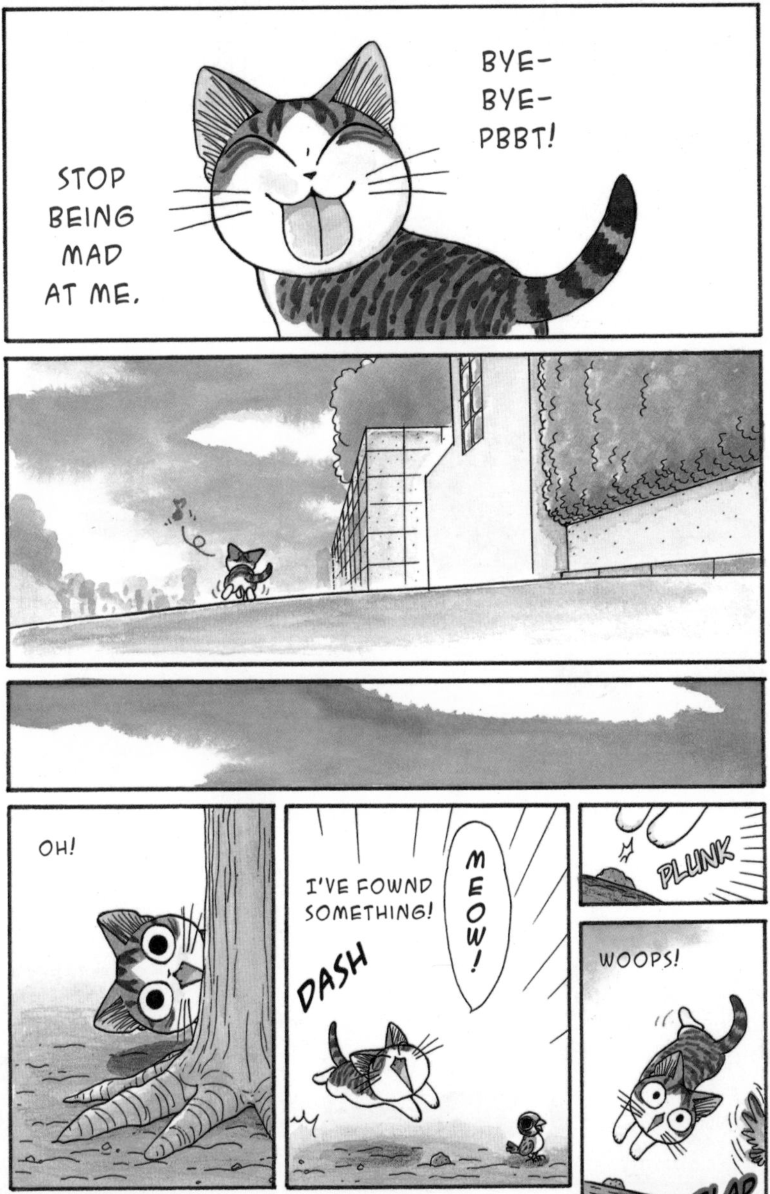
STOP BEING MAD AT ME.
BYE-BYE-PBBT!
OH!
I'VE FOWND SOMETHING!
MEOW!
DASH
PLUNK
WOOPS!
FLAP

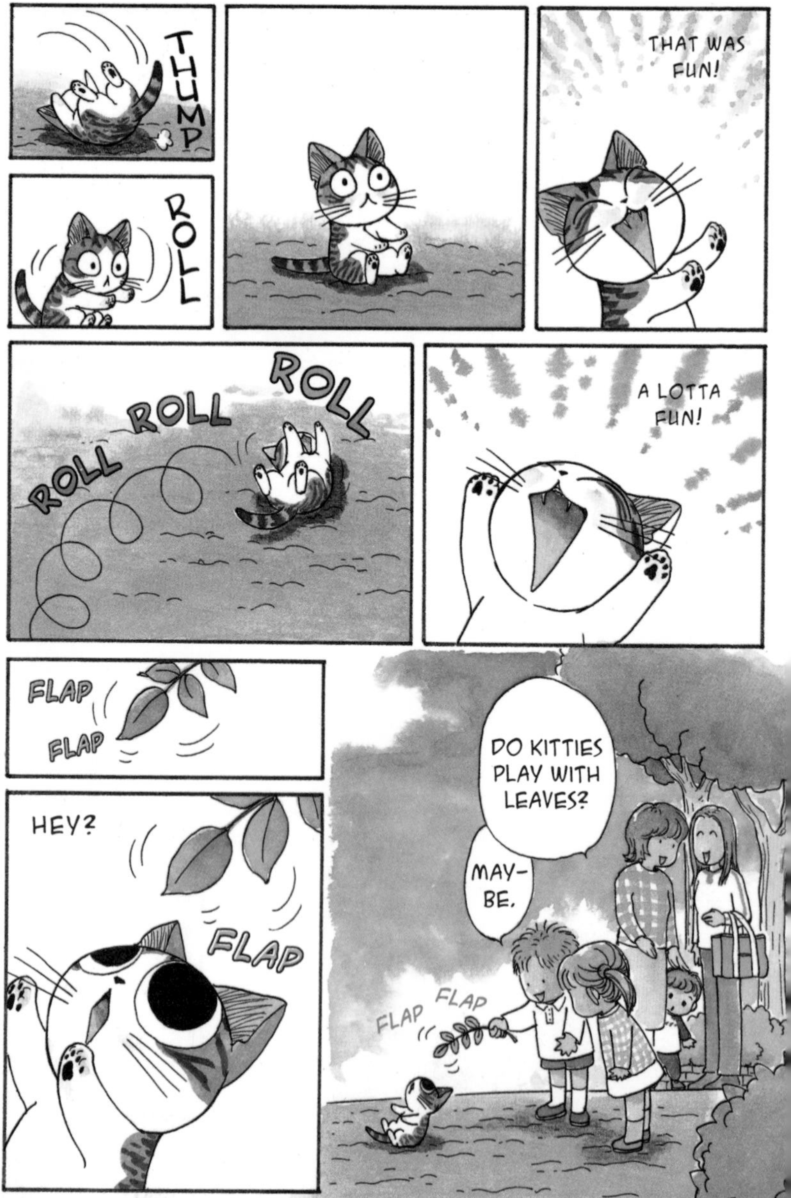
THUMP
ROLL
THAT WAS FUN!
ROLL
ROLL
ROLL
A LOTTA FUN!
FLAP
FLAP
HEY?
FLAP
DO KITTIES PLAY WITH LEAVES?
MAY-BE.
FLAP
FLAP

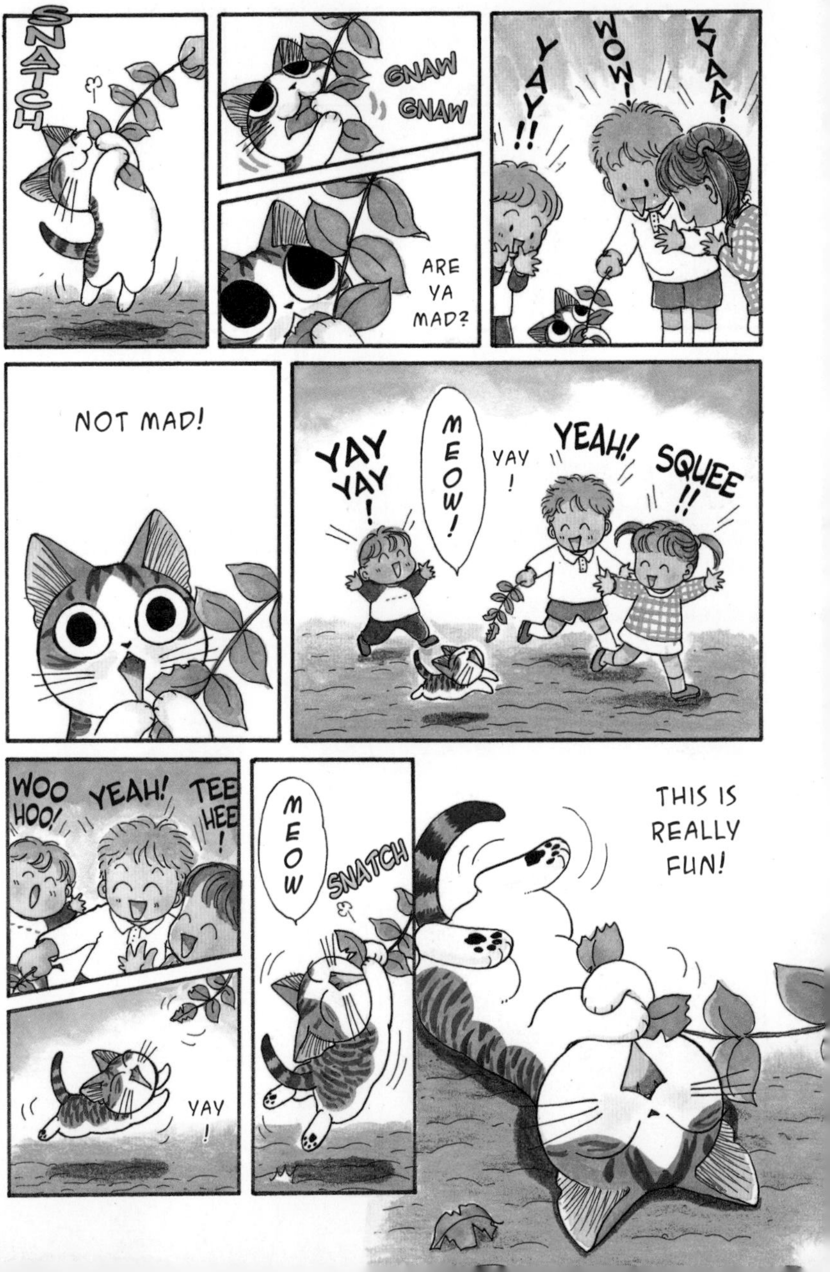
SNATCH
GNAW GNAW
ARE YA MAD?
YAY!!
WOW!
KYAA!
NOT MAD!
YAY YAY!
MEOW!
YAY!
YEAH!
SQUEE!!
WOO HOO!
YEAH!
TEE HEE!
YAY!
MEOW
SNATCH
THIS IS REALLY FUN!

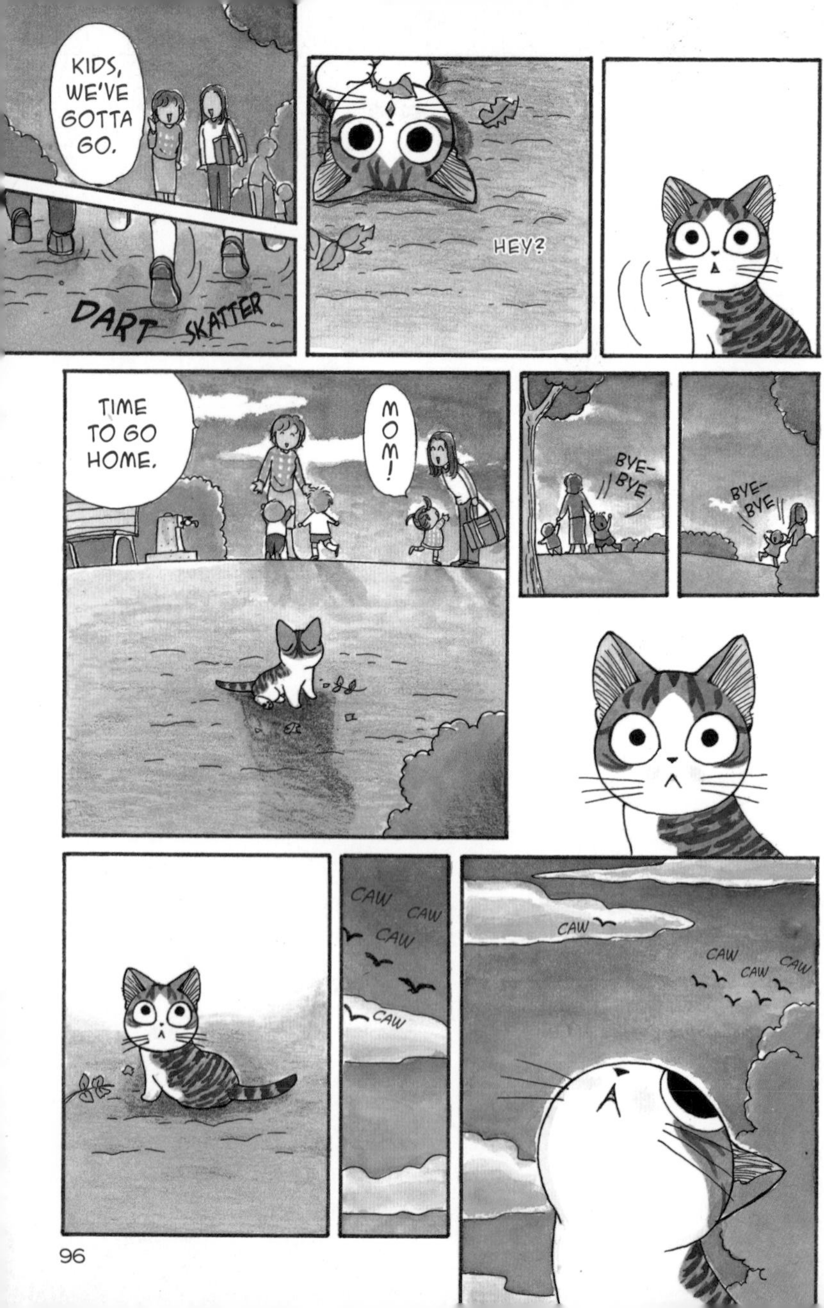
KIDS, WE'VE GOTTA GO.
DART
SKATTER
HEY?
TIME TO GO HOME.
MOM!
BYE-BYE
BYE-BYE
CAW
CAW
CAW
CAW
CAW
CAW
CAW
CAW

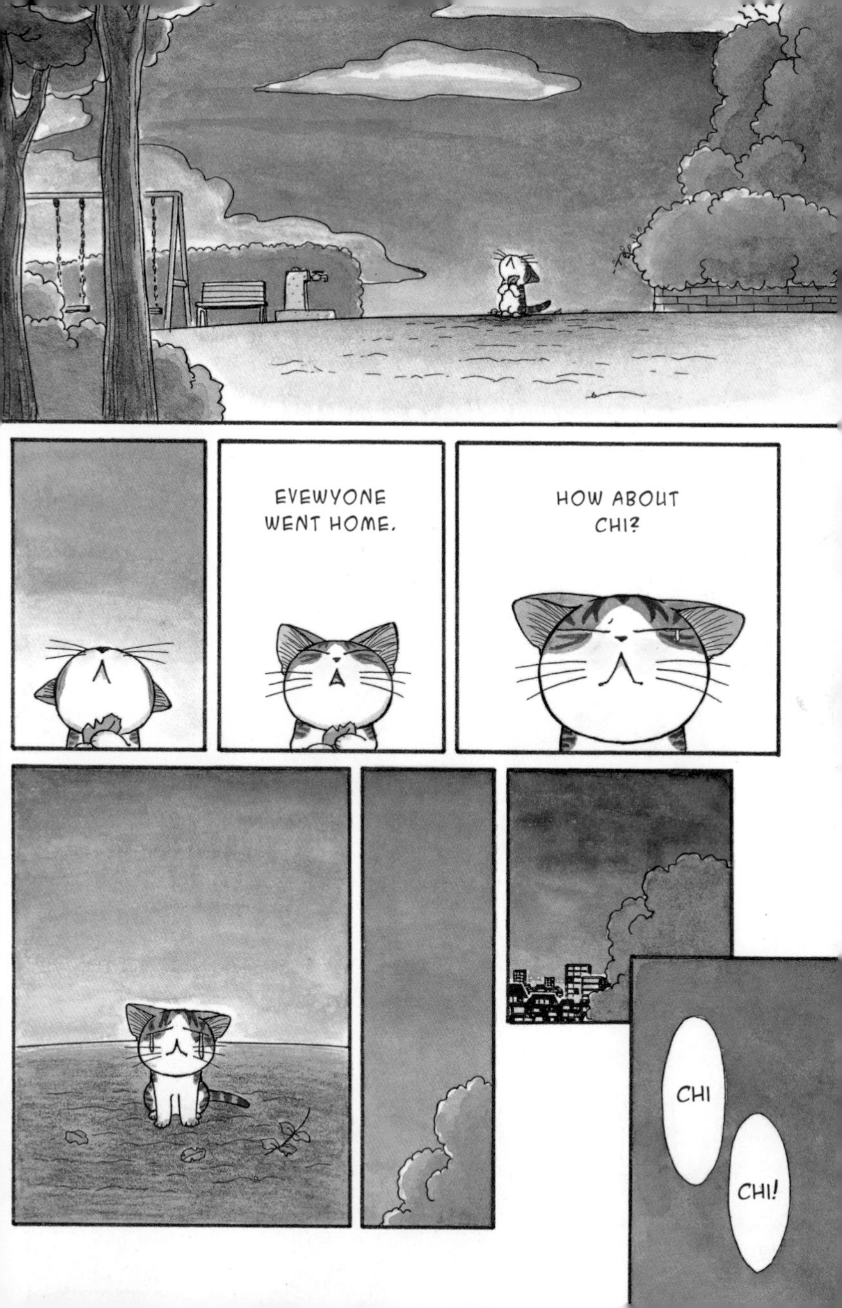
EVEWYONE WENT HOME.
HOW ABOUT CHI?
CHI
CHI!

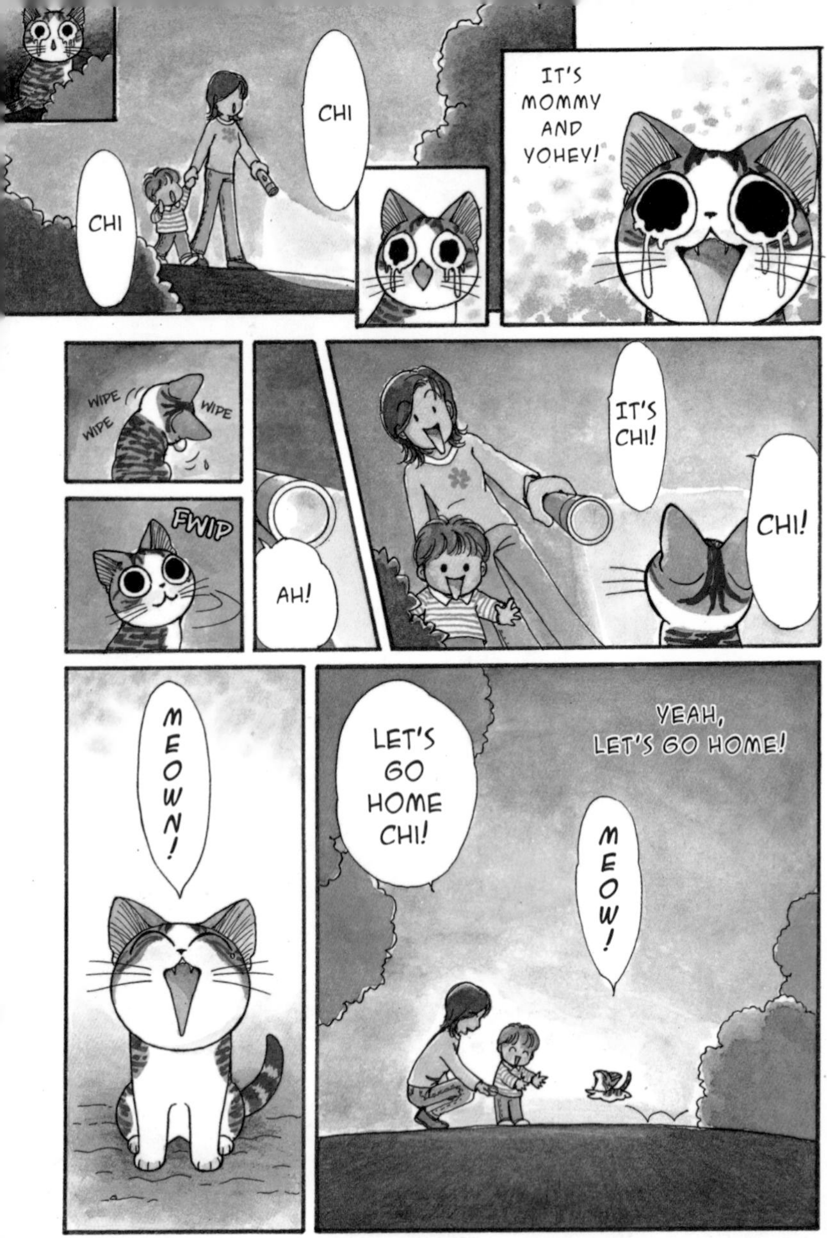
CHI
CHI
IT'S MOMMY AND YOHEY!
WIPE
WIPE
WIPE
FWIP
AH!
IT'S CHI!
CHI!
MEOWN!
LET'S GO HOME CHI!
YEAH, LET'S GO HOME!
MEOW!

the end

homemade 13: a cat fights!

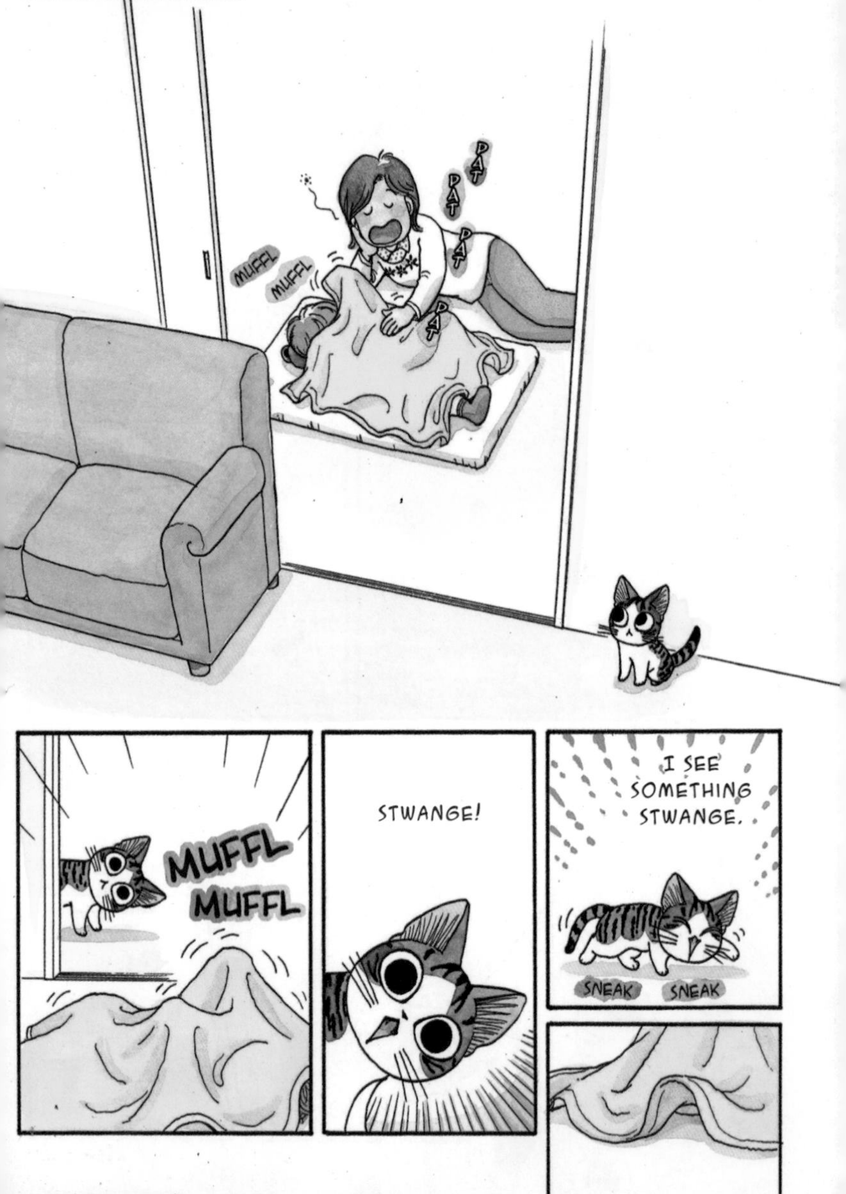
PAT
PAT
PAT
PAT
MUFFL
MUFFL
MUFFL
MUFFL
STWANGE!
I SEE SOMETHING STWANGE.
SNEAK
SNEAK

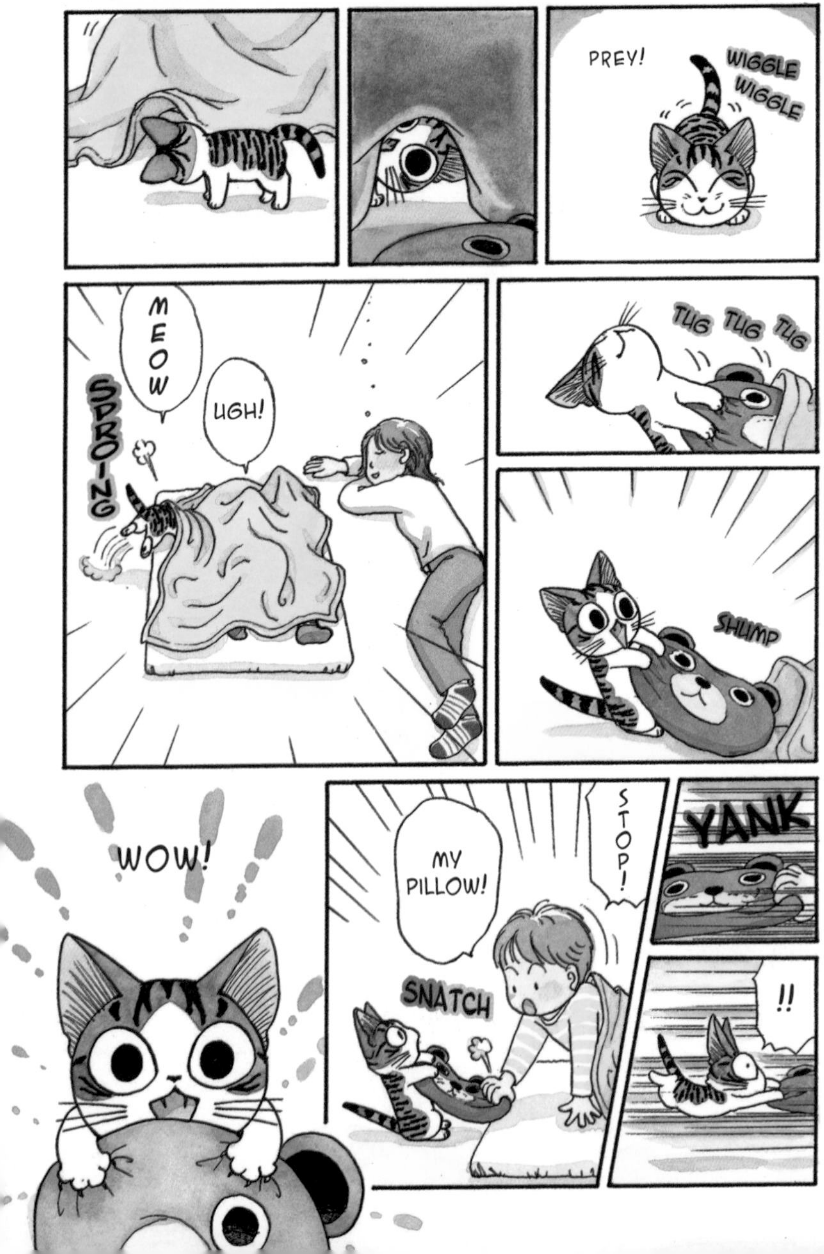
PREY!
WIGGLE WIGGLE
MEOW
UGH!
SPROING
TUG TUG TUG
SHUMP
WOW!
MY PILLOW!
STOP!
SNATCH
YANK
!!

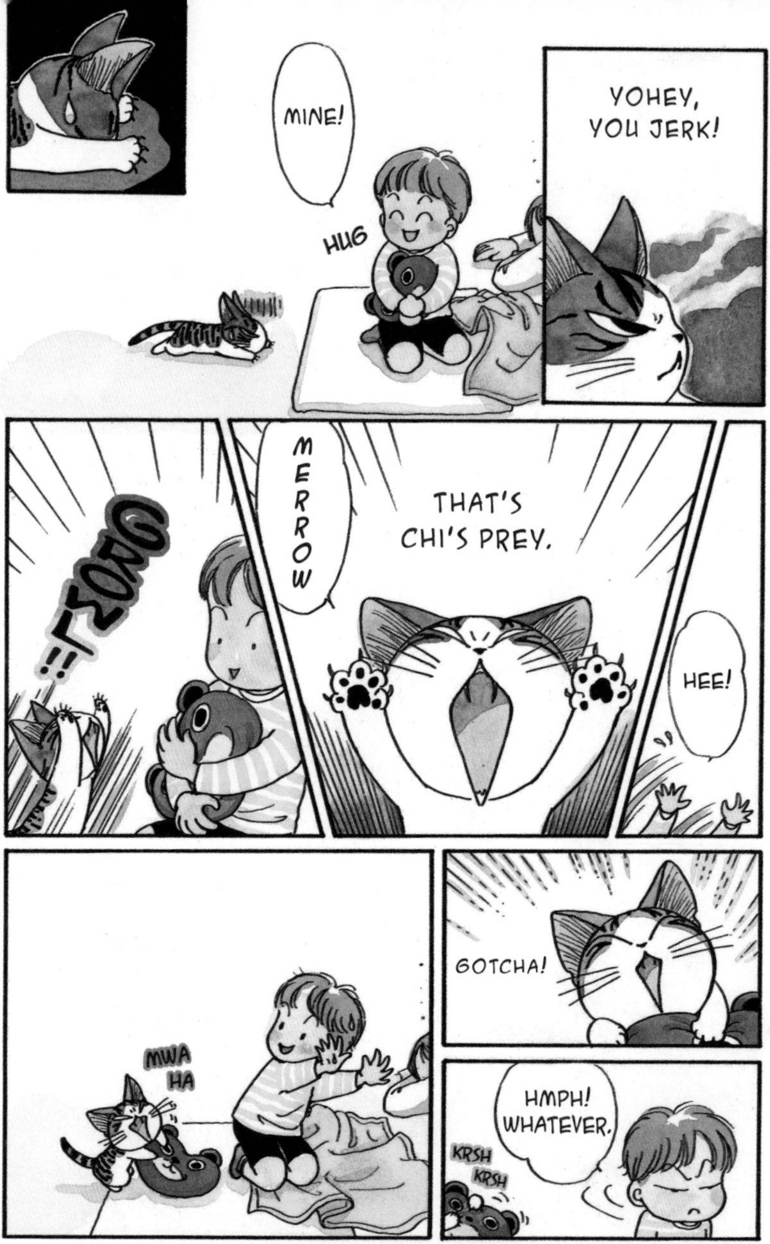
MINE!
HUG
YOHEY, YOU JERK!
GROWL!!
MERROW
THAT'S CHI'S PREY.
HEE!
MWA HA
GOTCHA!
HMPH! WHATEVER.
KRSH KRSH

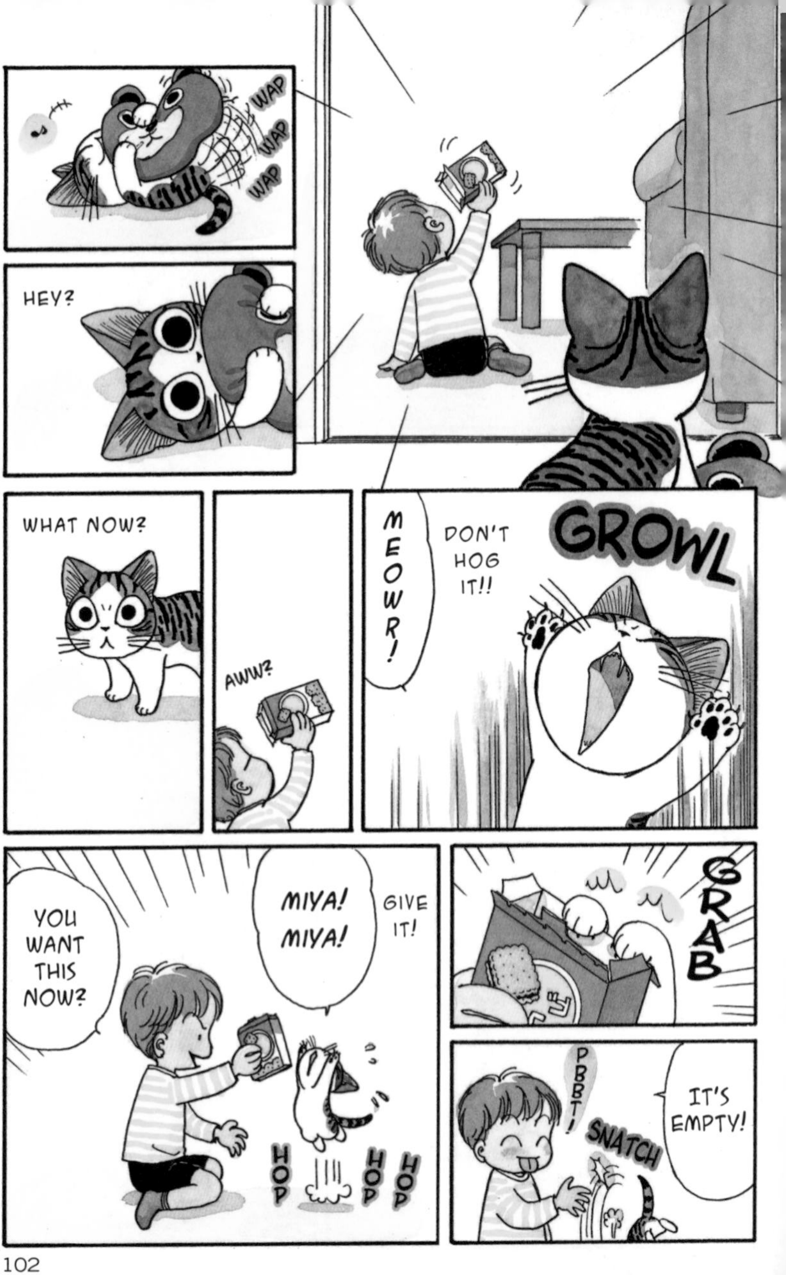
WAP
WAP
WAP
HEY?
WHAT NOW?
AWW?
MEOWR!
DON'T HOG IT!!
GROWL
YOU WANT THIS NOW?
MIYA! MIYA!
GIVE IT!
HOP
HOP
HOP
GRAB
PBBT!
SNATCH
IT'S EMPTY!

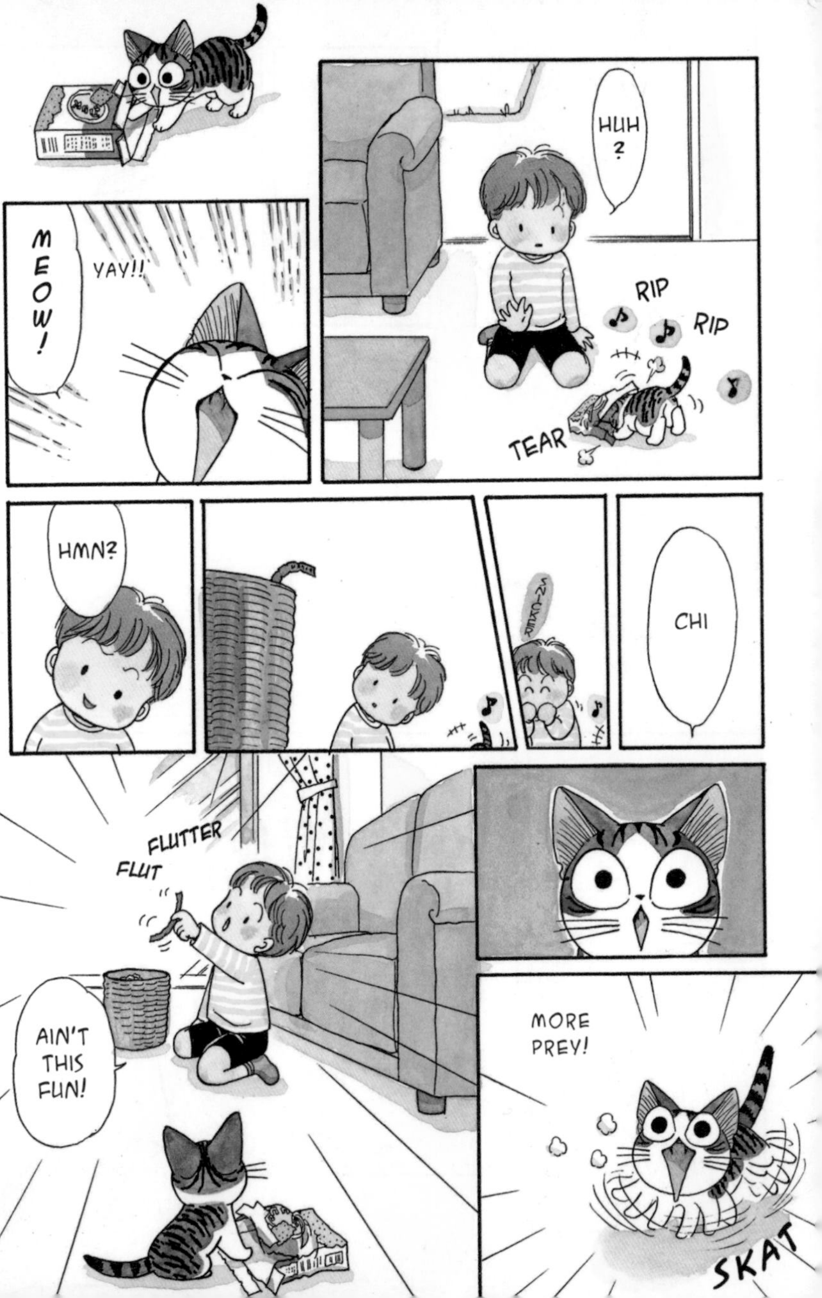
MEOW!
YAY!!
HUH?
RIP
RIP
TEAR
HMN?
SNICKER
CHI
FLUTTER
FLUT
AIN'T THIS FUN!
MORE PREY!
SKAT

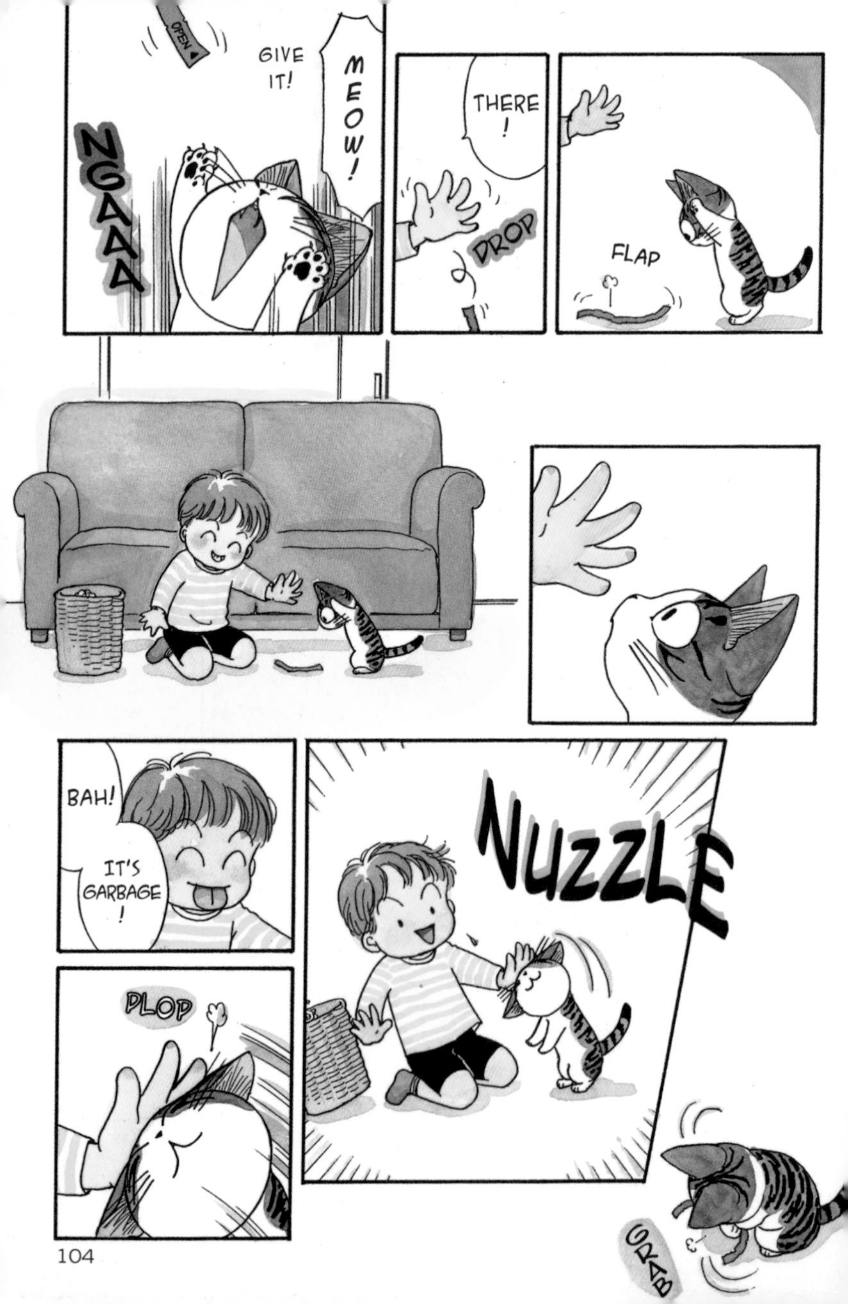
OPEN
GIVE IT!
MEOW!
NGAAA
THERE!
DROP
FLAP
BAH!
IT'S GARBAGE!
PLOP
NUZZLE
GRAB

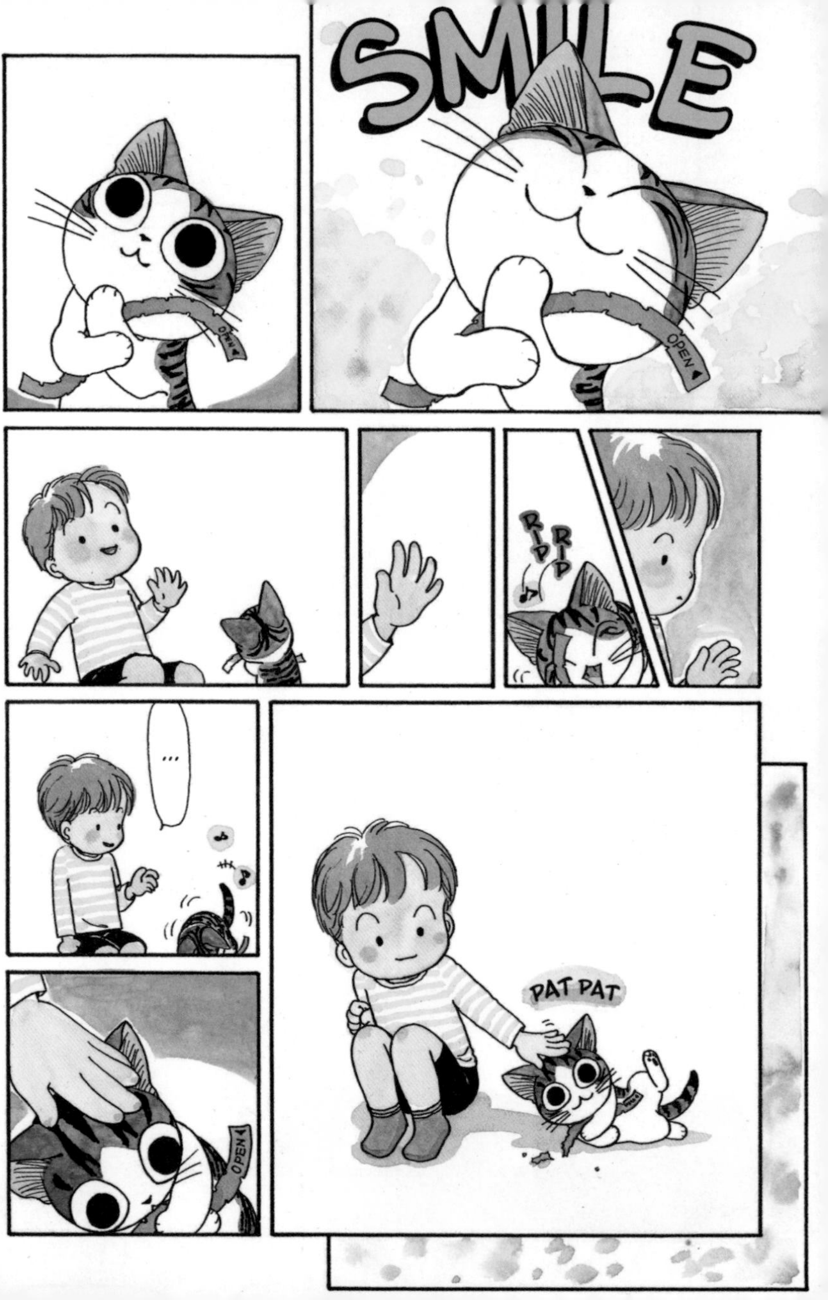
OPEN
SMILE
OPEN
RIP RIP
...
OPEN
PAT PAT

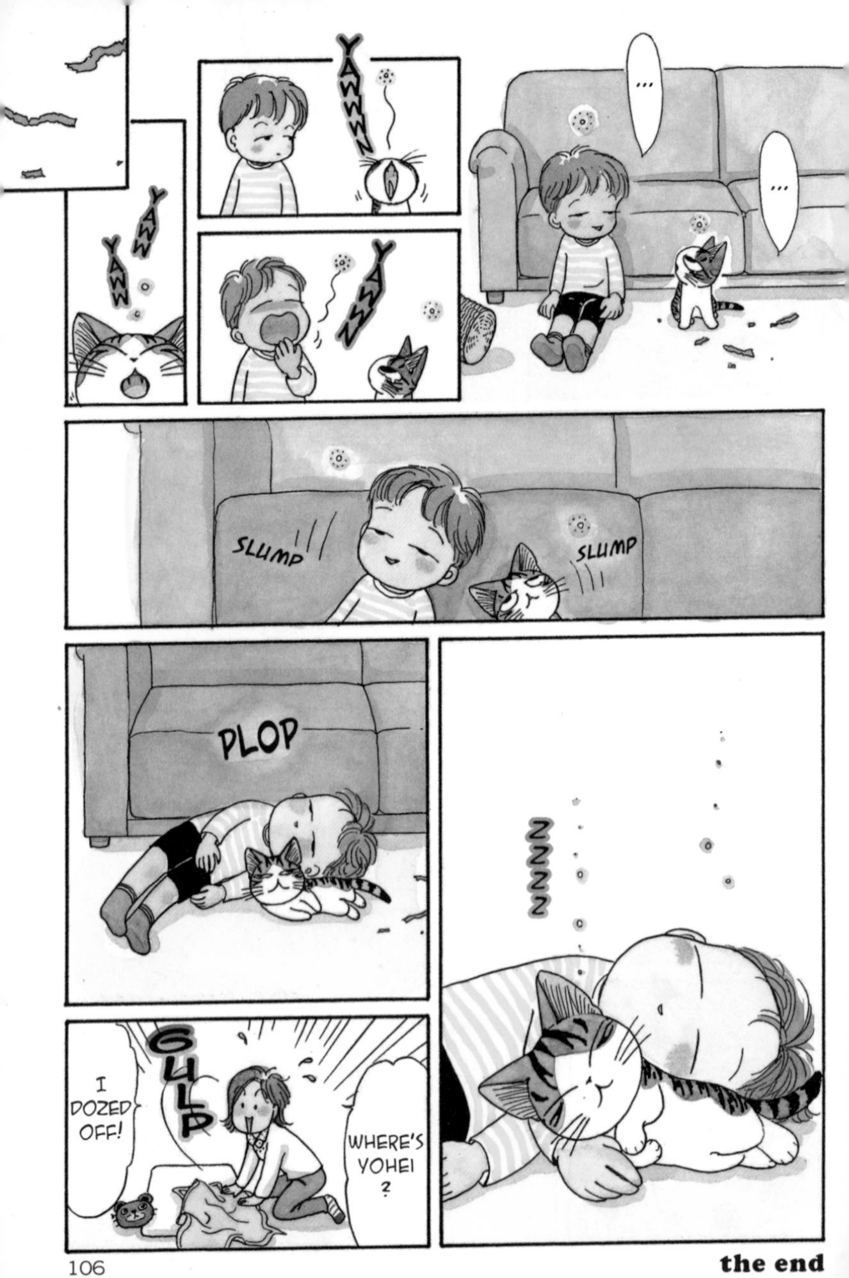
YAWN
YAWN
YAWWWN
YAWWN
...
...
SLUMP
SLUMP
PLOP
GULP
I DOZED OFF!
WHERE'S YOHEI?
ZZZZ

the end

homemade 14: a cat goes to the vet (part 1)

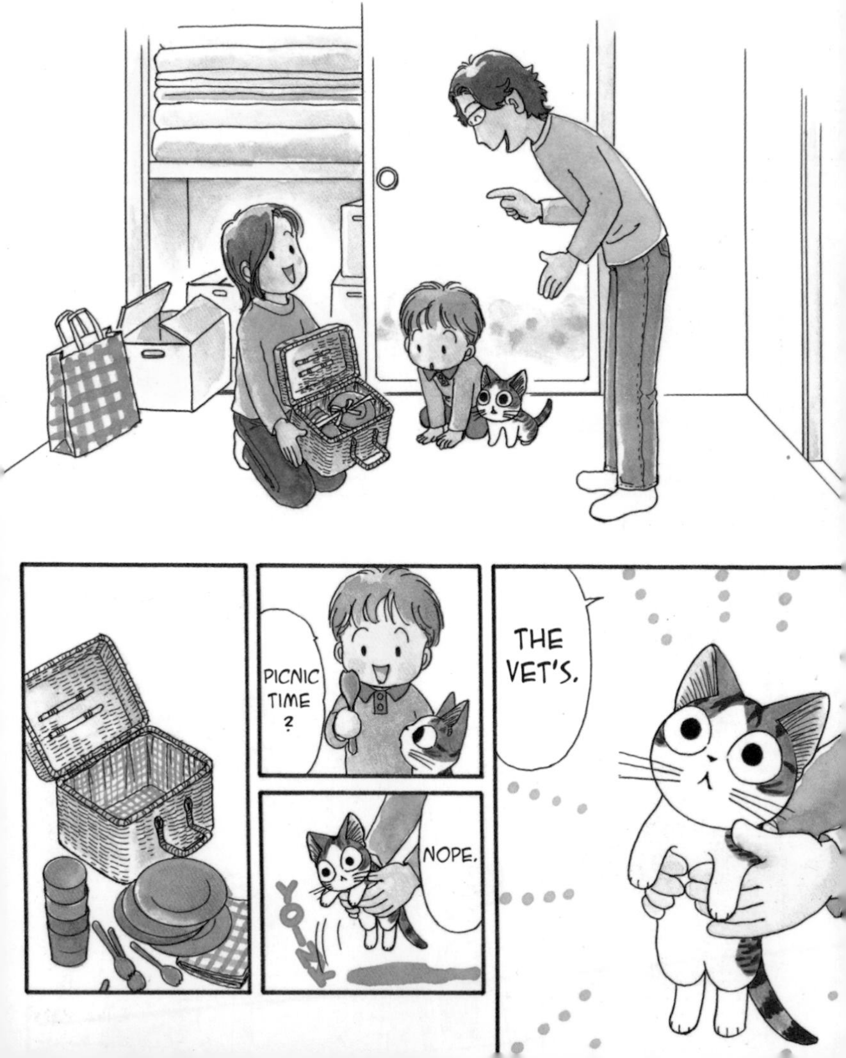
PICNIC TIME?
YOINK
NOPE.
THE VET'S.

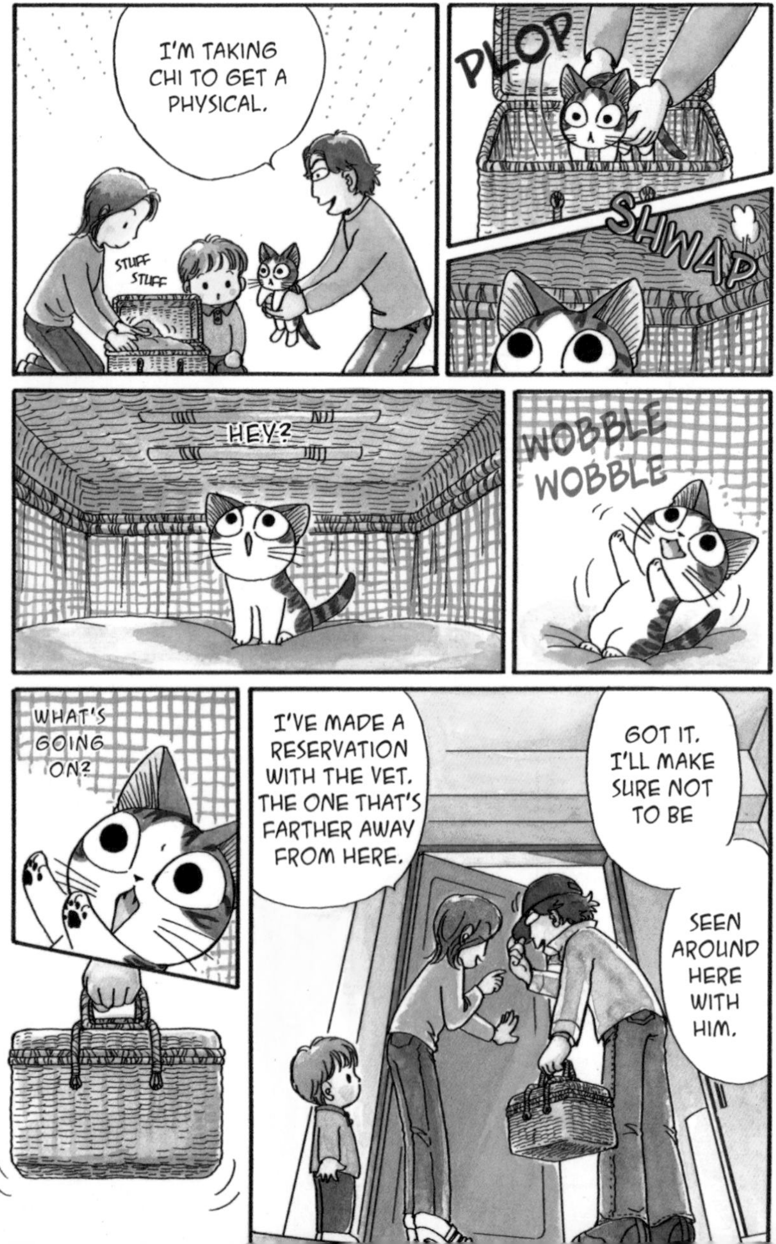
I'M TAKING CHI TO GET A PHYSICAL.
STUFF STUFF
PLOP
SHWAP
HEY?
WOBBLE WOBBLE
WHAT'S GOING ON?
I'VE MADE A RESERVATION WITH THE VET. THE ONE THAT'S FARTHER AWAY FROM HERE.
GOT IT. I'LL MAKE SURE NOT TO BE
SEEN AROUND HERE WITH HIM.

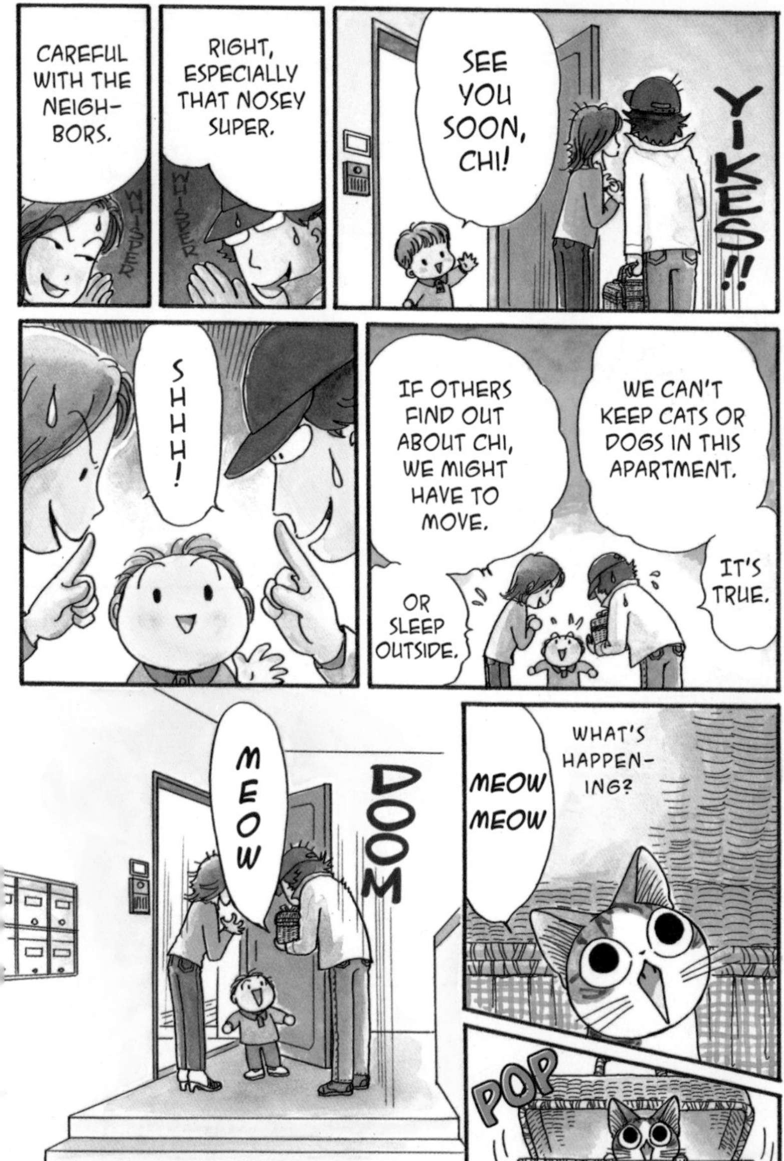
CAREFUL WITH THE NEIGH-BORS.
WHISPER
RIGHT, ESPECIALLY THAT NOSEY SUPER.
WHISPER
SEE YOU SOON, CHI!
YIKES!!
SHHH!
IF OTHERS FIND OUT ABOUT CHI, WE MIGHT HAVE TO MOVE.
WE CAN'T KEEP CATS OR DOGS IN THIS APARTMENT.
OR SLEEP OUTSIDE.
IT'S TRUE.
MEOW
DOOM
MEOW MEOW
WHAT'S HAPPEN-ING?
POP

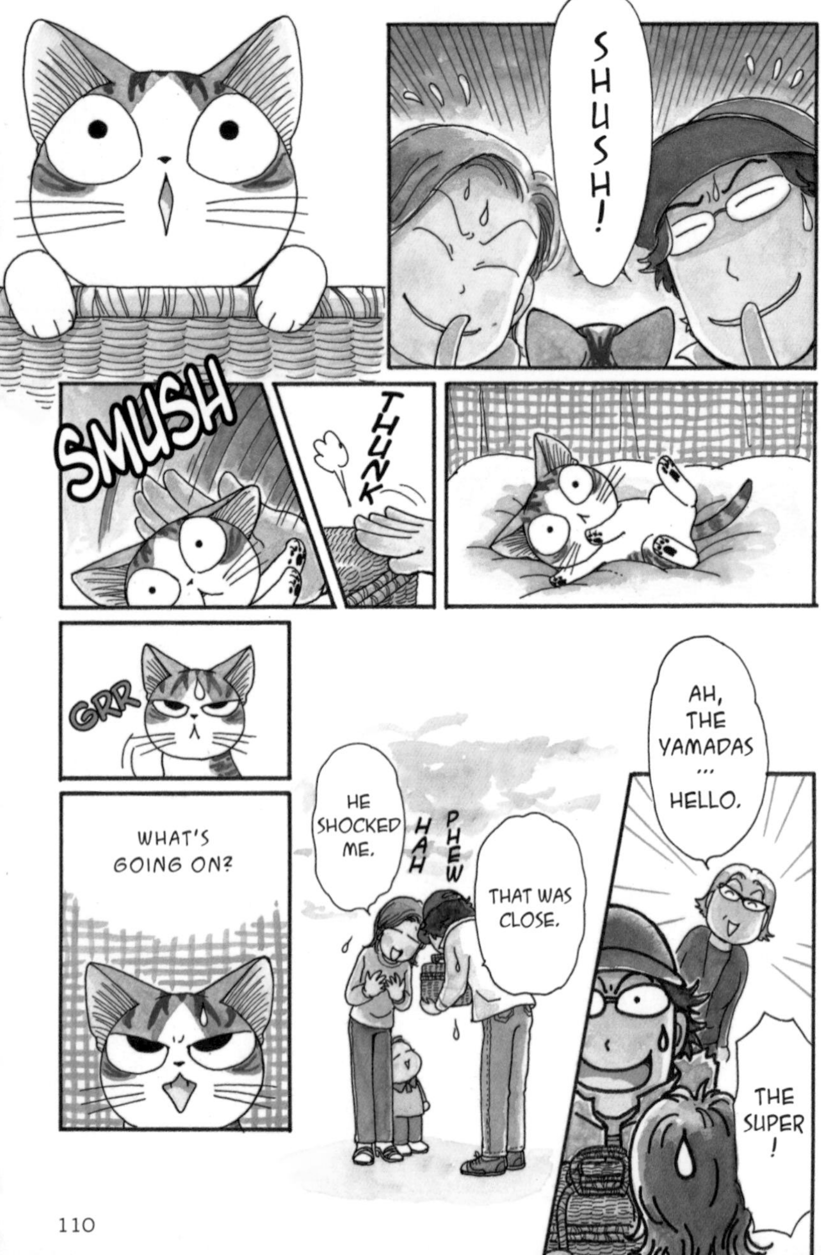
SHUSH!
SMUSH
THUNK
GRR
WHAT'S GOING ON?
HE SHOCKED ME.
HAH
PHEW
THAT WAS CLOSE.
AH, THE YAMADAS... HELLO.
THE SUPER!

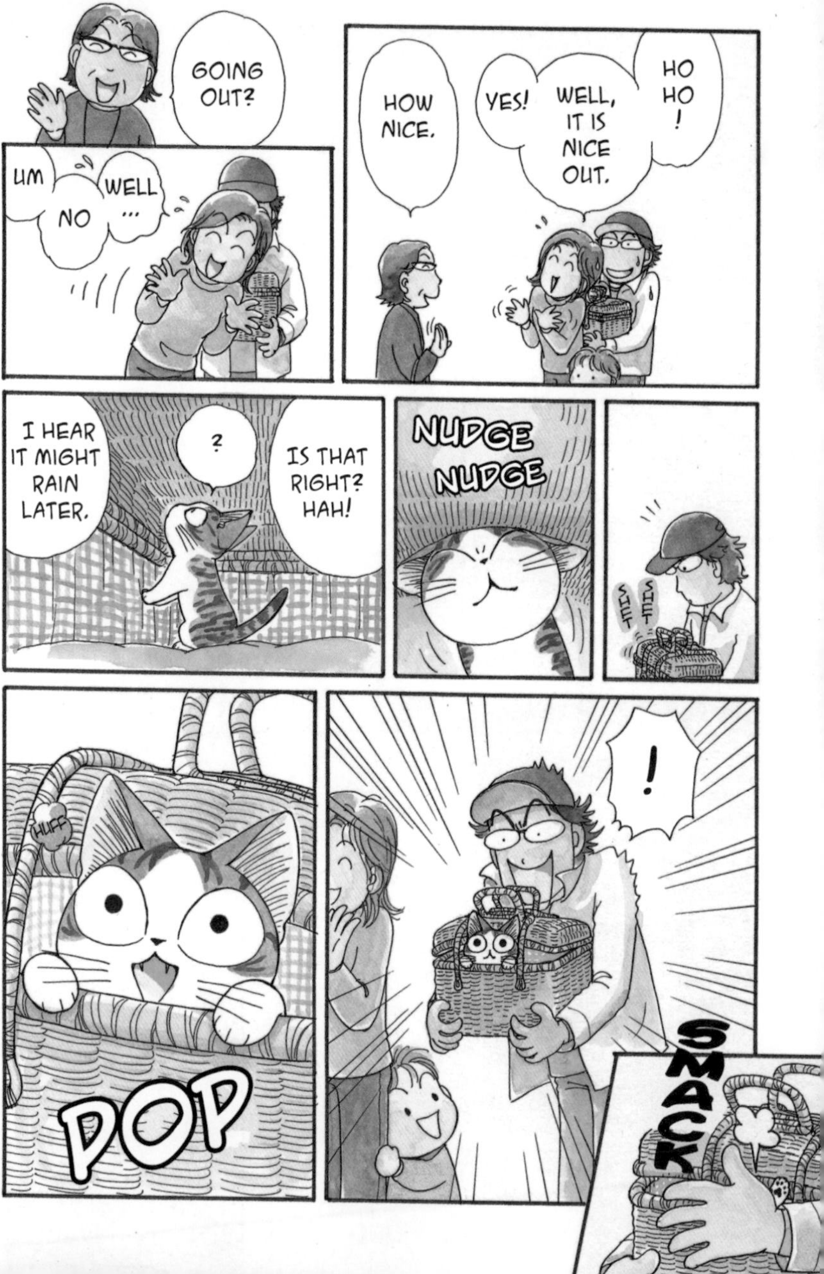
GOING OUT?
UM
NO
WELL ...
HOW NICE.
YES!
WELL, IT IS NICE OUT.
HO HO !
I HEAR IT MIGHT RAIN LATER.
?
IS THAT RIGHT? HAH!
NUDGE NUDGE
SHFT SHFT
HUFF
POP
!
SMACK

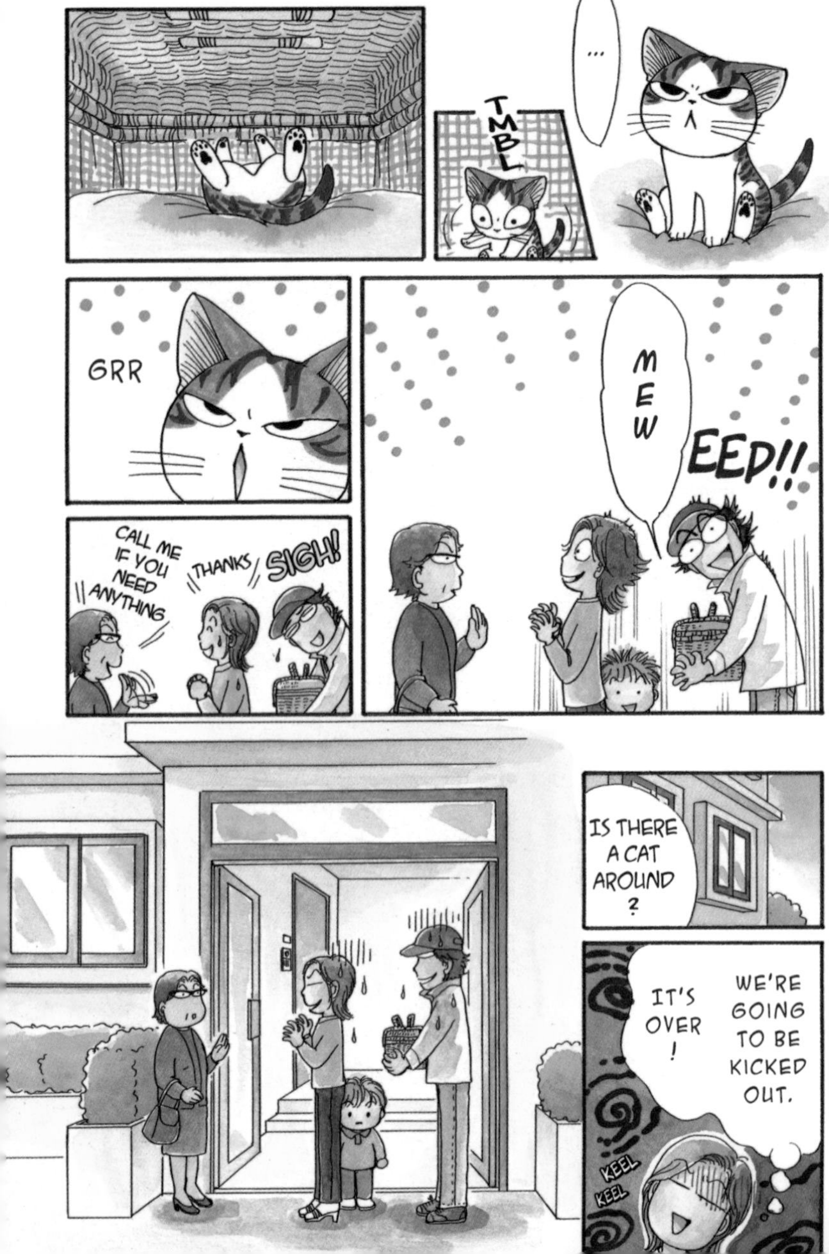

TMBL
...
GRR
CALL ME IF YOU NEED ANYTHING
THANKS
SIGH!
MEW
EED!!
IS THERE A CAT AROUND?
IT'S OVER!
WE'RE GOING TO BE KICKED OUT.
KEEL
KEEL

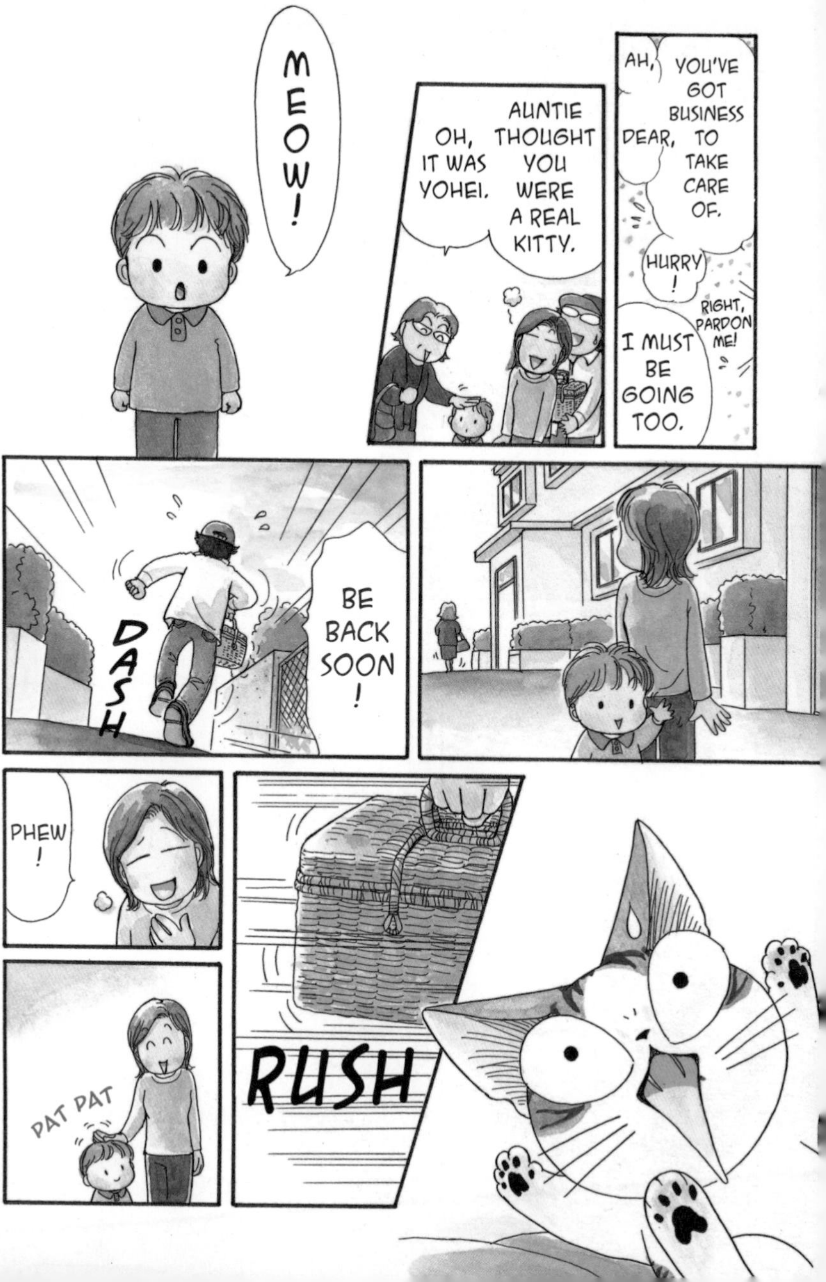
MEOW!
OH, IT WAS YOHEI.
AUNTIE THOUGHT YOU WERE A REAL KITTY.
AH, DEAR,
YOU'VE GOT BUSINESS TO TAKE CARE OF.
HURRY!
RIGHT, PARDON ME!
I MUST BE GOING TOO.
DASH
BE BACK SOON!
PHEW!
PAT PAT
RUSH

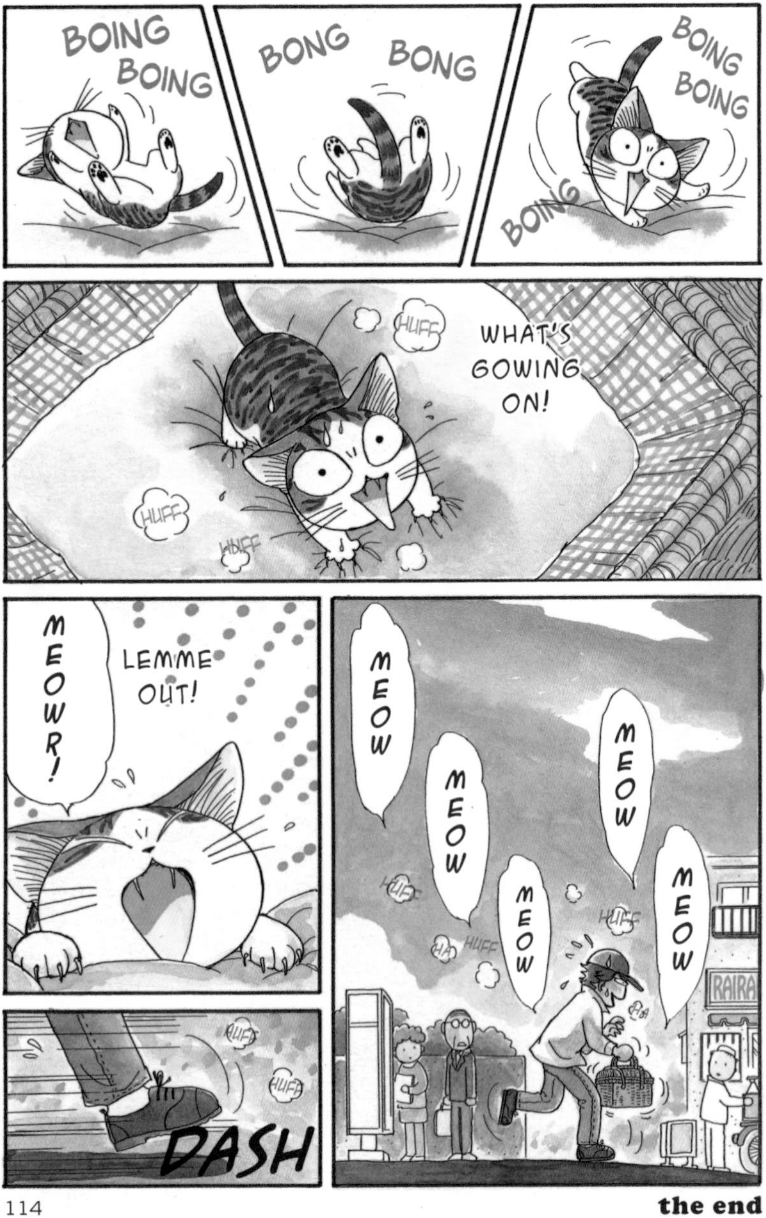
BOING
BOING
BONG
BONG
BOING
BOING
BOING
HUFF
WHAT'S GOWING ON!
HUFF
HUFF
LEMME OUT!
MEOWR!
HUFF
HUFF
DASH
MEOW
MEOW
MEOW
MEOW
MEOW
HUFF
HUFF
HA
HUFF
HA
RAIRA

the end

homemade 15: a cat goes to the vet (part 2)

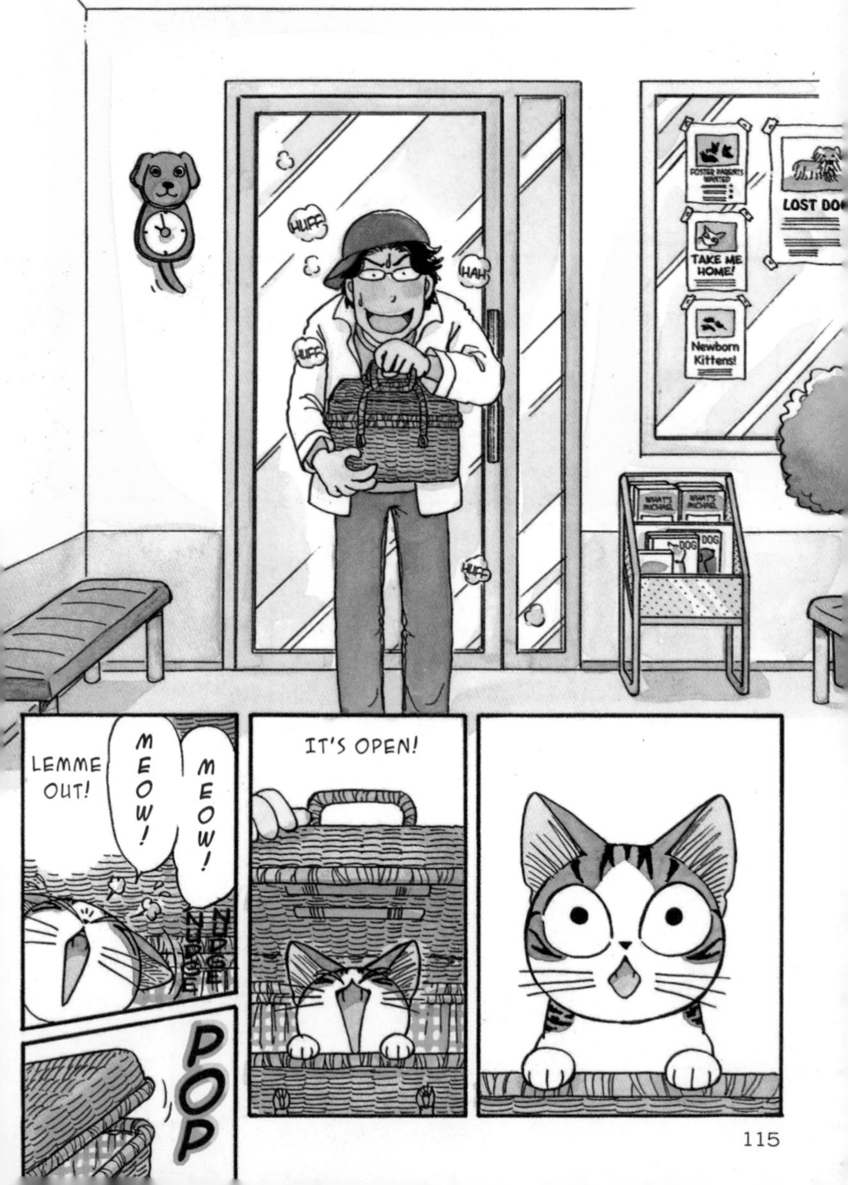
HUFF
HAH
HUFF
HUFF
FOSTER PARENTS WANTED
LOST DO
TAKE ME HOME!
Newborn Kittens!
WHAT'S MICHAEL
WHAT'S MICHAEL
DOG
DOG
LEMME OUT!
MEOW!
MEOW!
NUDGE
NUDGE
POP
IT'S OPEN!

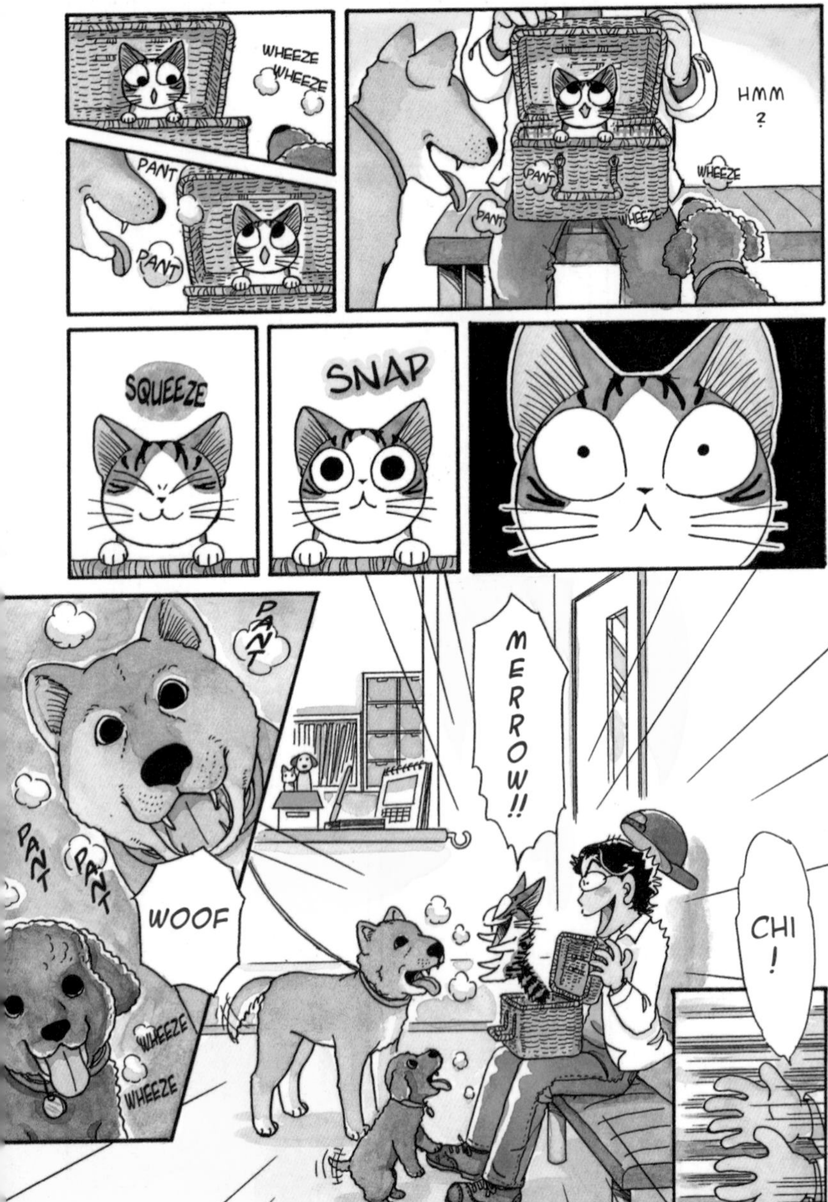

WHEEZE
WHEEZE
PANT
PANT
HMM ?
PANT
PANT
WHEEZE
WHEEZE
SQUEEZE
SNAP
PANT
PANT
PANT
WOOF
WHEEZE
WHEEZE
MERROW!!
CHI!

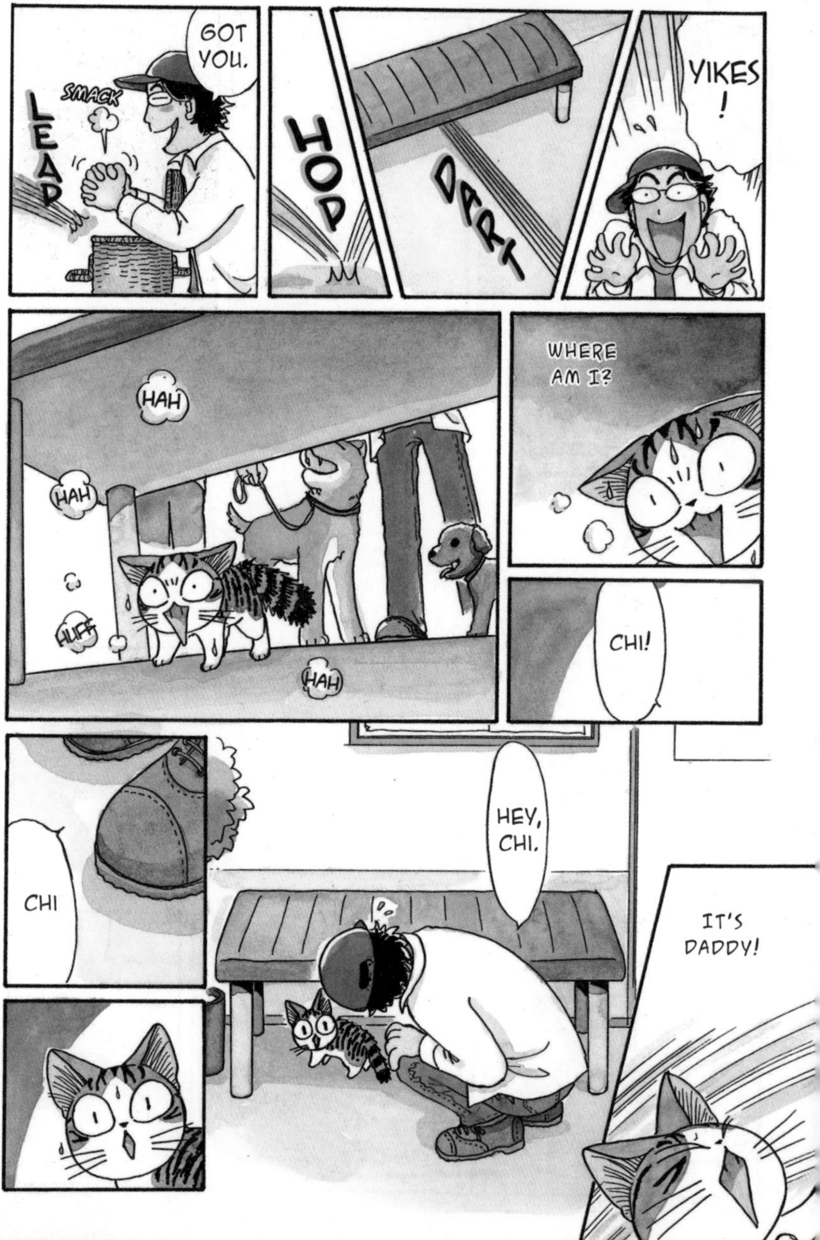
LEAP
SMACK
GOT YOU.
HOP
DART
YIKES!
HAH
HAH
HUFF
HAH
WHERE AM I?
CHI!
CHI
HEY, CHI.
IT'S DADDY!

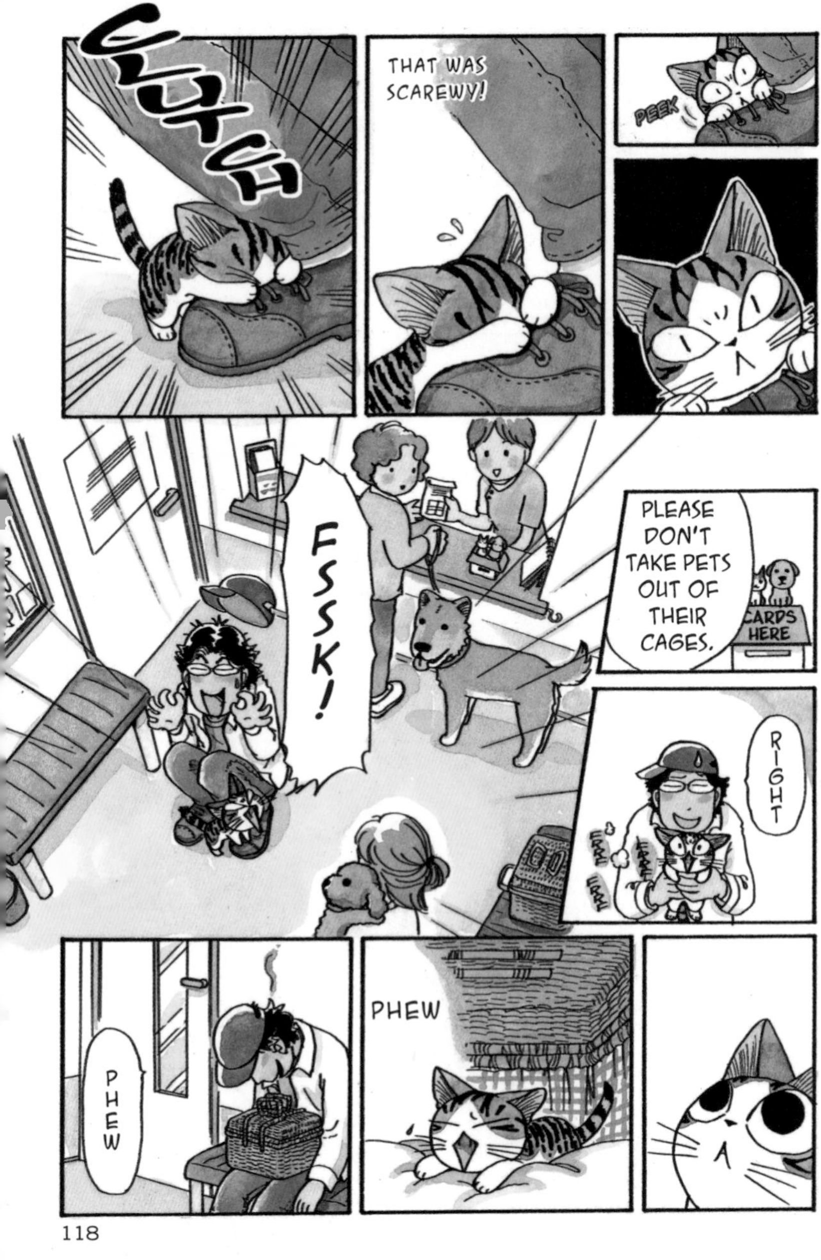
CLUTCH
THAT WAS SCAREWY!
PEEK
FSSK!
PLEASE DON'T TAKE PETS OUT OF THEIR CAGES.
CARDS HERE
RIGHT
ERRK
ERRK
ERRK
PHEW PHEW
PHEW

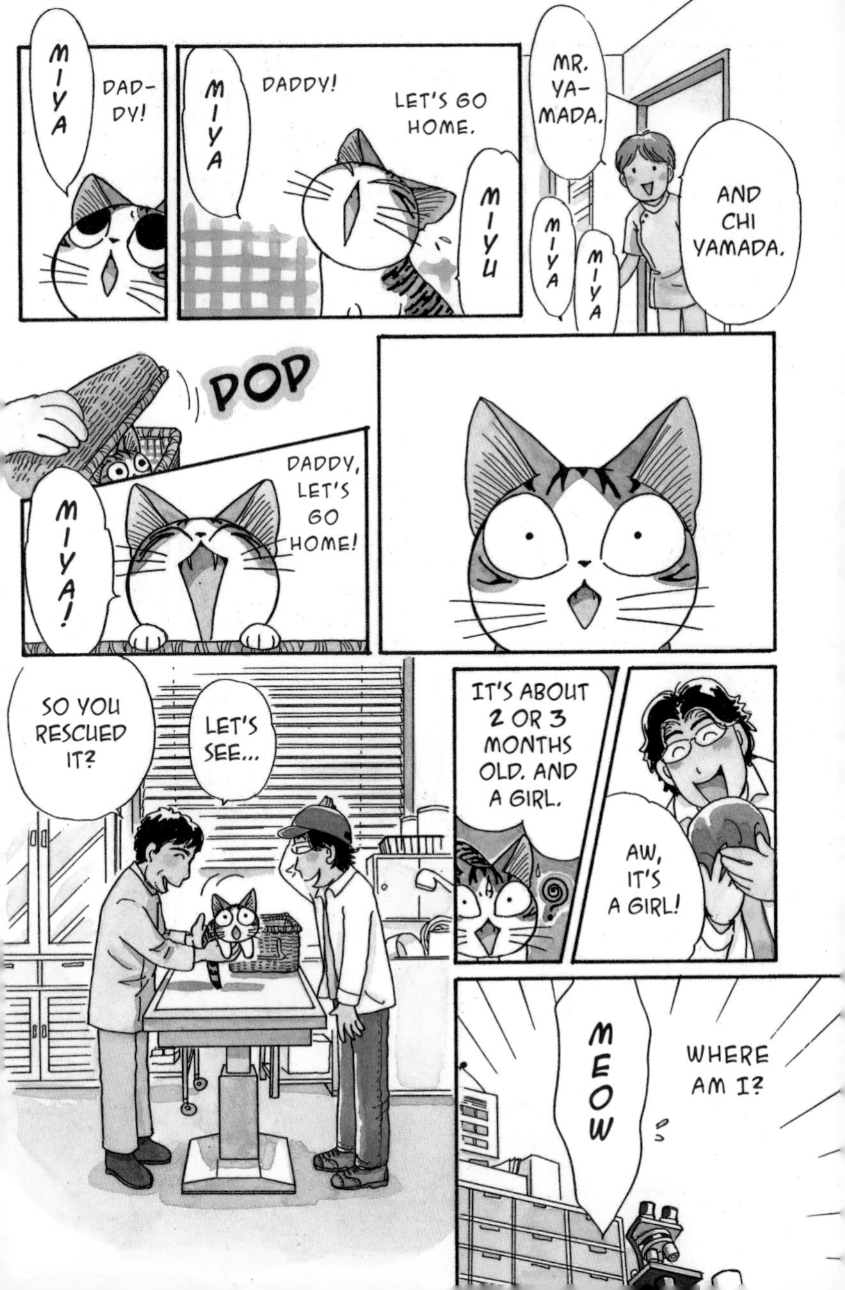
MIYA
DAD-DY!
MIYA
DADDY!
LET'S GO HOME.
MIYU
MR. YA-MADA.
MIYA
MIYA
AND CHI YAMADA.
POP
DADDY, LET'S GO HOME!
MIYA!
SO YOU RESCUED IT?
LET'S SEE...
IT'S ABOUT 2 OR 3 MONTHS OLD. AND A GIRL.
AW, IT'S A GIRL!
MEOW
WHERE AM I?

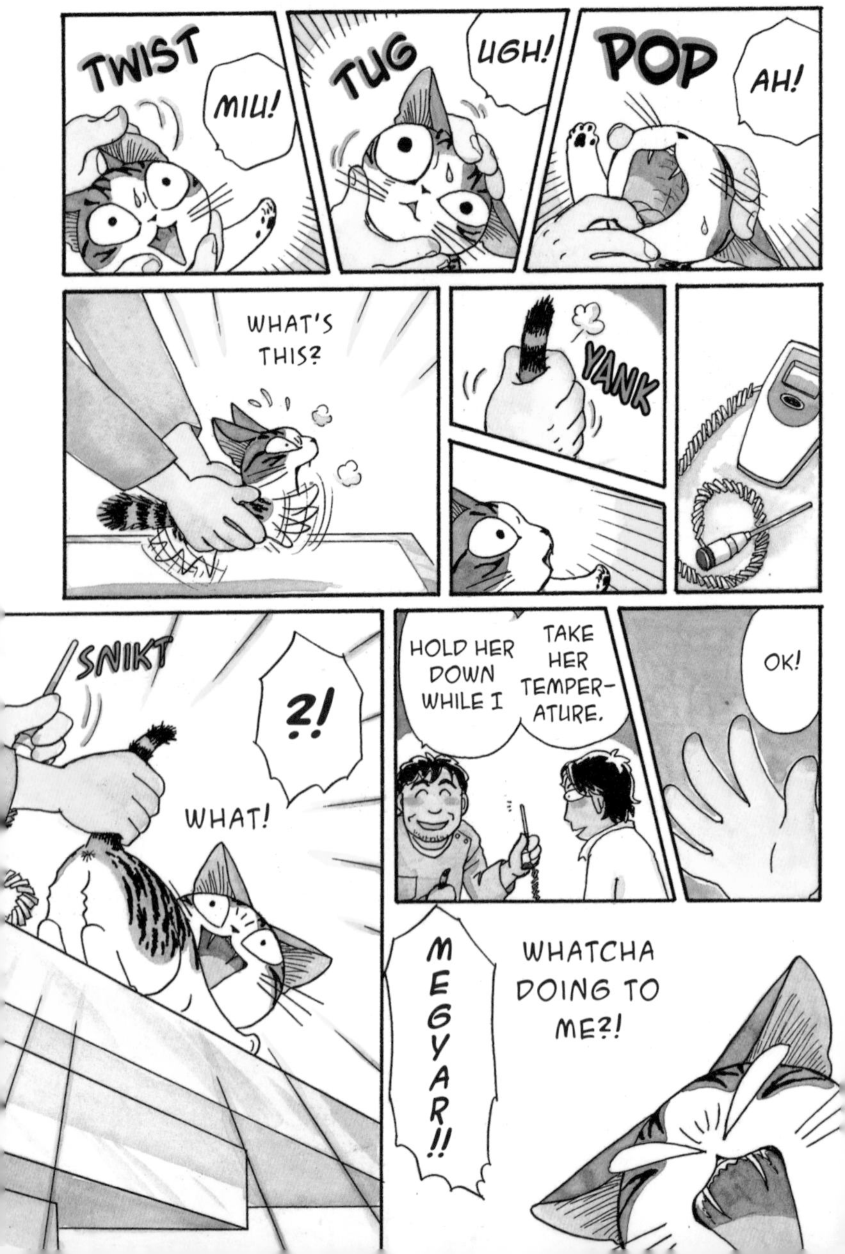
TWIST
MIU!
TUG
UGH!
POP
AH!
WHAT'S THIS?
YANK
SNIKT
?!
WHAT!
HOLD HER DOWN WHILE I
TAKE HER TEMPERATURE.
OK!
MEGYAR!!
WHATCHA DOING TO ME?!

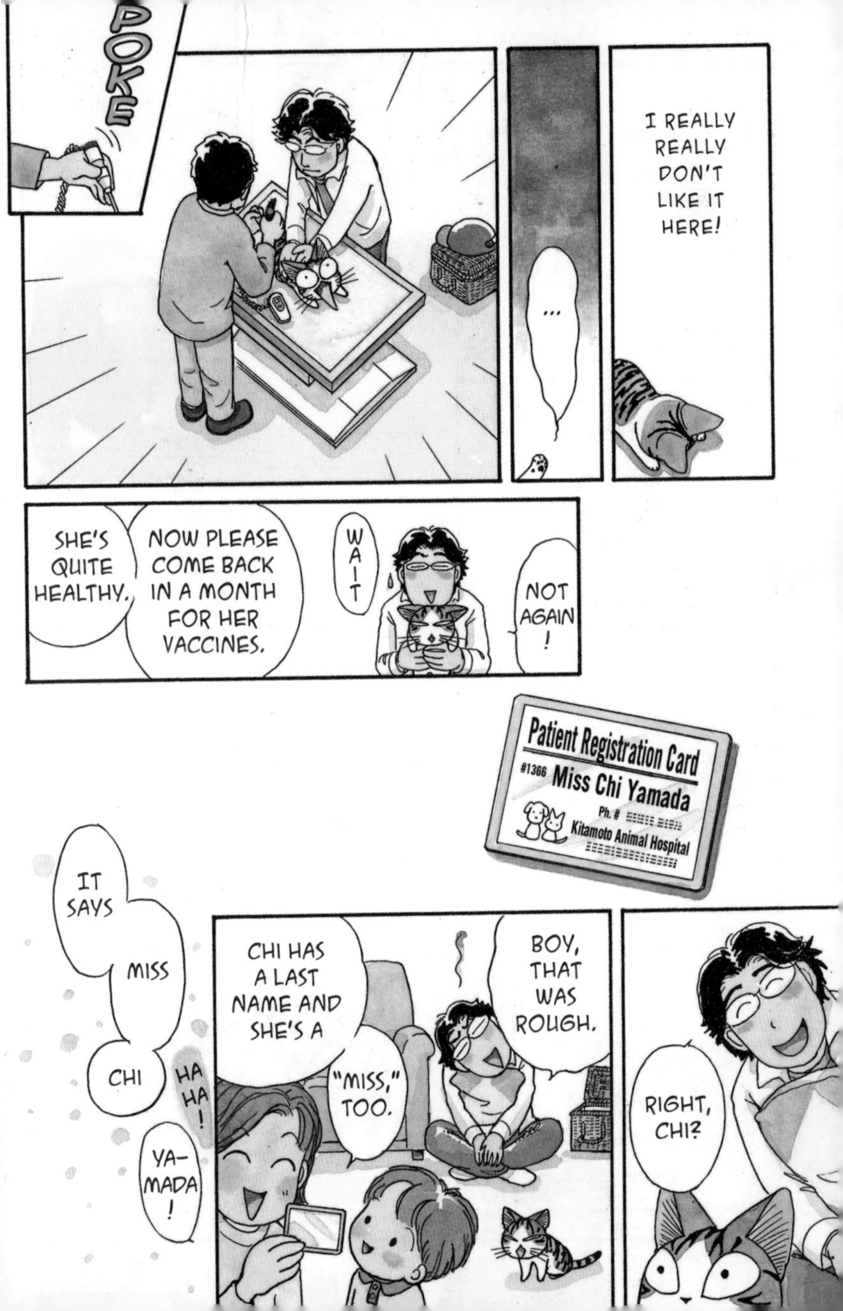
POKE
...
I REALLY REALLY DON'T LIKE IT HERE!
SHE'S QUITE HEALTHY.
NOW PLEASE COME BACK IN A MONTH FOR HER VACCINES.
WAIT
NOT AGAIN!
Patient Registration Card
#1366 Miss Chi Yamada
Ph. #
Kitamoto Animal Hospital
IT SAYS
MISS
CHI
YA-MADA!
HA HA!
CHI HAS A LAST NAME AND SHE'S A
"MISS," TOO.
BOY, THAT WAS ROUGH.
RIGHT, CHI?

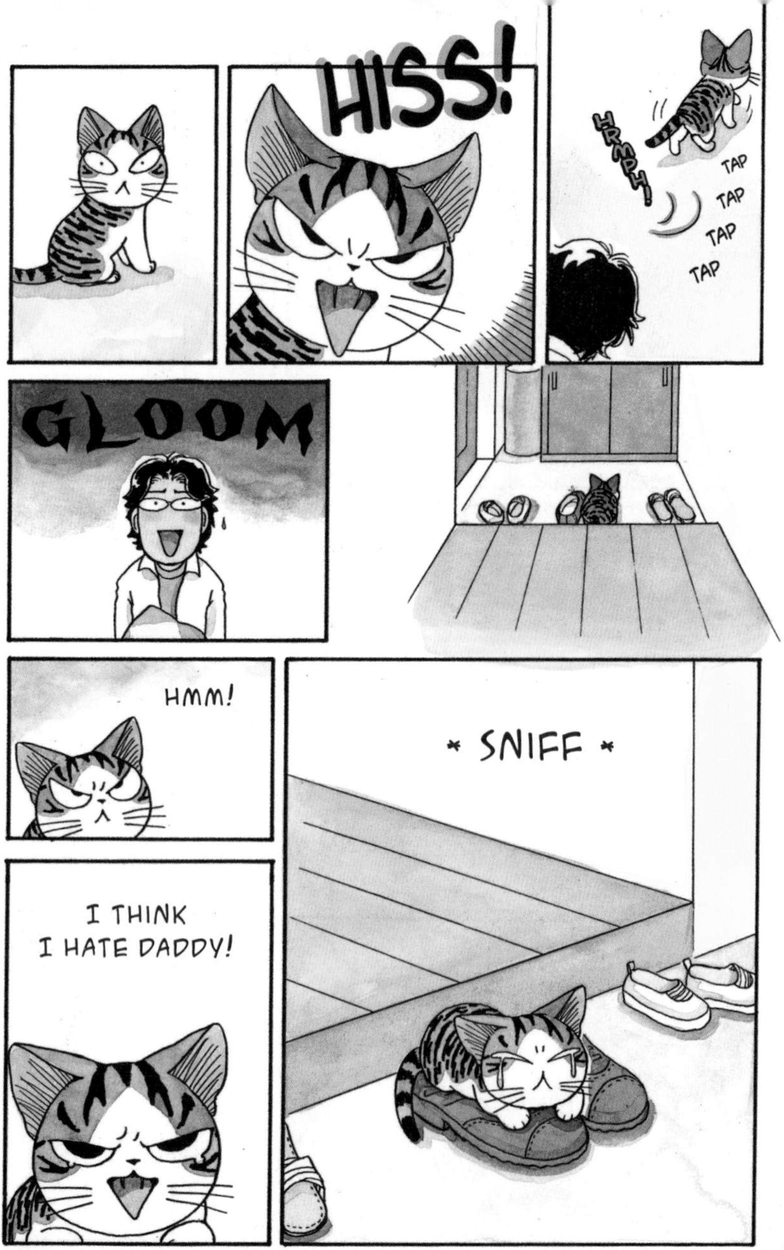
HISS!
HRMPH!
TAP
TAP
TAP
TAP
GLOOM
HMM!
I THINK
I HATE DADDY!
* SNIFF *

the end

homemade 16: a cat fears

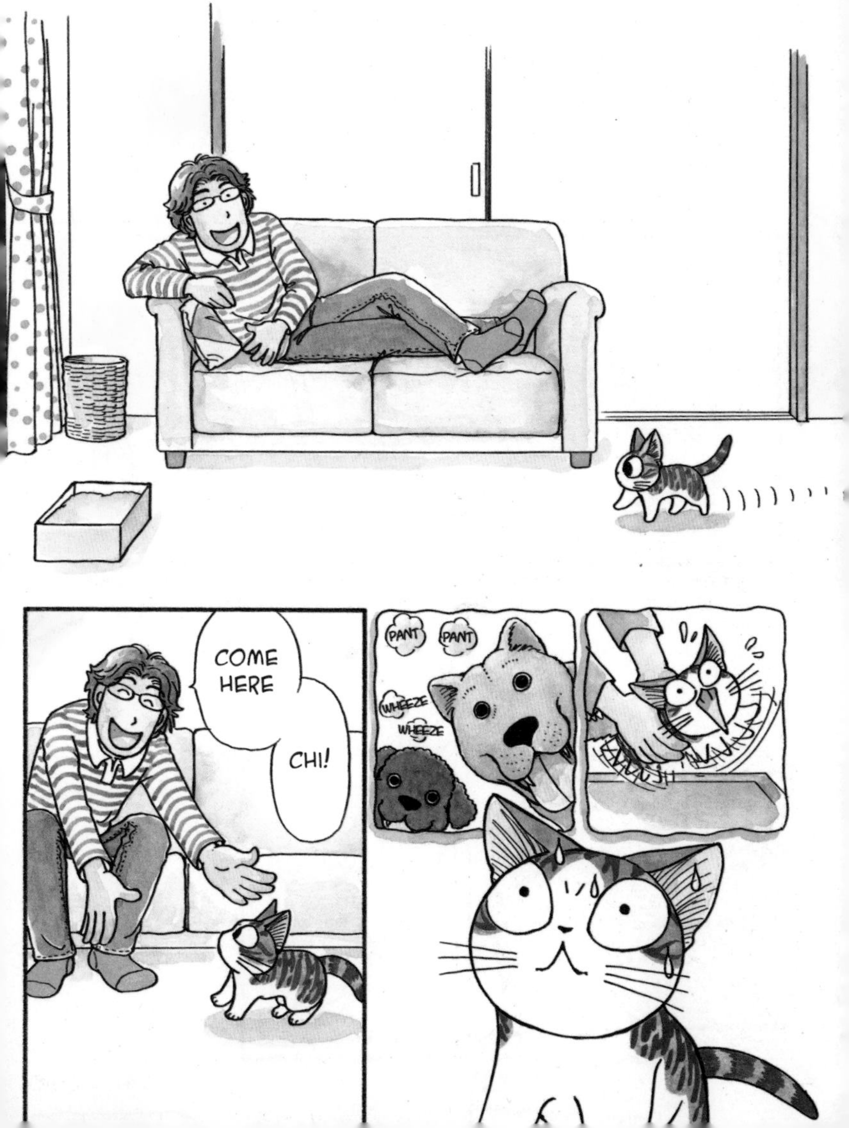
COME HERE
CHI!
PANT
PANT
WHEEZE
WHEEZE

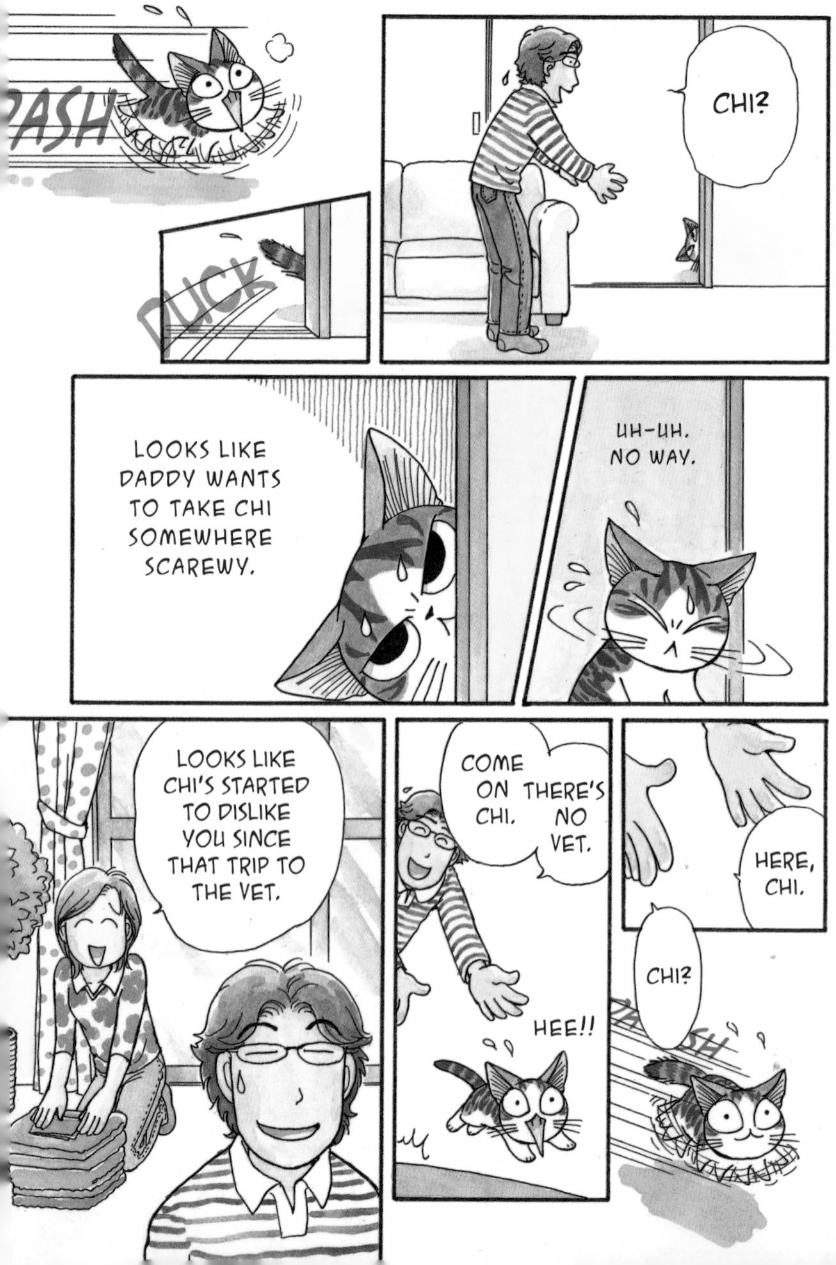
PASH
DUCK
CHI?
LOOKS LIKE DADDY WANTS TO TAKE CHI SOMEWHERE SCAREWY.
UH-UH. NO WAY.
LOOKS LIKE CHI'S STARTED TO DISLIKE YOU SINCE THAT TRIP TO THE VET.
COME ON CHI.
THERE'S NO VET.
HEE!!
HERE, CHI.
CHI?

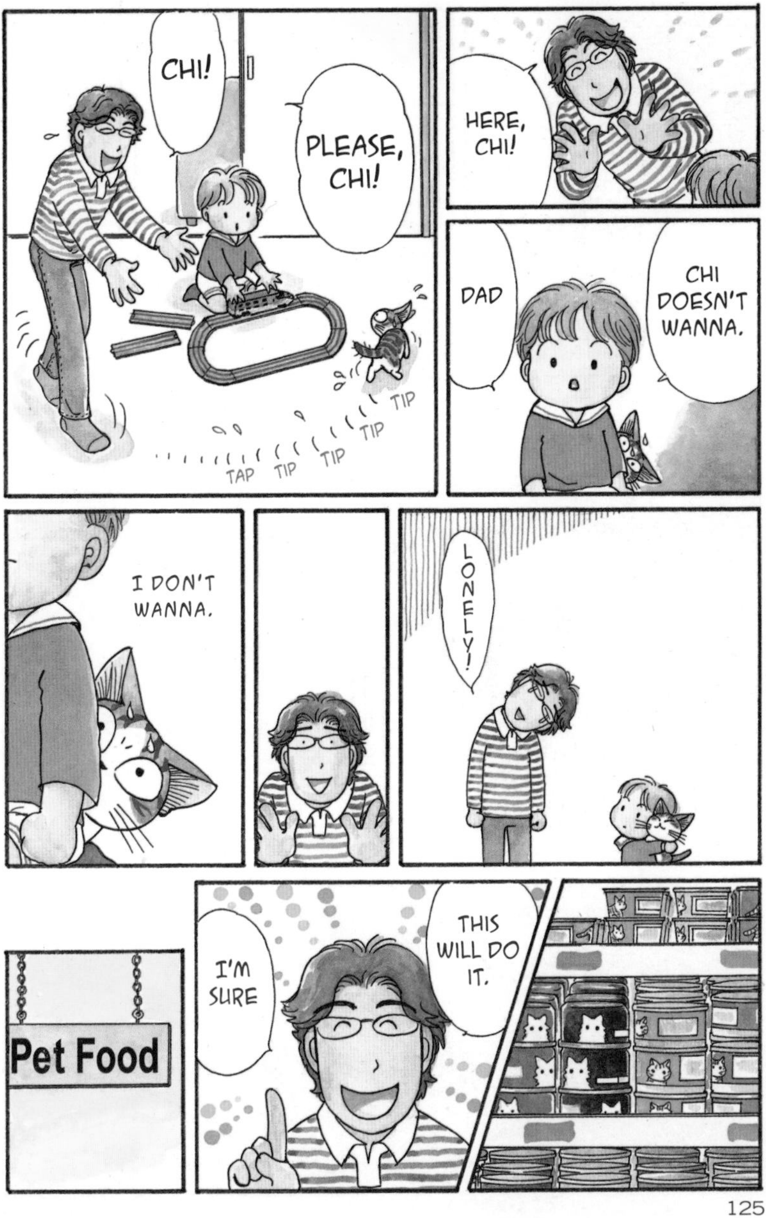
CHI!
PLEASE, CHI!
TAP TIP TIP TIP TIP
HERE, CHI!
DAD
CHI DOESN'T WANNA.
I DON'T WANNA.
LONELY!
Pet Food
I'M SURE
THIS WILL DO IT.

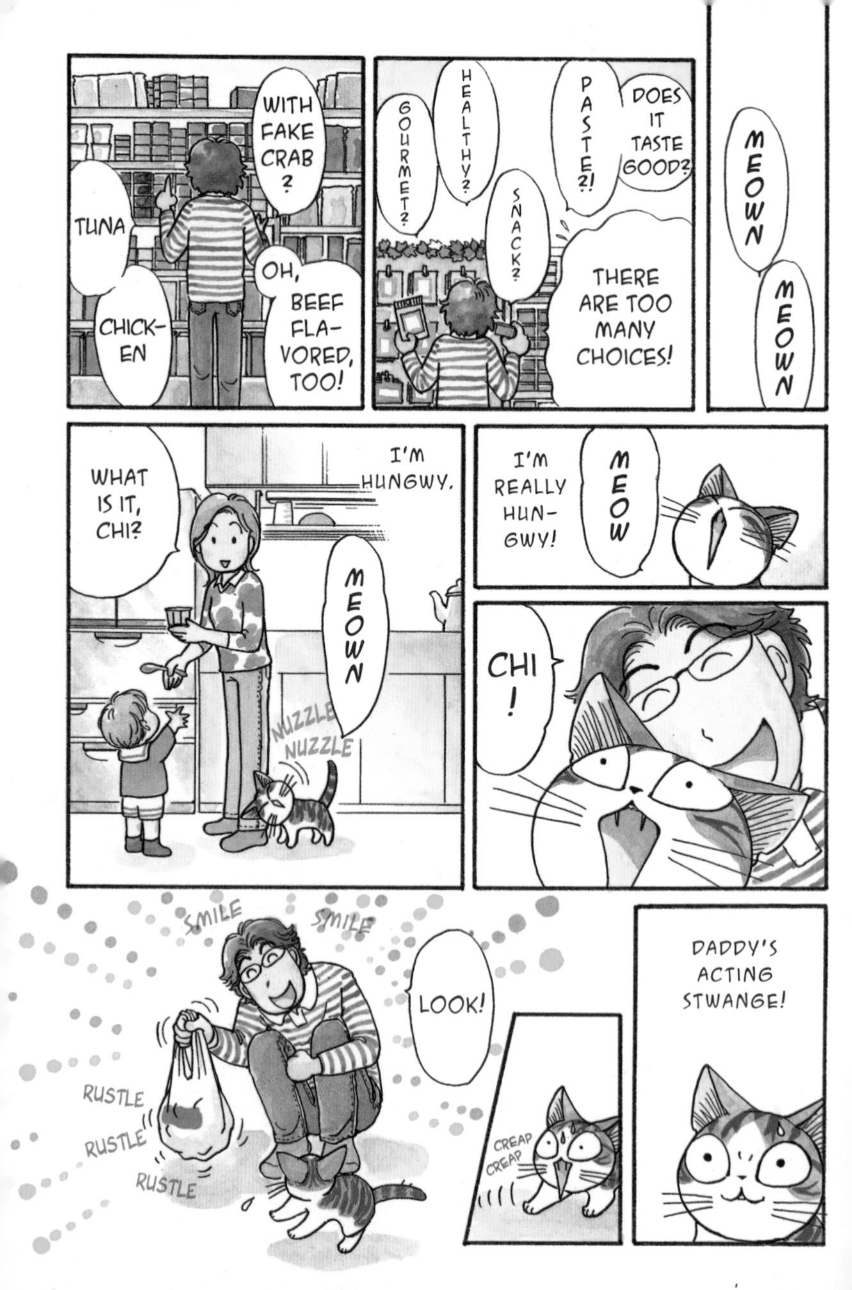
WITH FAKE CRAB?
TUNA
OH, BEEF FLA-VORED, TOO!
CHICK-EN
GOURMET?
HEALTHY?
PASTE?!
DOES IT TASTE GOOD?
SNACK?
THERE ARE TOO MANY CHOICES!
MEOWN
MEOWN
WHAT IS IT, CHI?
I'M HUNGWY.
MEOWN
NUZZLE NUZZLE
I'M REALLY HUN-GWY!
MEOW
CHI!
SMILE
SMILE
RUSTLE
RUSTLE
RUSTLE
LOOK!
CREAP CREAP
DADDY'S ACTING STWANGE!

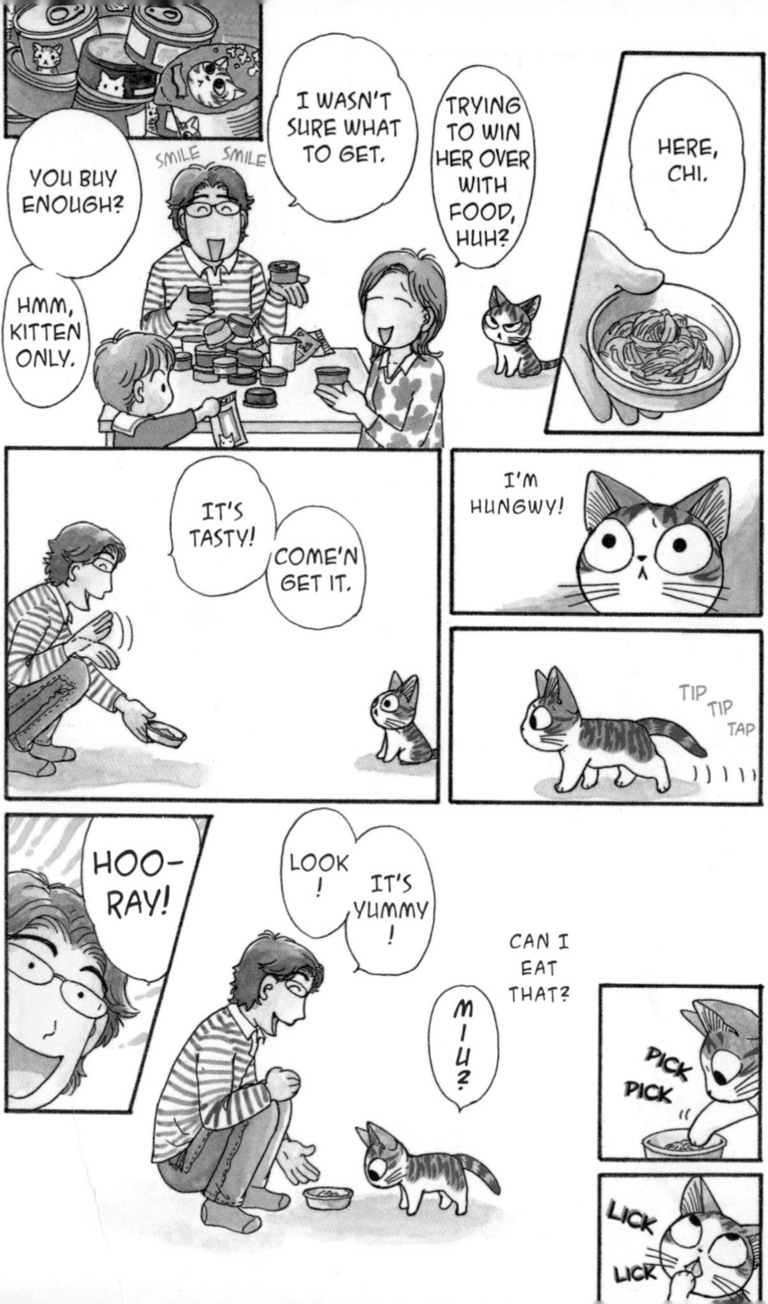
YOU BUY ENOUGH?
HMM, KITTEN ONLY.
SMILE SMILE
I WASN'T SURE WHAT TO GET.
TRYING TO WIN HER OVER WITH FOOD, HUH?
HERE, CHI.
IT'S TASTY!
COME'N GET IT.
I'M HUNGWY!
TIP TIP TAP
HOO-RAY!
LOOK!
IT'S YUMMY!
CAN I EAT THAT?
MIU?
PICK PICK
LICK LICK

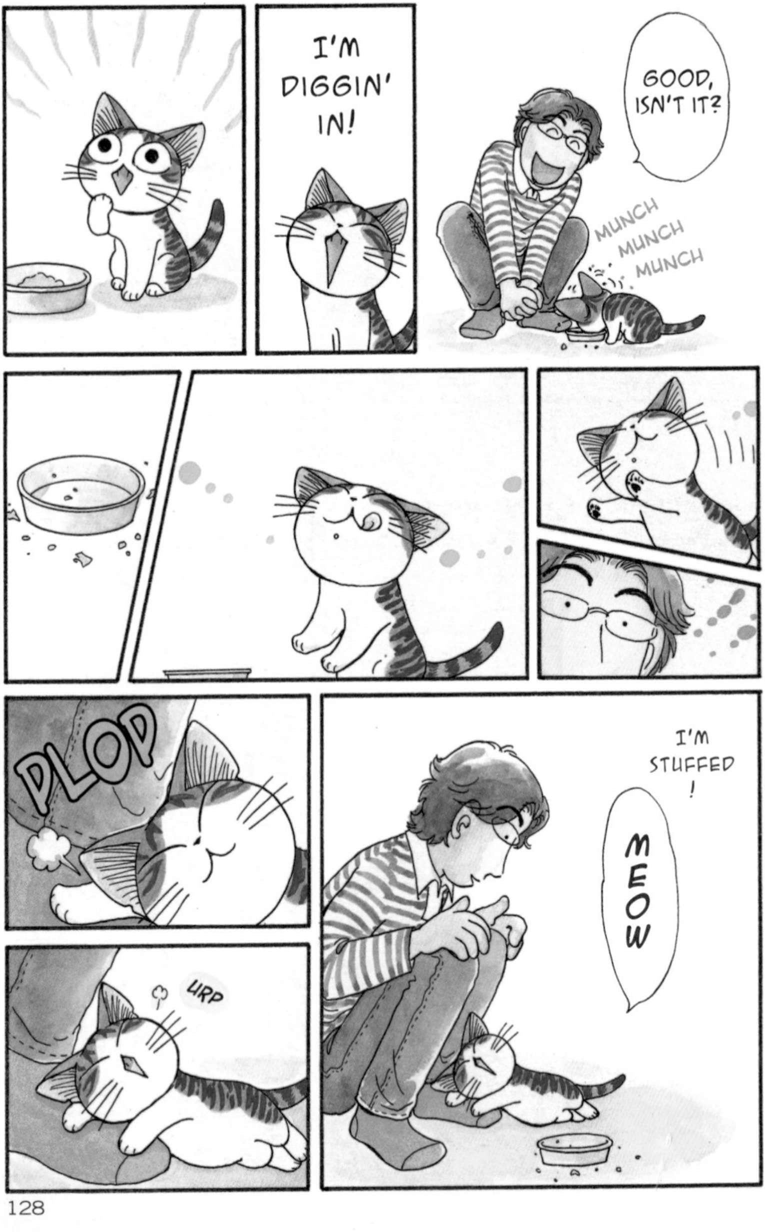
I'M DIGGIN' IN!
GOOD, ISN'T IT?
MUNCH MUNCH MUNCH
PLOP
URP
I'M STUFFED!
MEOW

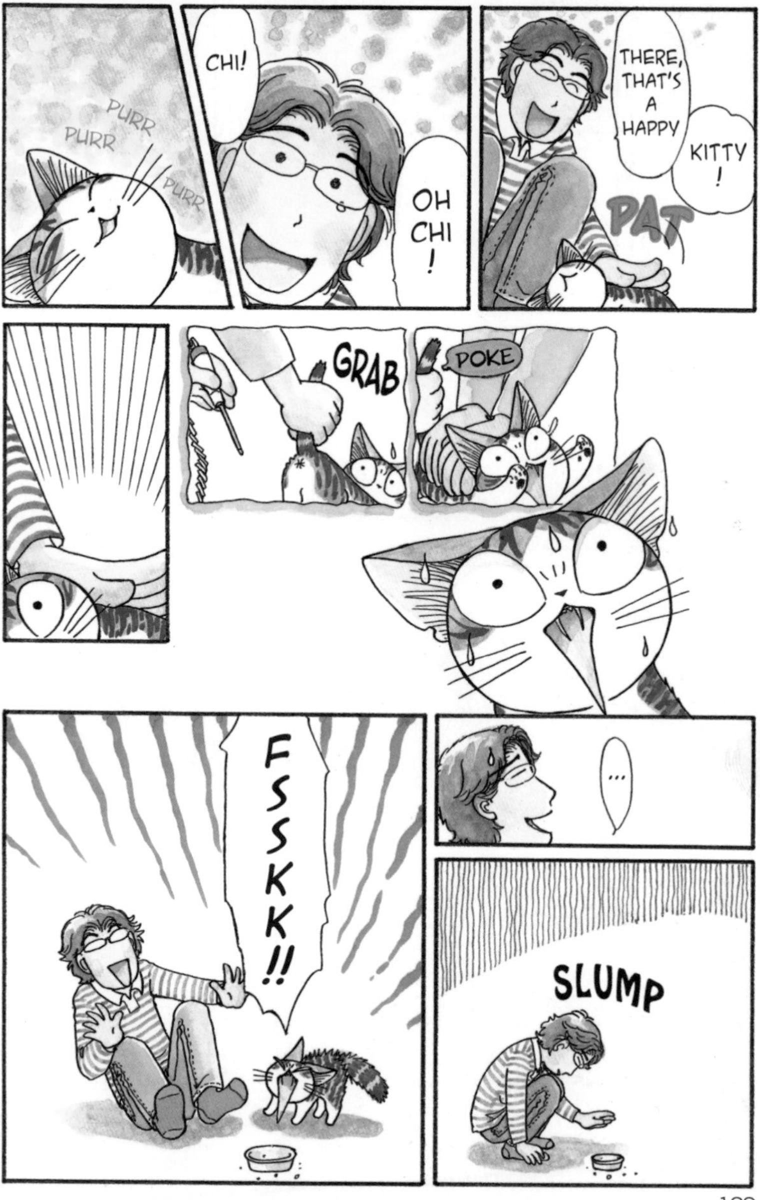
PURR
PURR
PURR
CHI!
OH CHI!
THERE, THAT'S A HAPPY
KITTY!
PAT
GRAB
POKE
FSSKK!!
...
SLUMP

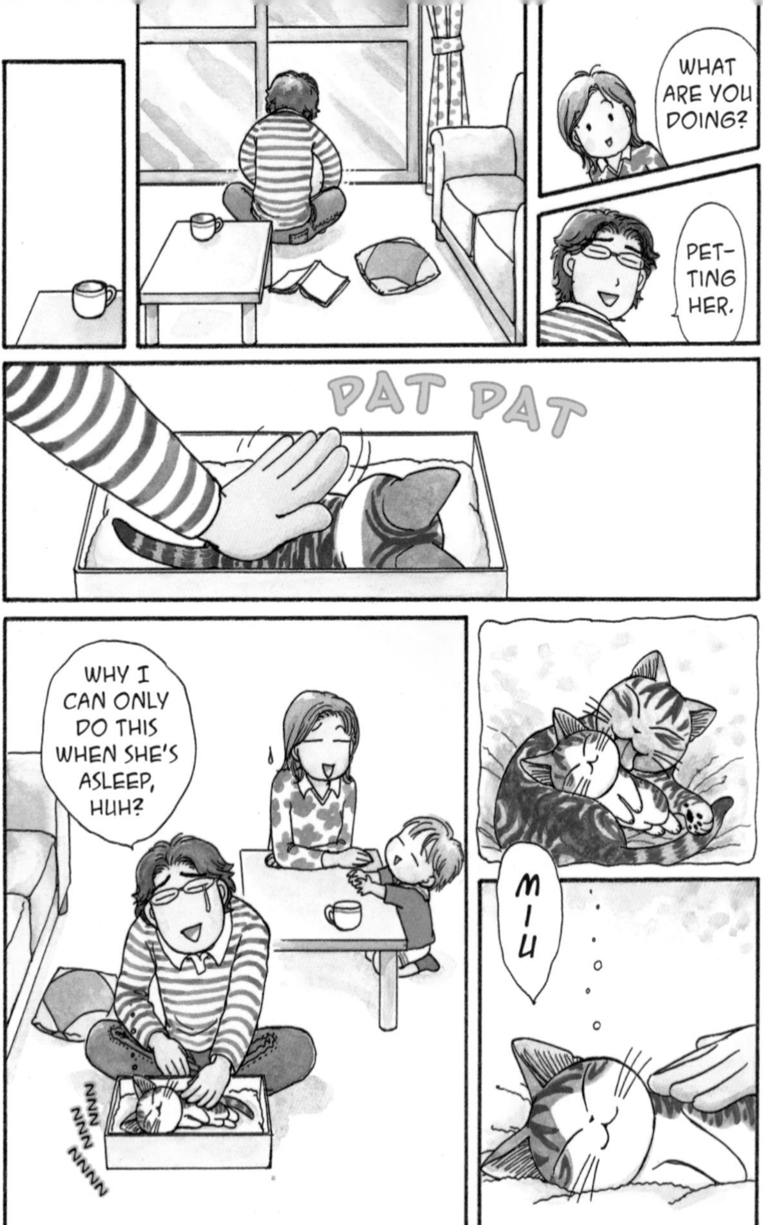
WHAT ARE YOU DOING?
PET-TING HER.
PAT PAT
WHY I CAN ONLY DO THIS WHEN SHE'S ASLEEP, HUH?
MIU

the end

homemade 17: a cat discovers

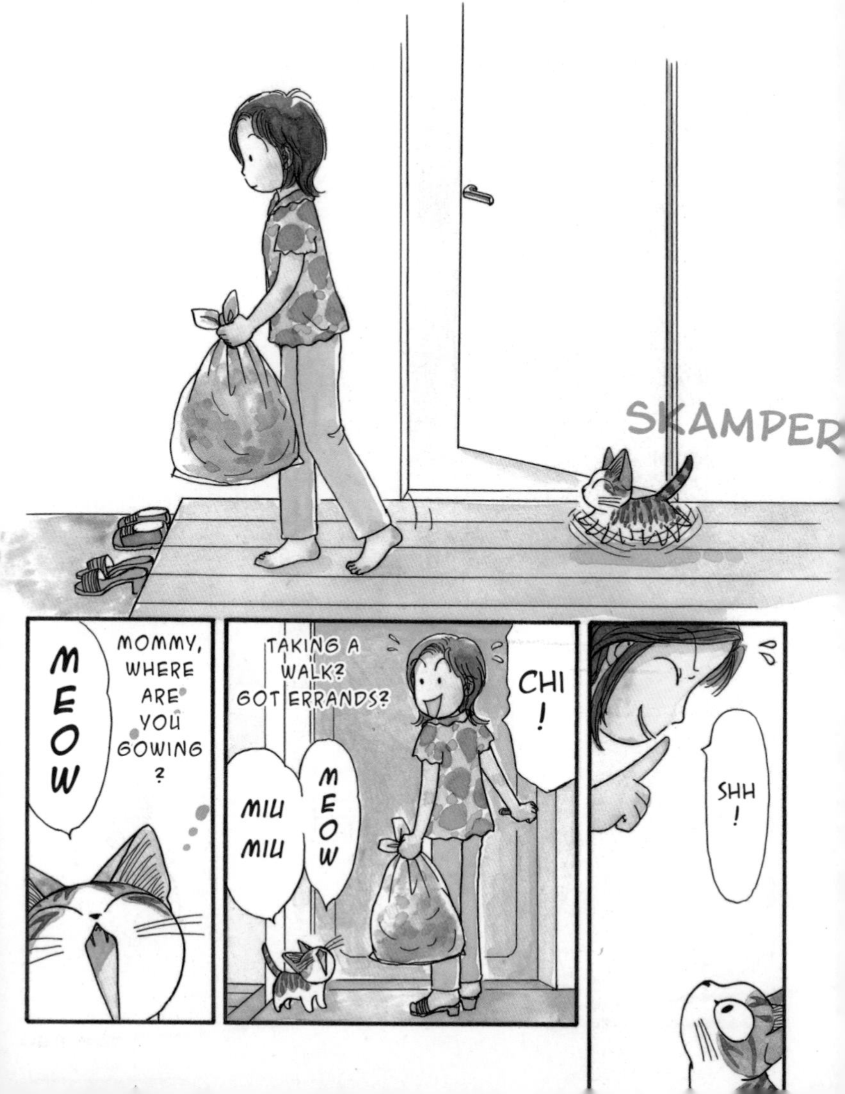
SKAMPER
MEOW
MOMMY, WHERE ARE YOU GOWING ?
TAKING A WALK? GOT ERRANDS?
MIU MIU
MEOW
CHI!
SHH!

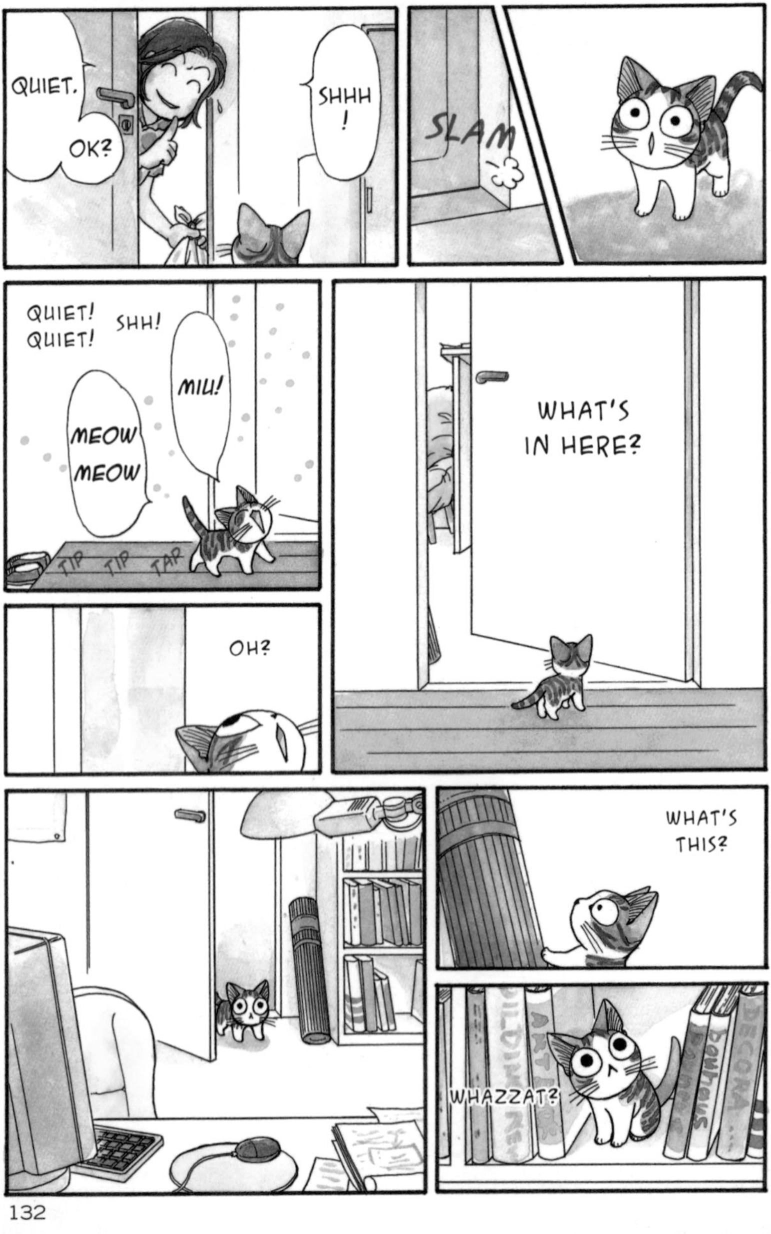
QUIET.
OK?
SHHH!
SLAM
QUIET! QUIET!
SHH!
MIU!
MEOW MEOW
TIP TIP TAP
OH?
WHAT'S IN HERE?
WHAT'S THIS?
WHAZZAT?

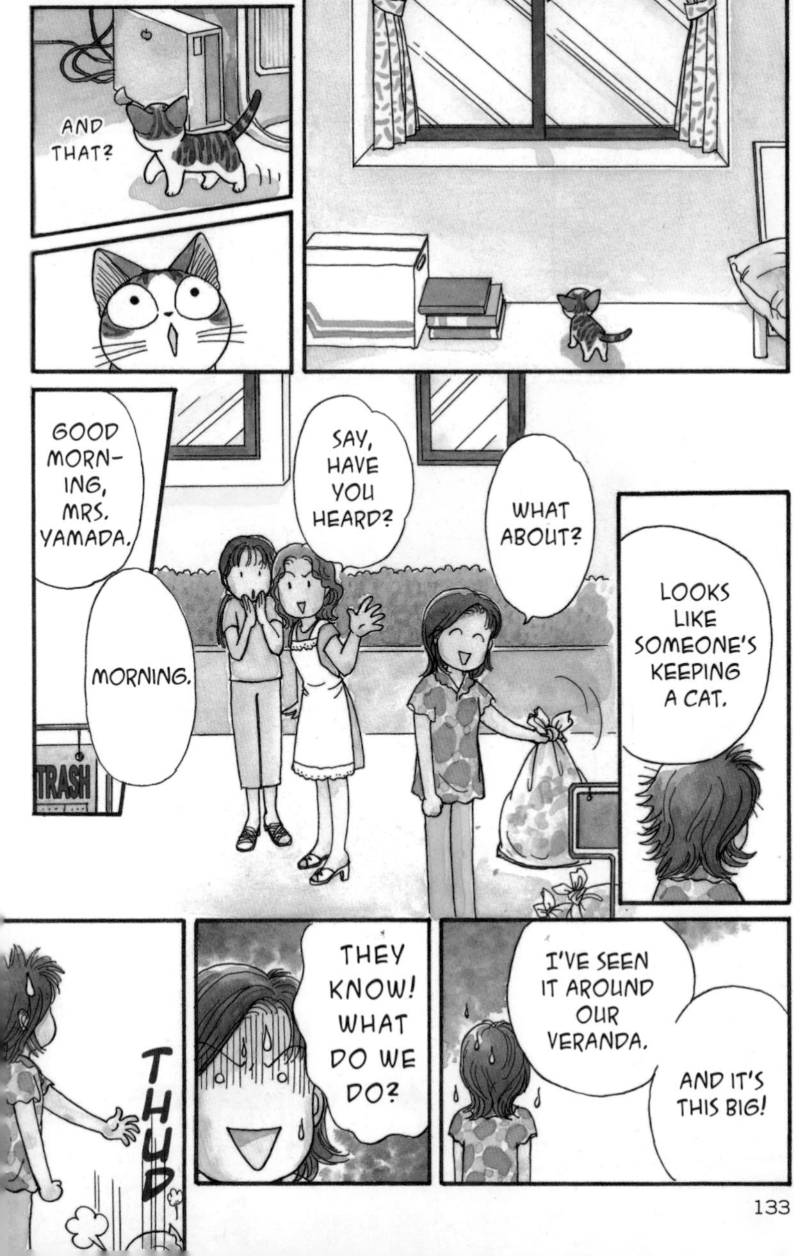
AND THAT?
GOOD MORNING, MRS. YAMADA.
MORNING.
SAY, HAVE YOU HEARD?
WHAT ABOUT?
TRASH
LOOKS LIKE SOMEONE'S KEEPING A CAT.
THUD
THEY KNOW! WHAT DO WE DO?
I'VE SEEN IT AROUND OUR VERANDA.
AND IT'S THIS BIG!

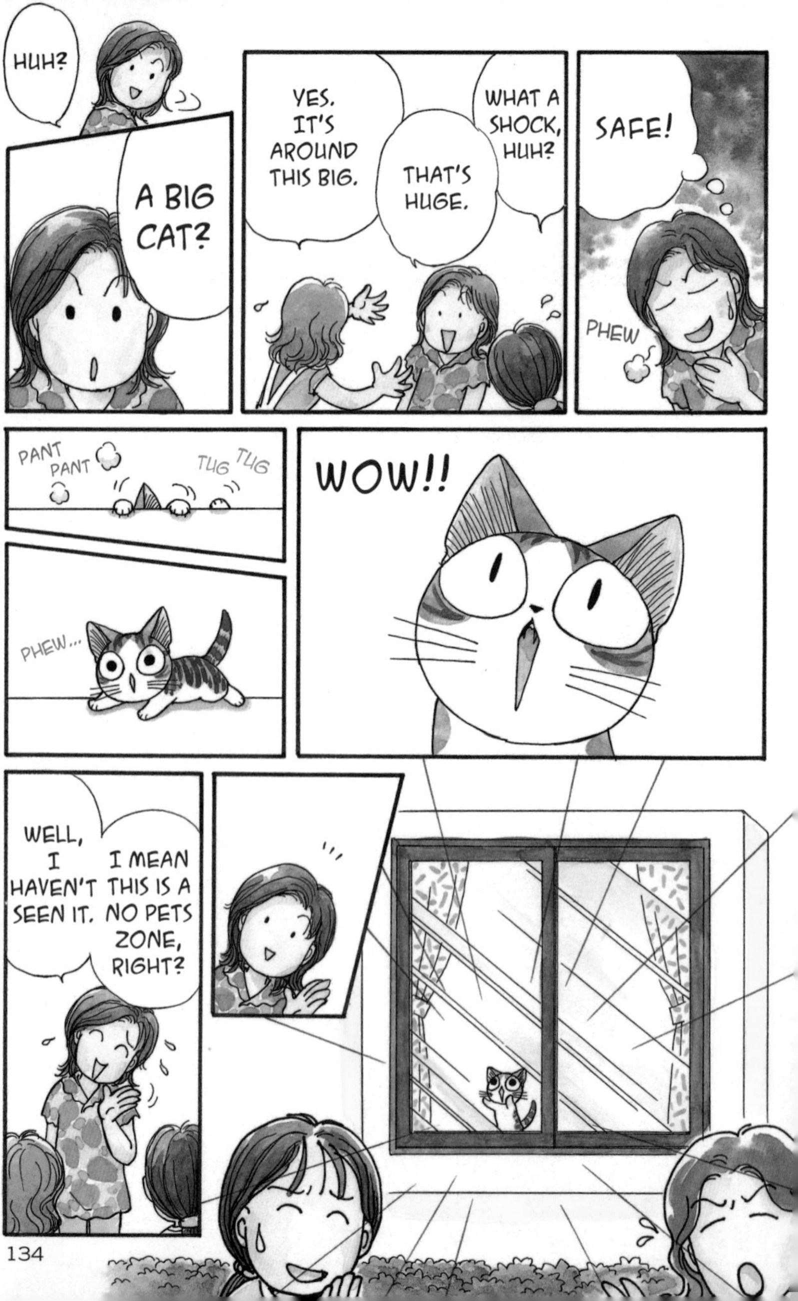
HUH?
A BIG CAT?
YES. IT'S AROUND THIS BIG.
THAT'S HUGE.
WHAT A SHOCK, HUH?
SAFE!
PHEW
PANT PANT
TUG TUG
PHEW...
WOW!!
WELL, I HAVEN'T SEEN IT.
I MEAN THIS IS A NO PETS ZONE, RIGHT?

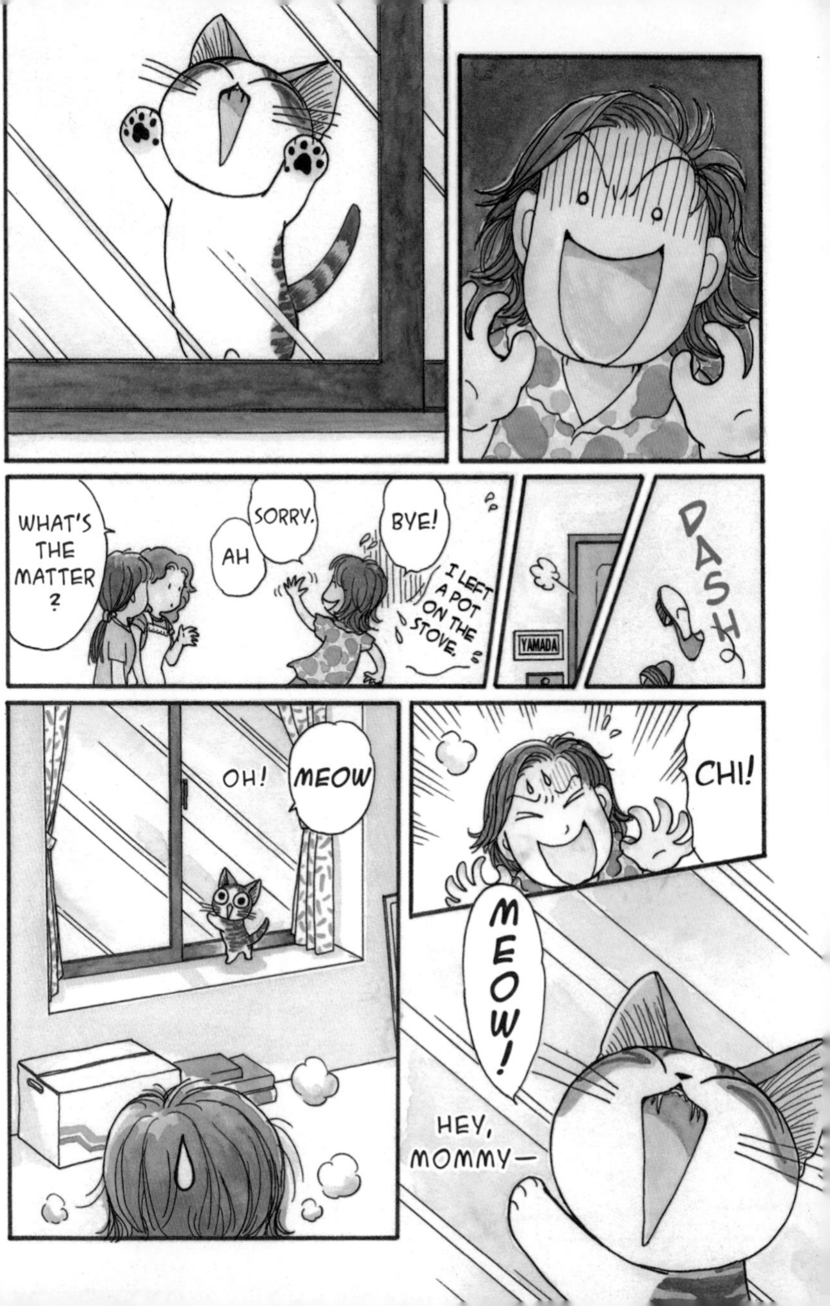
WHAT'S THE MATTER ?
AH
SORRY.
BYE!
I LEFT A POT ON THE STOVE.
YAMADA
DASH
OH!
MEOW
CHI!
MEOW!
HEY, MOMMY—

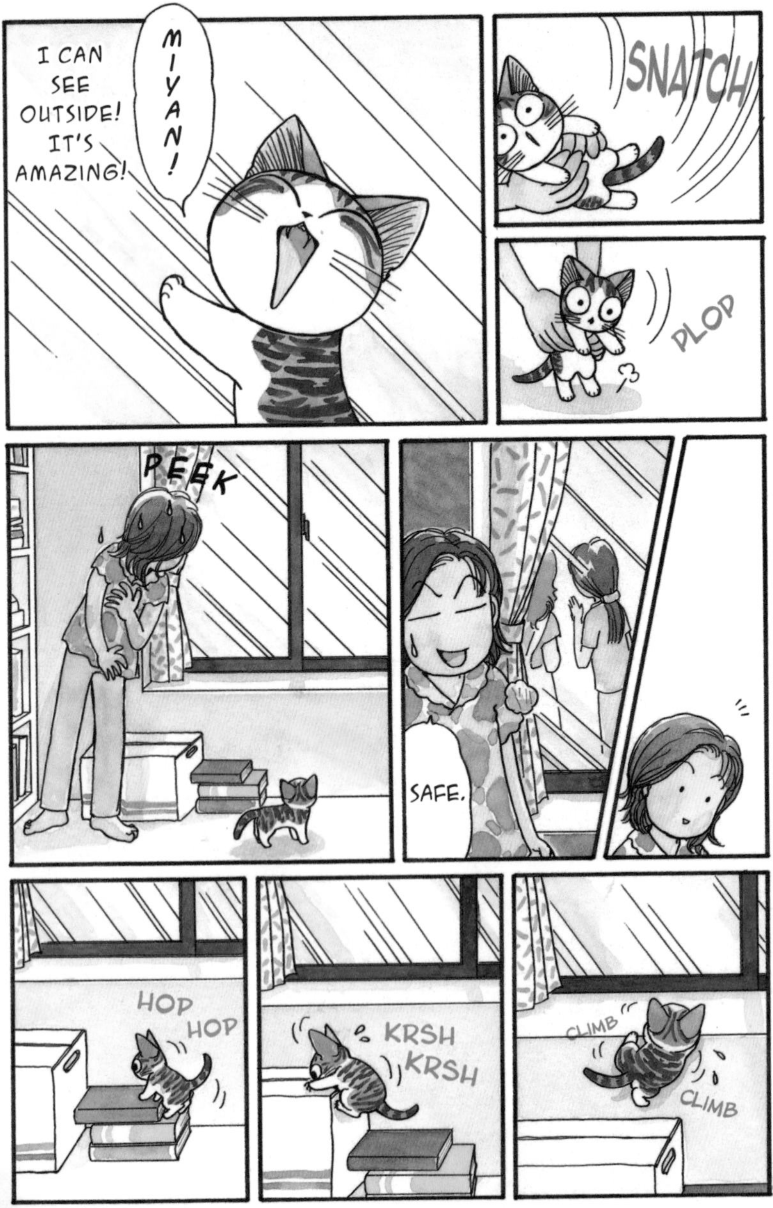
I CAN SEE OUTSIDE! IT'S AMAZING!
MIYAN!
SNATCH
PLOP
PEEK
SAFE.
HOP HOP
KRSH KRSH
CLIMB
CLIMB

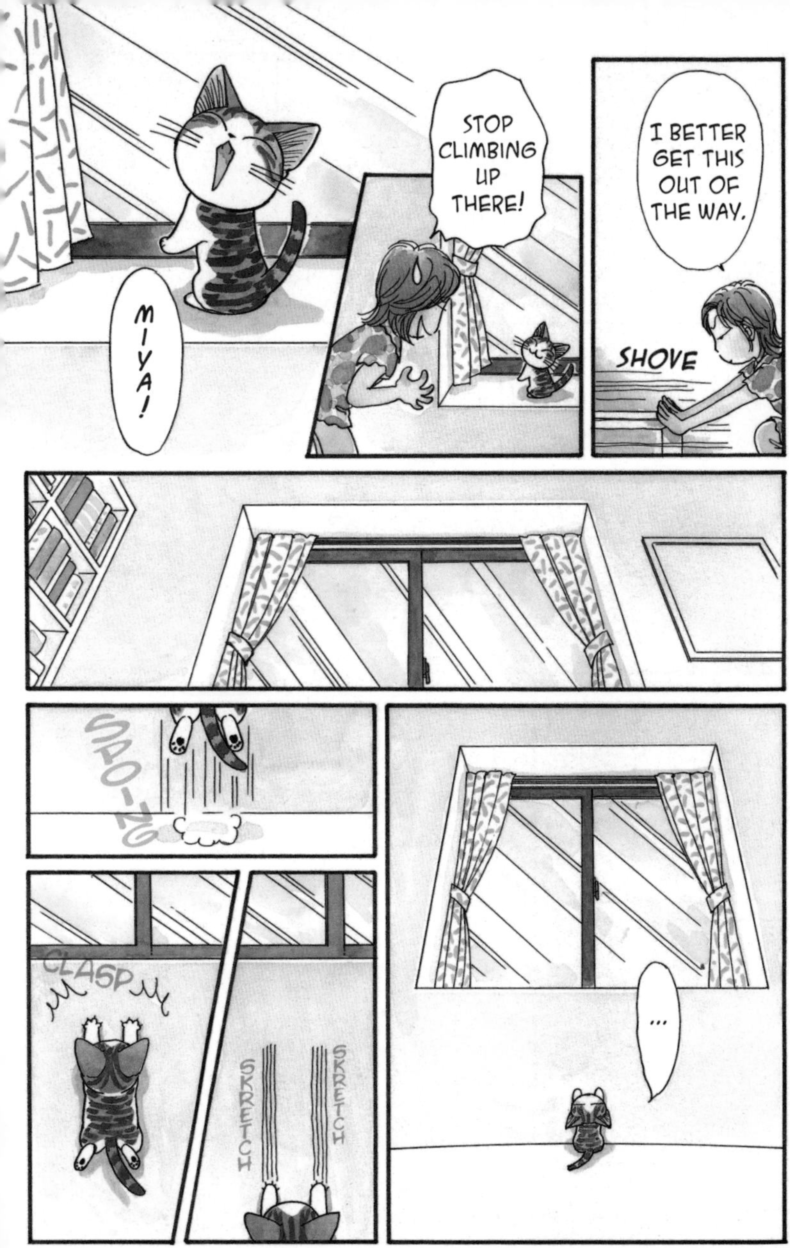
MIYA!
STOP CLIMBING UP THERE!
I BETTER GET THIS OUT OF THE WAY.
SHOVE
SPOING
CLASP
SKRETCH
SKRETCH
...

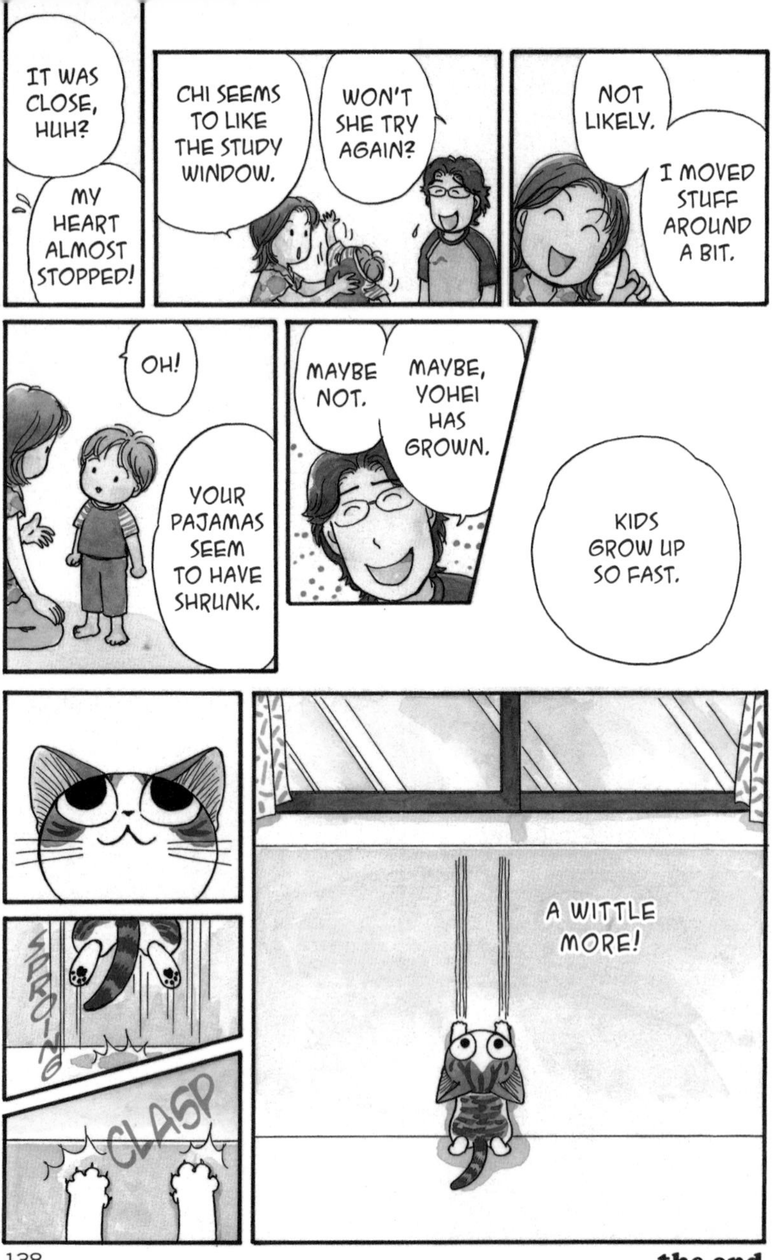
IT WAS CLOSE, HUH?
MY HEART ALMOST STOPPED!
CHI SEEMS TO LIKE THE STUDY WINDOW.
WON'T SHE TRY AGAIN?
NOT LIKELY.
I MOVED STUFF AROUND A BIT.
OH!
YOUR PAJAMAS SEEM TO HAVE SHRUNK.
MAYBE NOT.
MAYBE, YOHEI HAS GROWN.
KIDS GROW UP SO FAST.
SPROING
CLASP
A WITTLE MORE!

the end

homemade 18: a cat is discovered

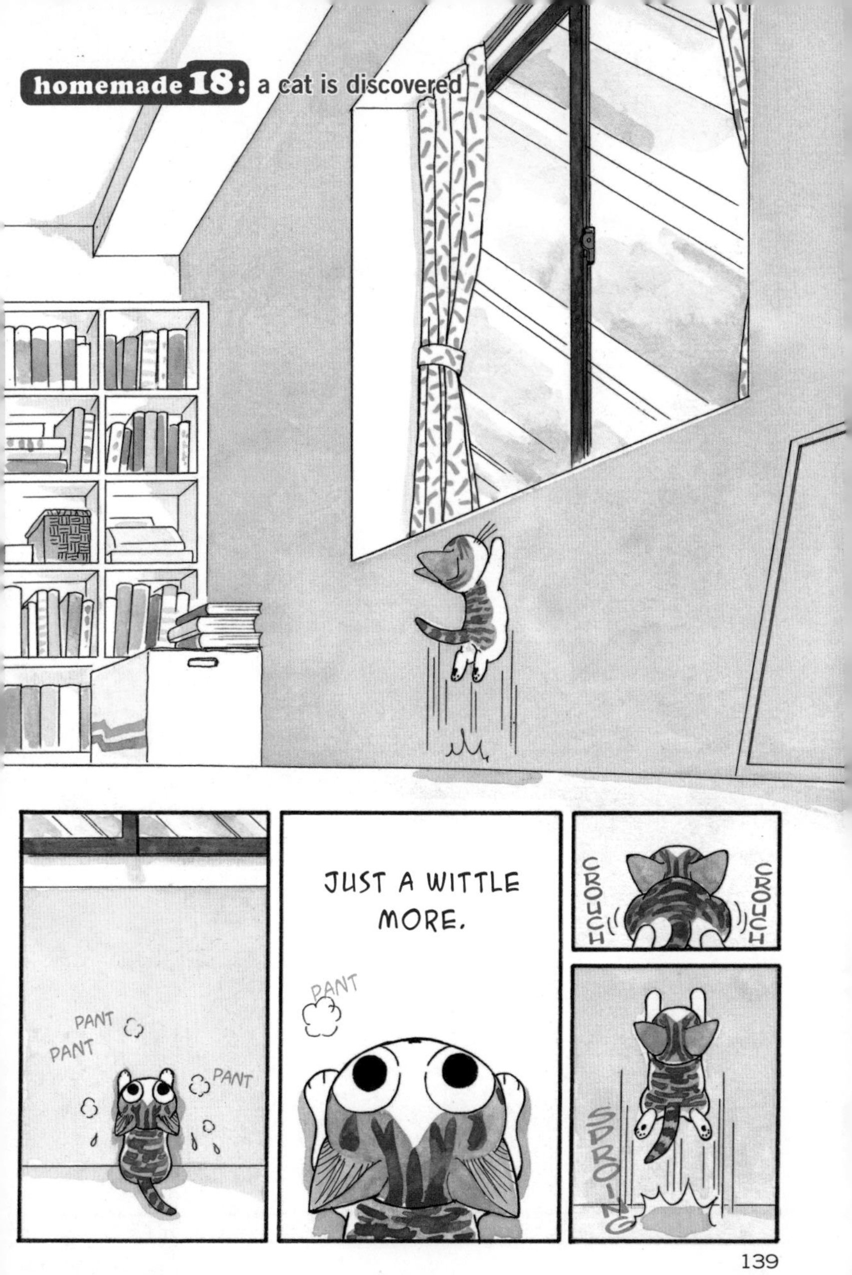

PANT
PANT
PANT
JUST A WITTLE MORE.
PANT
CROUCH
CROUCH
SPROING

SMACK

CLIMB CLIMB

SKTCH SKTCH

PANT

I CWIMBED IT!

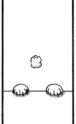

MEOW!

TINK

WOW!

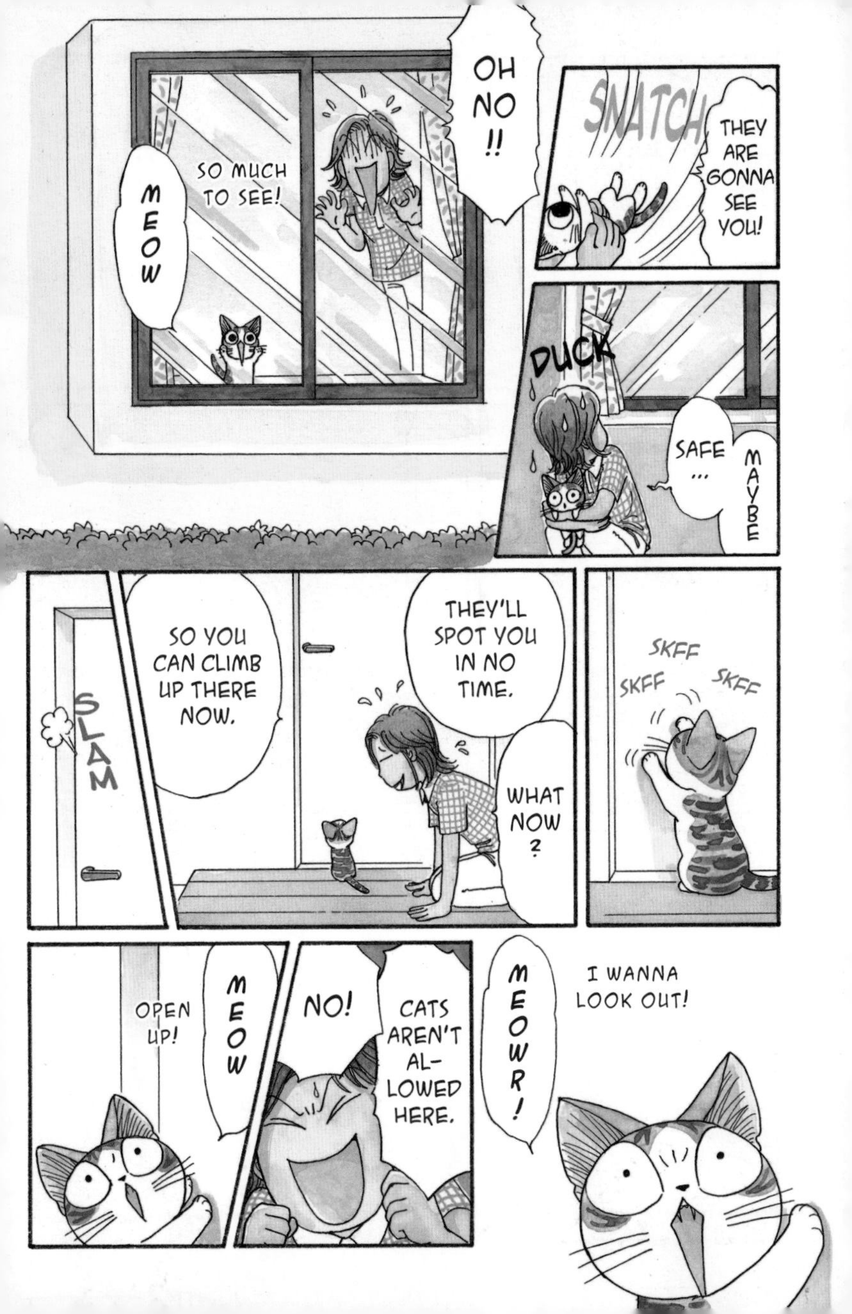
MEOW
SO MUCH TO SEE!
OH NO !!
SNATCH
THEY ARE GONNA SEE YOU!
DUCK
SAFE ...
MAYBE
SLAM
SO YOU CAN CLIMB UP THERE NOW.
THEY'LL SPOT YOU IN NO TIME.
WHAT NOW ?
SKFF
SKFF
SKFF
OPEN UP!
MEOW
NO!
CATS AREN'T AL- LOWED HERE.
MEOWR!
I WANNA LOOK OUT!

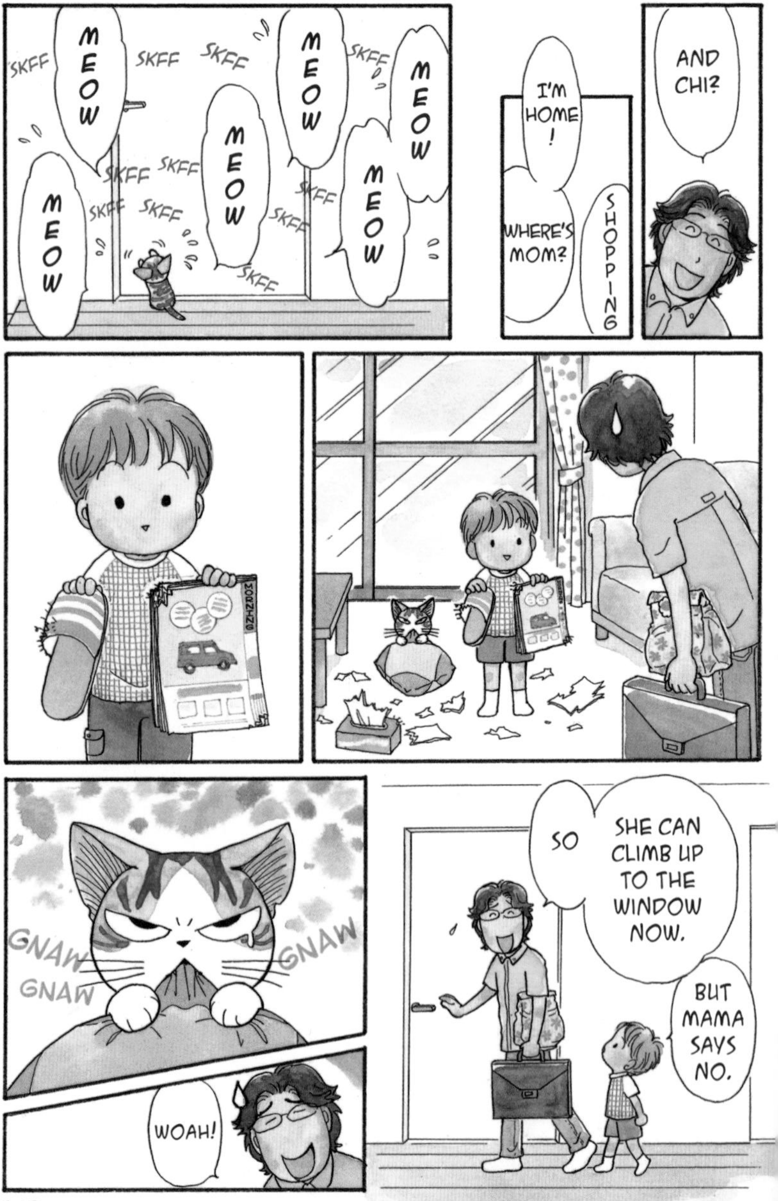
SKFF
MEOW
SKFF
SKFF
MEOW
SKFF
MEOW
SKFF
MEOW
SKFF
SKFF
MEOW
SKFF
MEOW
SKFF
SKFF
SKFF
I'M HOME!
WHERE'S MOM?
SHOPPING
AND CHI?
MORNING
GNAW
GNAW
GNAW
WOAH!
SO
SHE CAN CLIMB UP TO THE WINDOW NOW.
BUT MAMA SAYS NO.

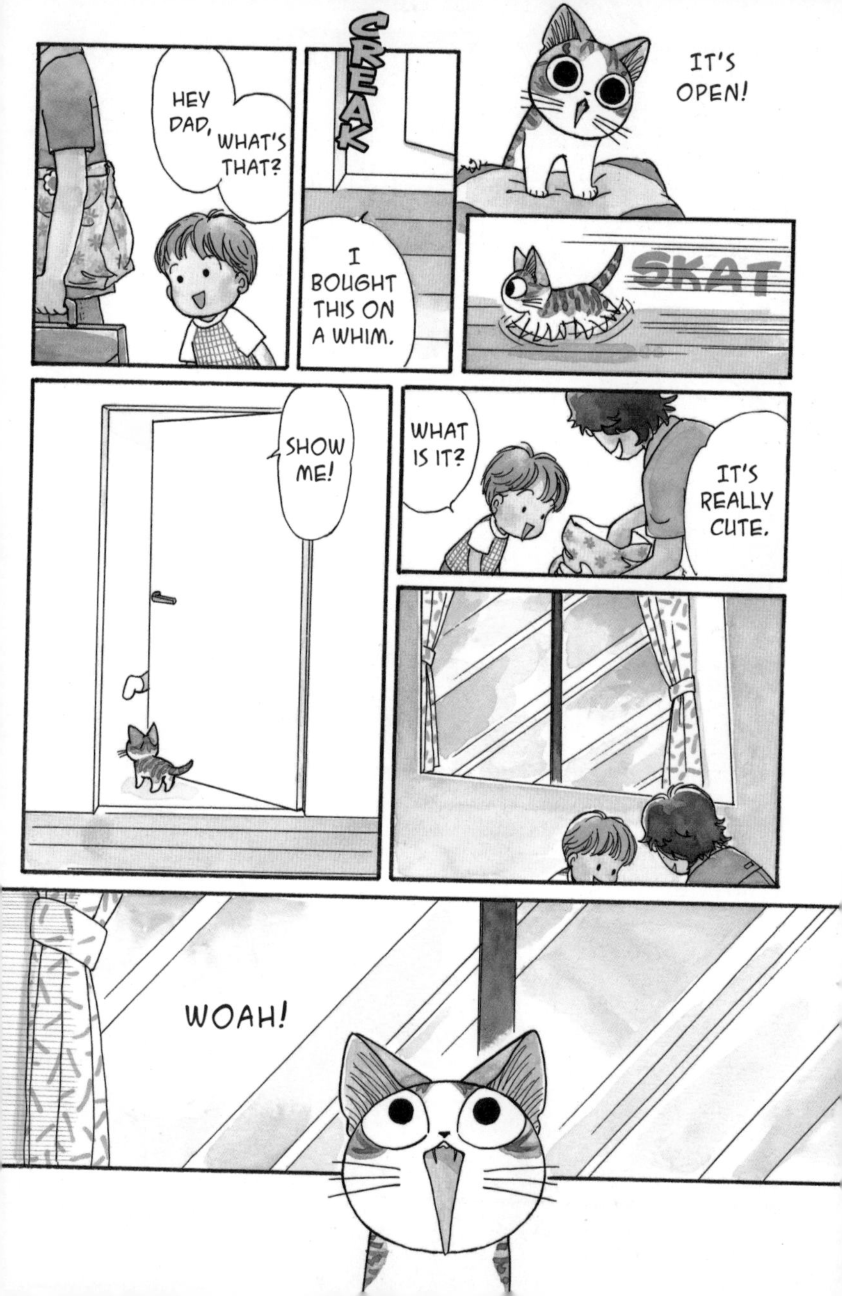
HEY DAD, WHAT'S THAT?
CREAK
I BOUGHT THIS ON A WHIM.
IT'S OPEN!
SKAT
SHOW ME!
WHAT IS IT?
IT'S REALLY CUTE.
WOAH!

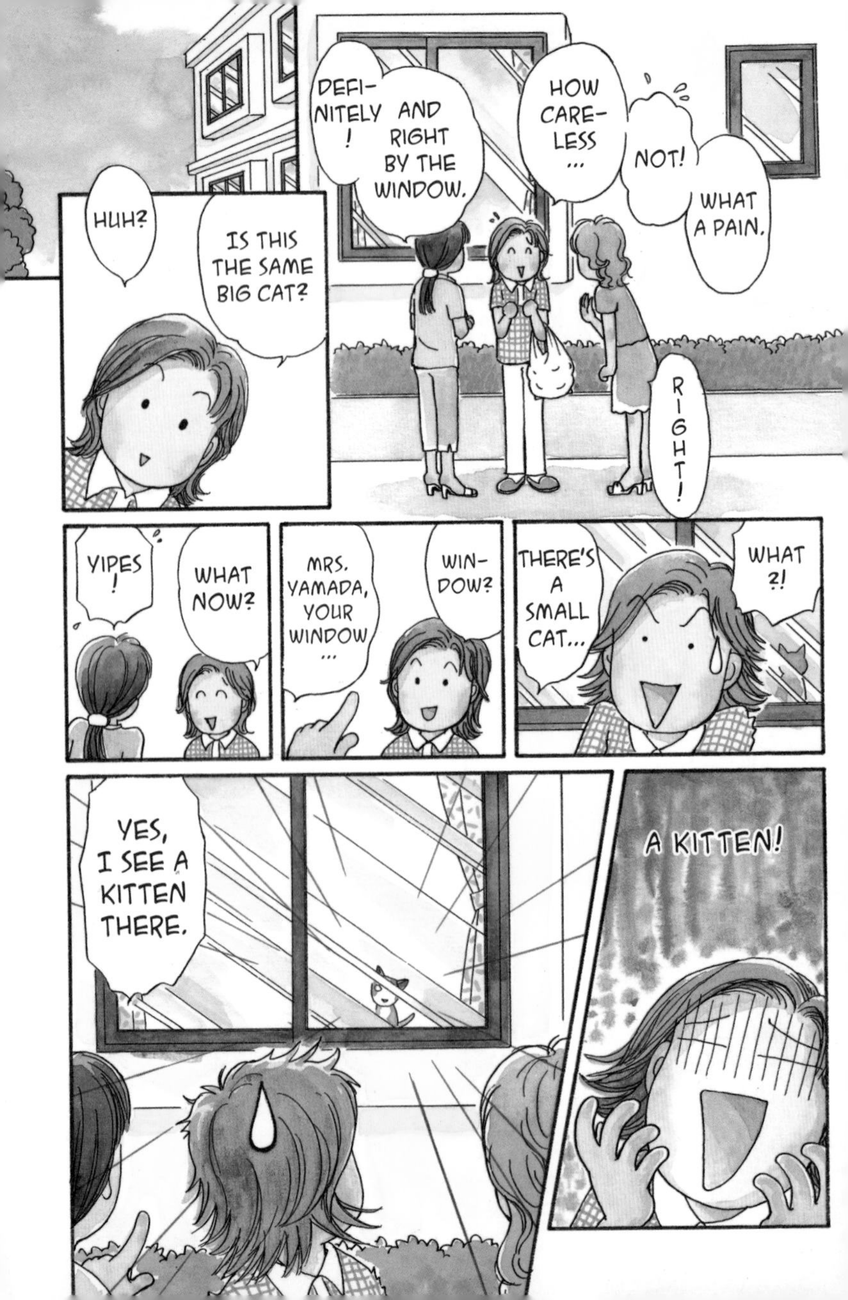
DEFI-NITELY!
AND RIGHT BY THE WINDOW.
HOW CARE-LESS...
NOT!
WHAT A PAIN.
RIGHT!
HUH?
IS THIS THE SAME BIG CAT?
YIPES!
WHAT NOW?
MRS. YAMADA, YOUR WINDOW...
WIN-DOW?
THERE'S A SMALL CAT...
WHAT?!
YES, I SEE A KITTEN THERE.
A KITTEN!

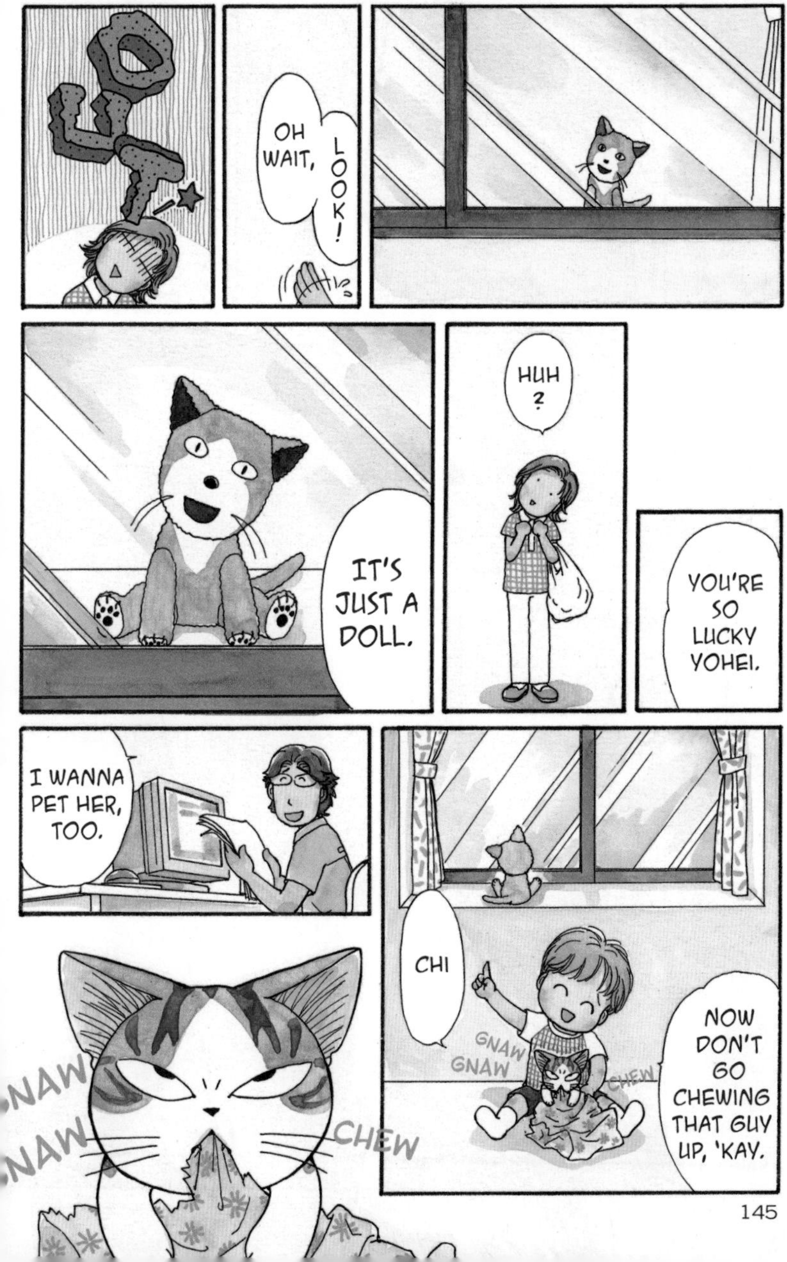
LOL
OH WAIT, LOOK!
IT'S JUST A DOLL.
HUH?
YOU'RE SO LUCKY YOHEI.
I WANNA PET HER, TOO.
CHI
NOW DON'T GO CHEWING THAT GUY UP, 'KAY.
GNAW GNAW
CHEW
GNAW GNAW
CHEW

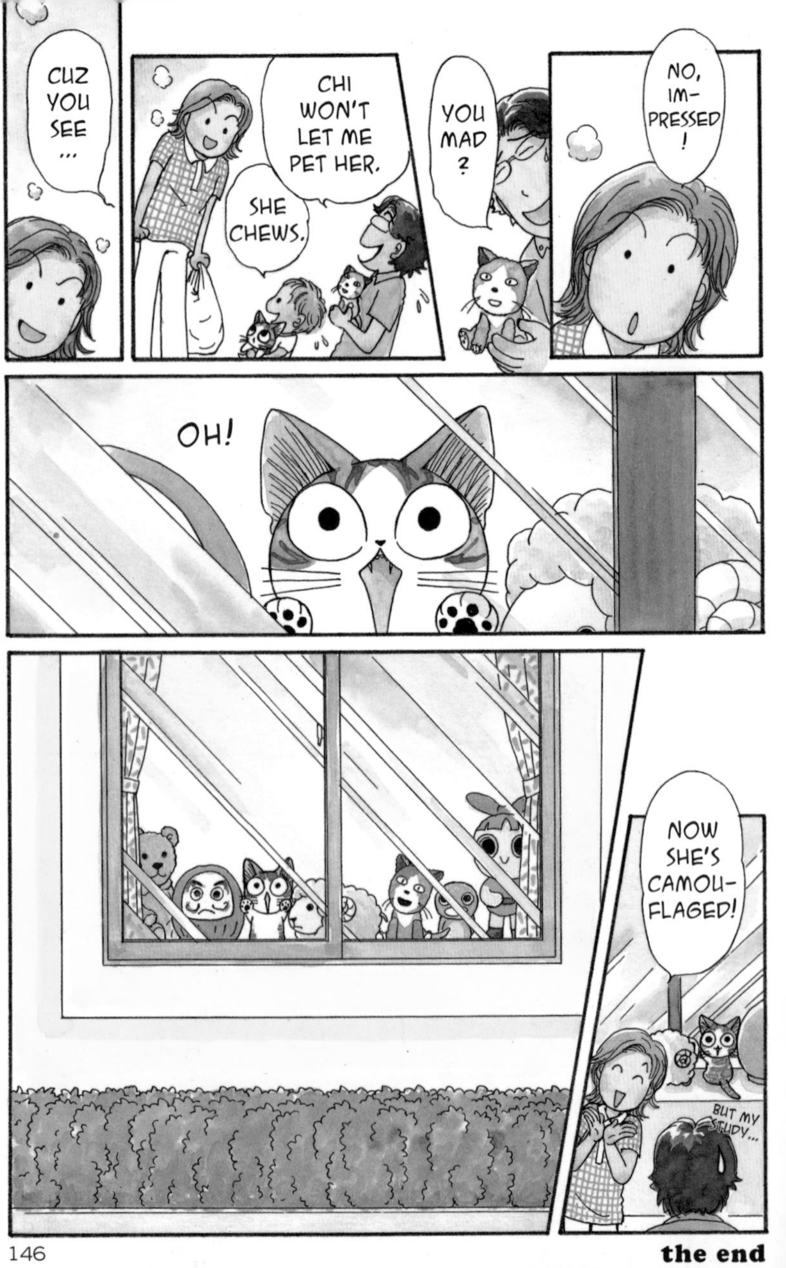
CUZ YOU SEE ...
CHI WON'T LET ME PET HER.
SHE CHEWS.
YOU MAD?
NO, IM-PRESSED!
OH!
NOW SHE'S CAMOU-FLAGED!
BUT MY STUDY...

the end

homemade 19: a cat obsesses

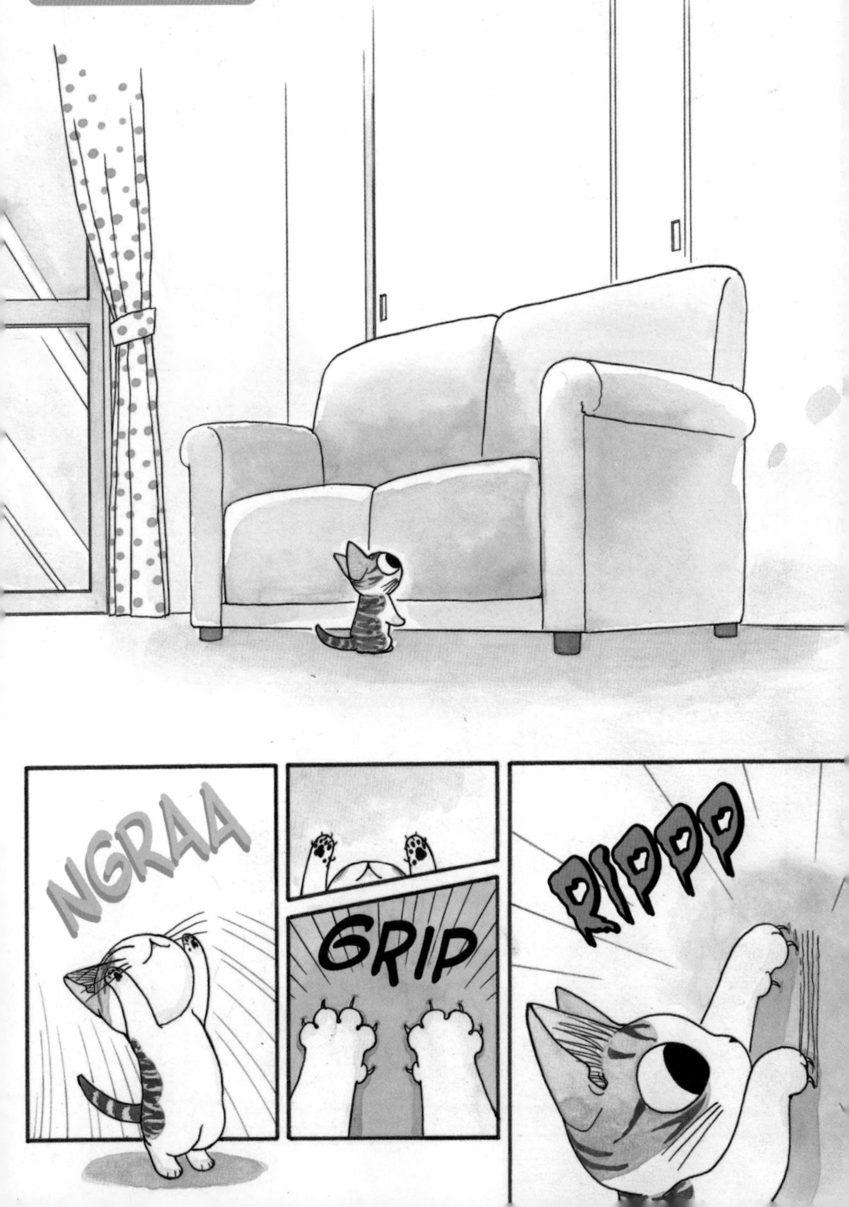
NGRAA
GRIP
RIPPP

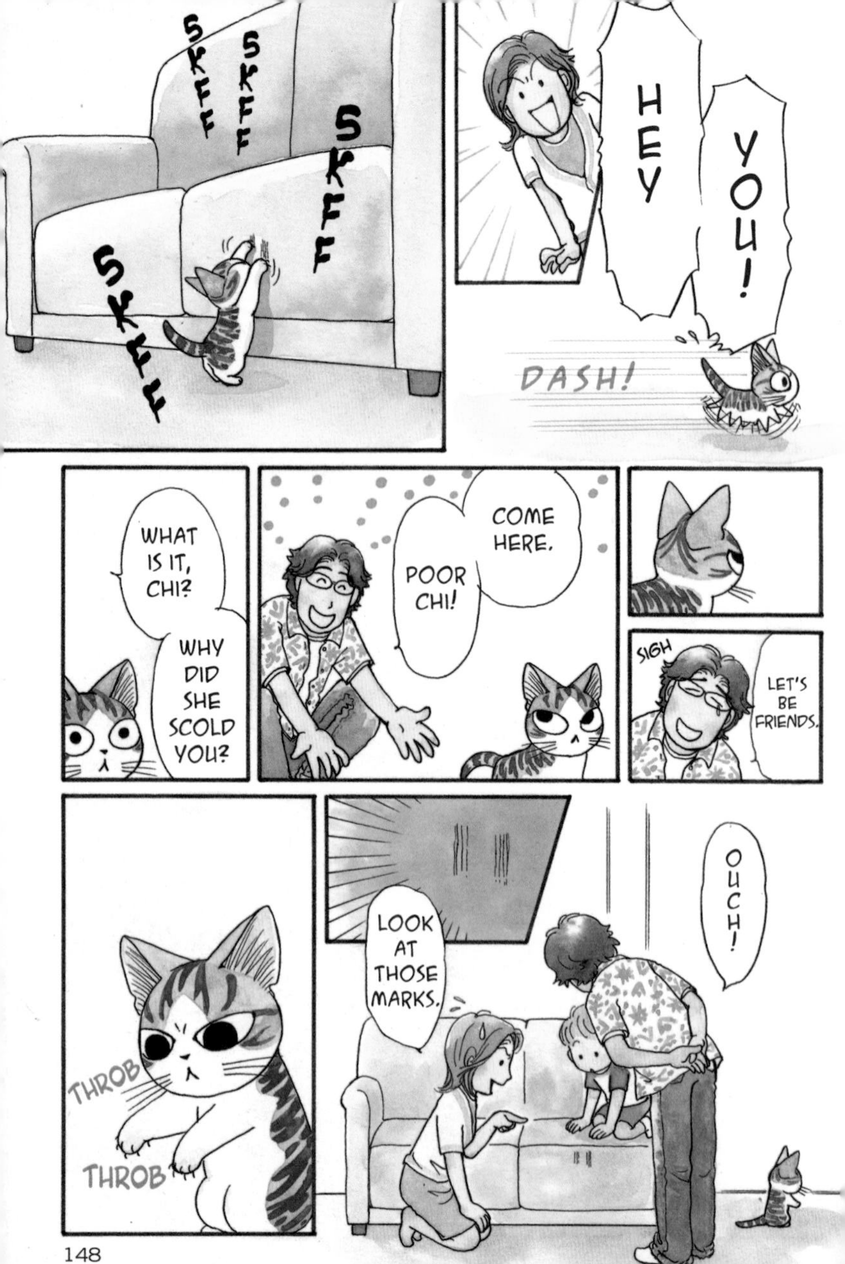
SKFF SKFF SKFF SKFF
HEY YOU!
DASH!
WHAT IS IT, CHI?
WHY DID SHE SCOLD YOU?
COME HERE.
POOR CHI!
SIGH
LET'S BE FRIENDS.
THROB
THROB
LOOK AT THOSE MARKS.
OUCH!

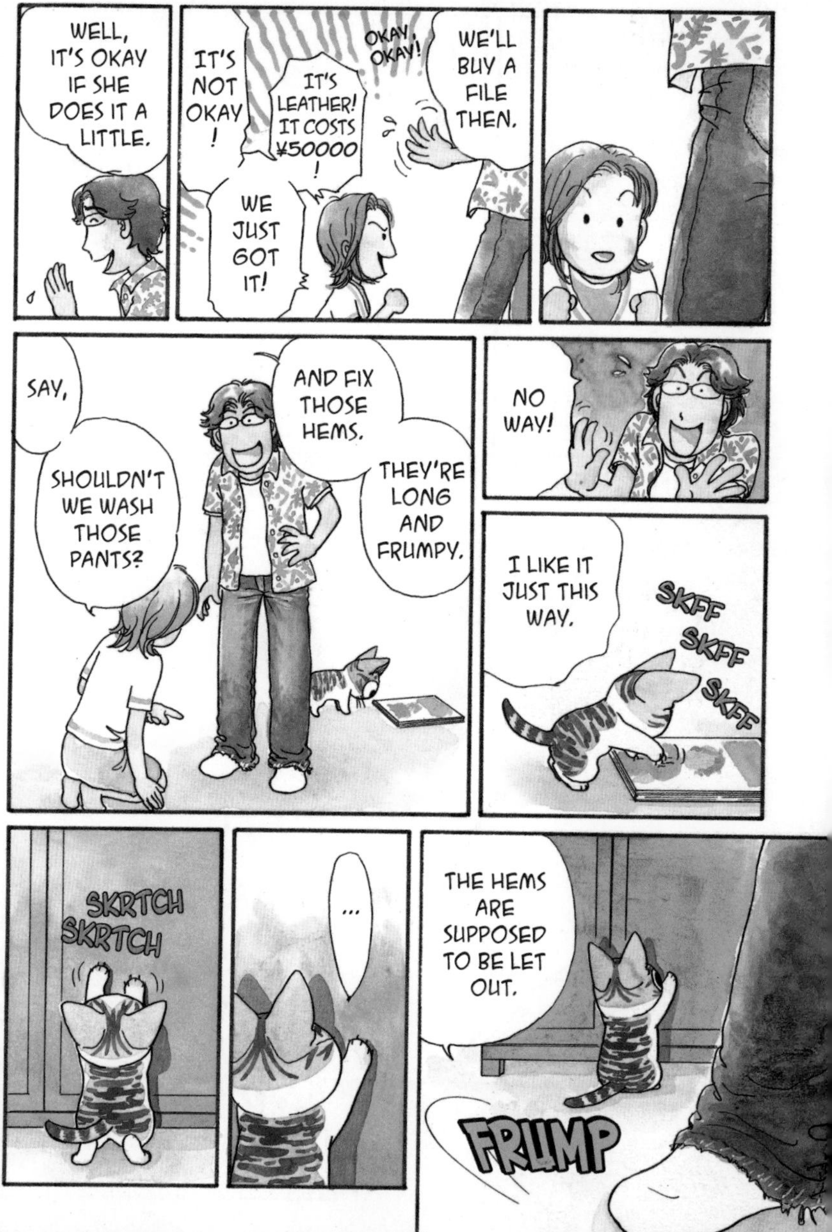
WELL, IT'S OKAY IF SHE DOES IT A LITTLE.
IT'S NOT OKAY!
IT'S LEATHER! IT COSTS ¥50000!
WE JUST GOT IT!
OKAY, OKAY!
WE'LL BUY A FILE THEN.
SAY,
SHOULDN'T WE WASH THOSE PANTS?
AND FIX THOSE HEMS.
THEY'RE LONG AND FRUMPY.
NO WAY!
I LIKE IT JUST THIS WAY.
SKFF SKFF SKFF
SKRTCH SKRTCH
...
THE HEMS ARE SUPPOSED TO BE LET OUT.
FRUMP

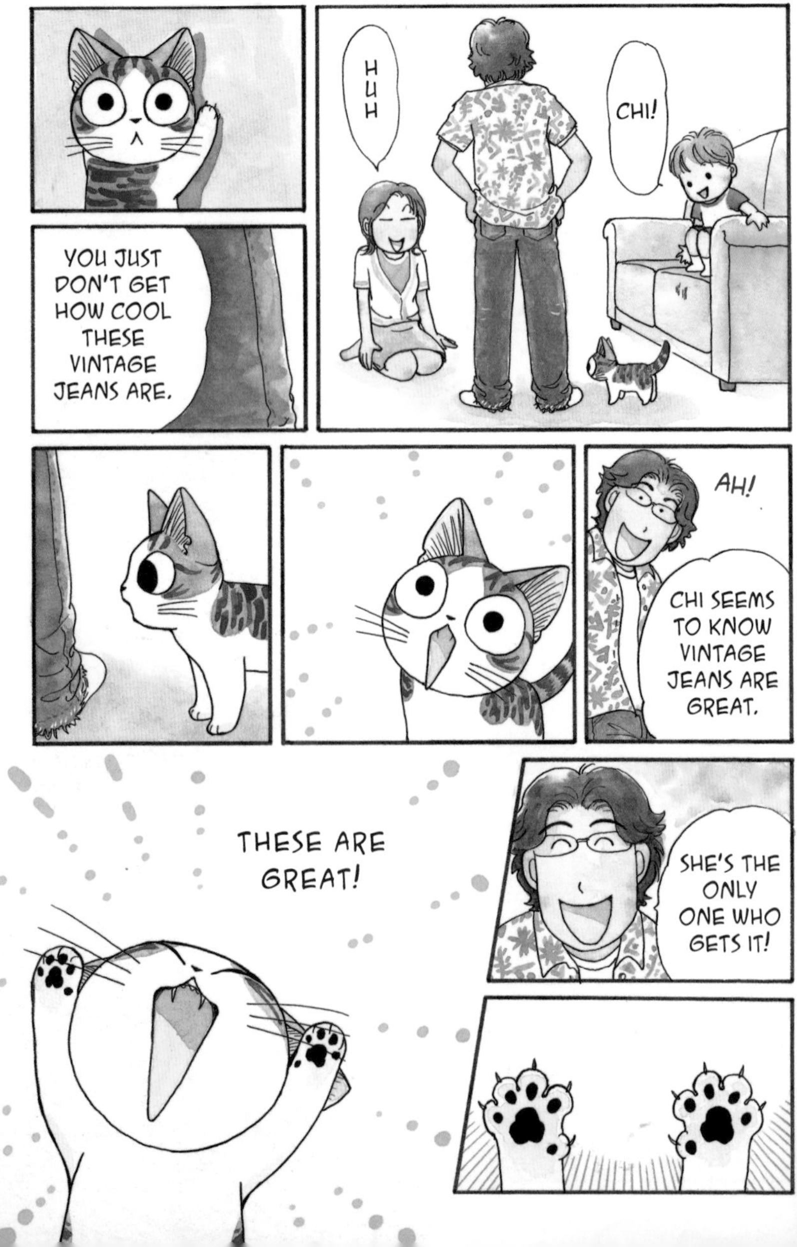
YOU JUST DON'T GET HOW COOL THESE VINTAGE JEANS ARE.
HUH
CHI!
AH!
CHI SEEMS TO KNOW VINTAGE JEANS ARE GREAT.
THESE ARE GREAT!
SHE'S THE ONLY ONE WHO GETS IT!

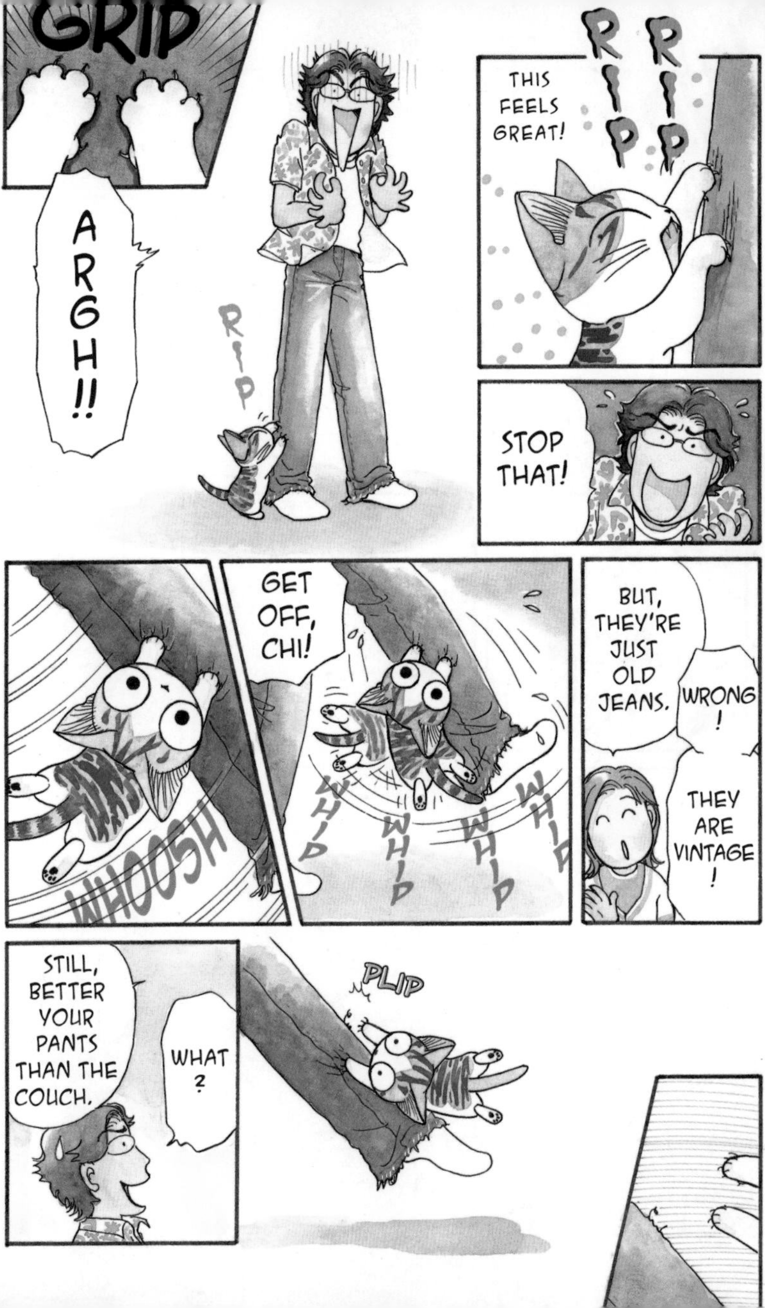
GRIP
ARGH!!
RIP
RIP
THIS FEELS GREAT!
RIP RIP
STOP THAT!
WHOOSH
GET OFF, CHI!
WHIP
WHIP
WHIP
WHIP
BUT, THEY'RE JUST OLD JEANS.
WRONG!
THEY ARE VINTAGE!
STILL, BETTER YOUR PANTS THAN THE COUCH.
WHAT?
PLIP

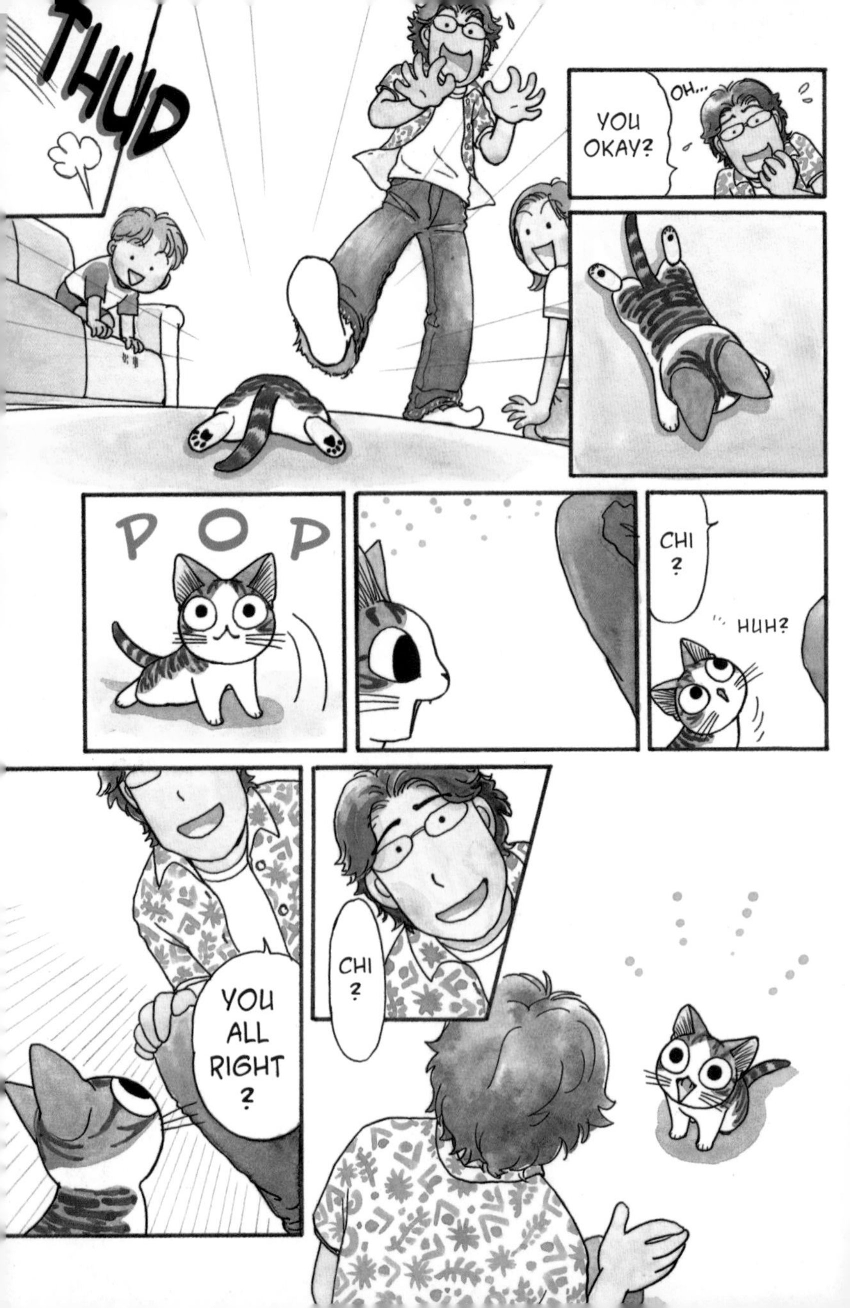
THUD
OH...
YOU OKAY?
POP
CHI?
HUH?
YOU ALL RIGHT?
CHI?

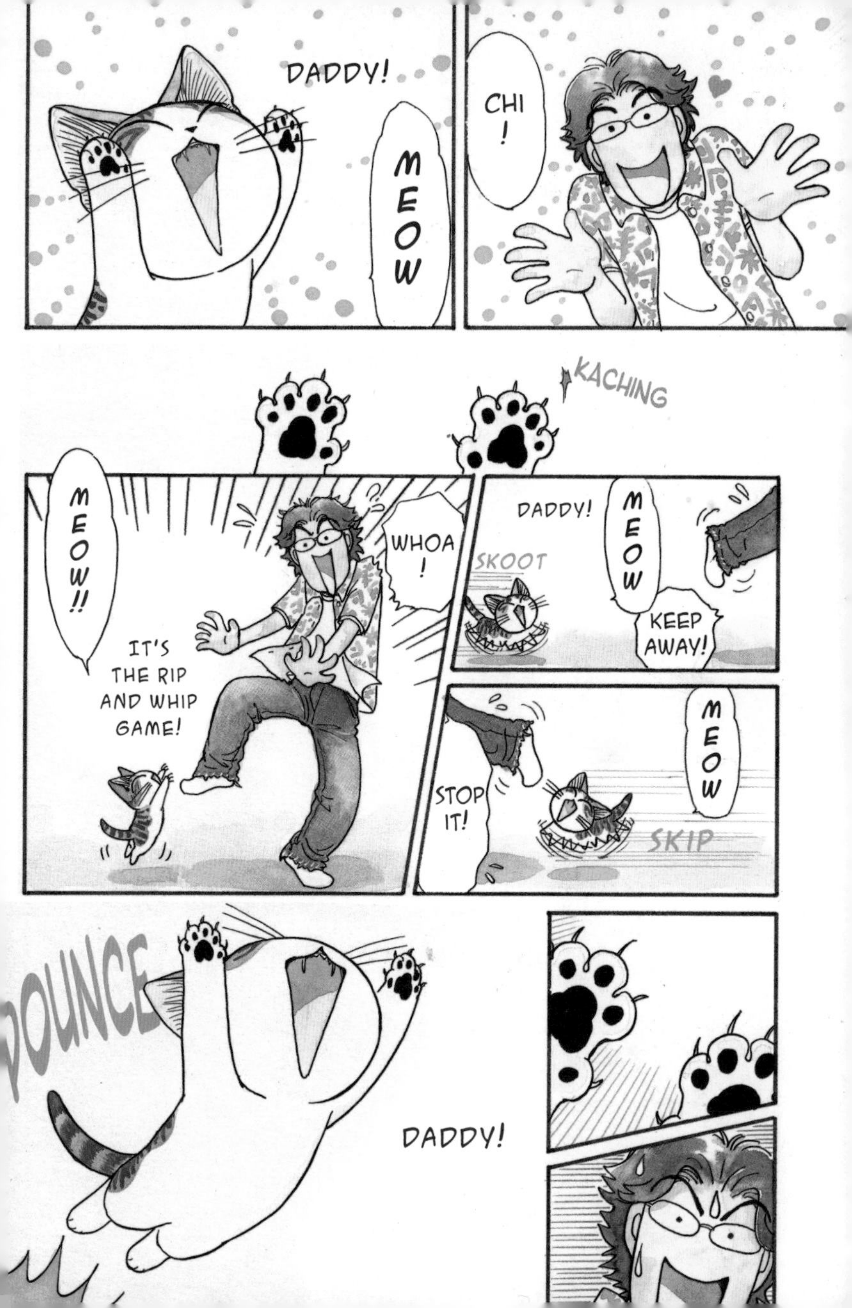
DADDY!
MEOW
CHI!
KACHING
MEOW!!
IT'S THE RIP AND WHIP GAME!
WHOA!
DADDY!
MEOW
SKOOT
KEEP AWAY!
STOP IT!
MEOW
SKIP
POUNCE
DADDY!

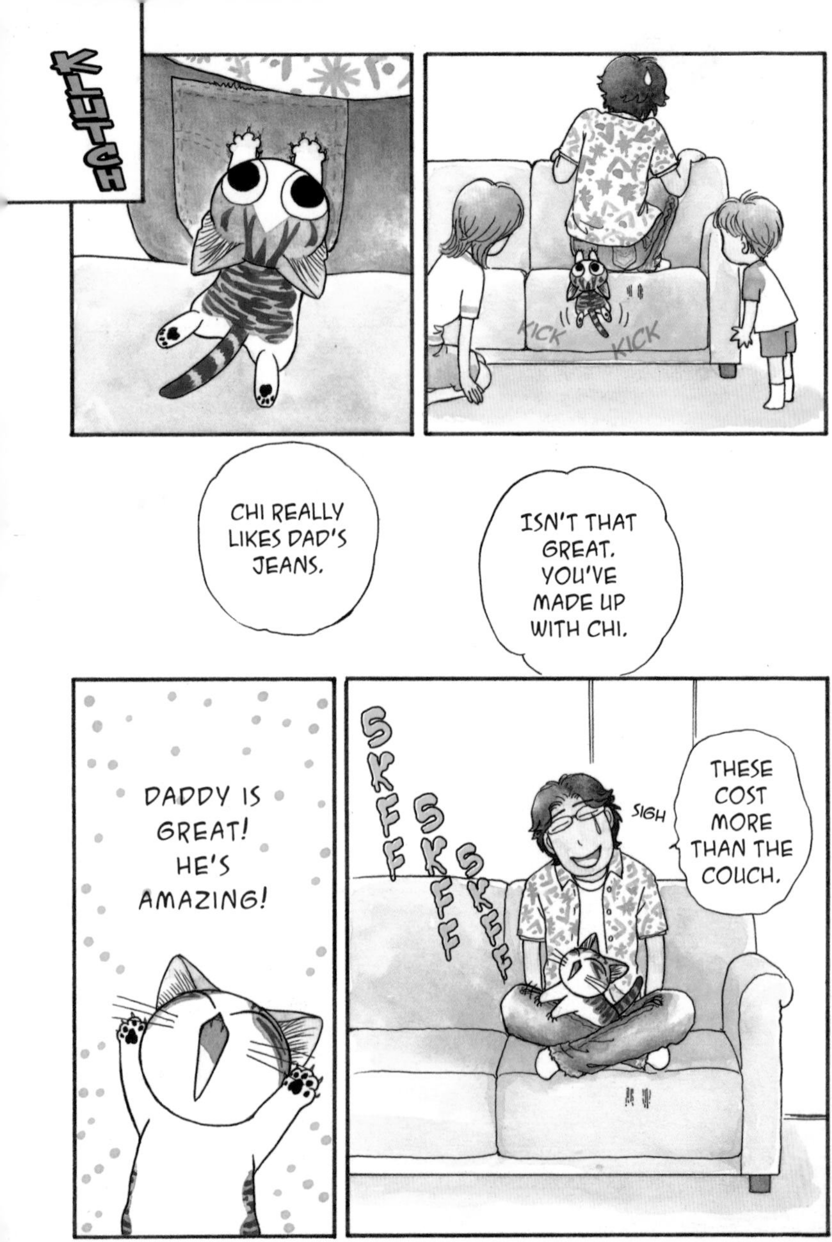
KLUTCH
KICK
KICK
CHI REALLY LIKES DAD'S JEANS.
ISN'T THAT GREAT. YOU'VE MADE UP WITH CHI.
DADDY IS GREAT! HE'S AMAZING!
SKFF
SKFF
SKFF
SIGH
THESE COST MORE THAN THE COUCH.

the end

homemade 20: a cat is home alone

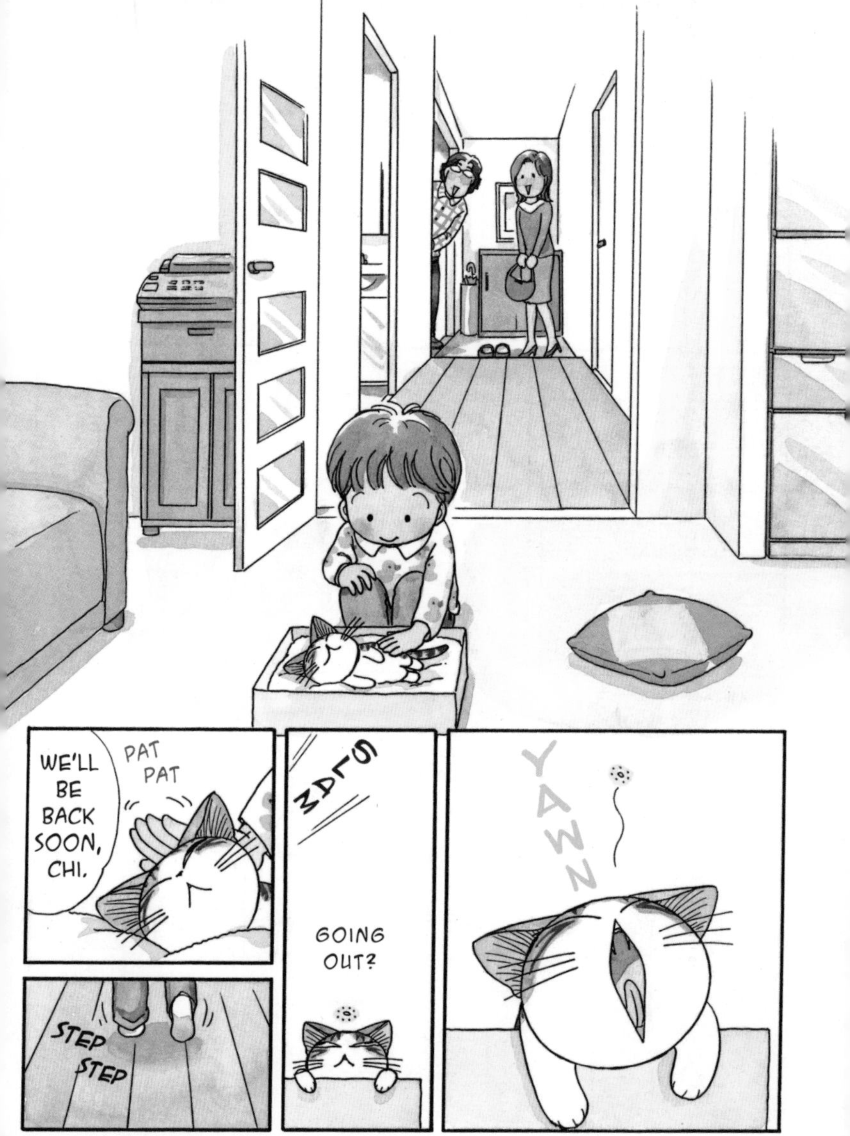
WE'LL BE BACK SOON, CHI.
PAT PAT
STEP STEP
SLAM
GOING OUT?
YAWN

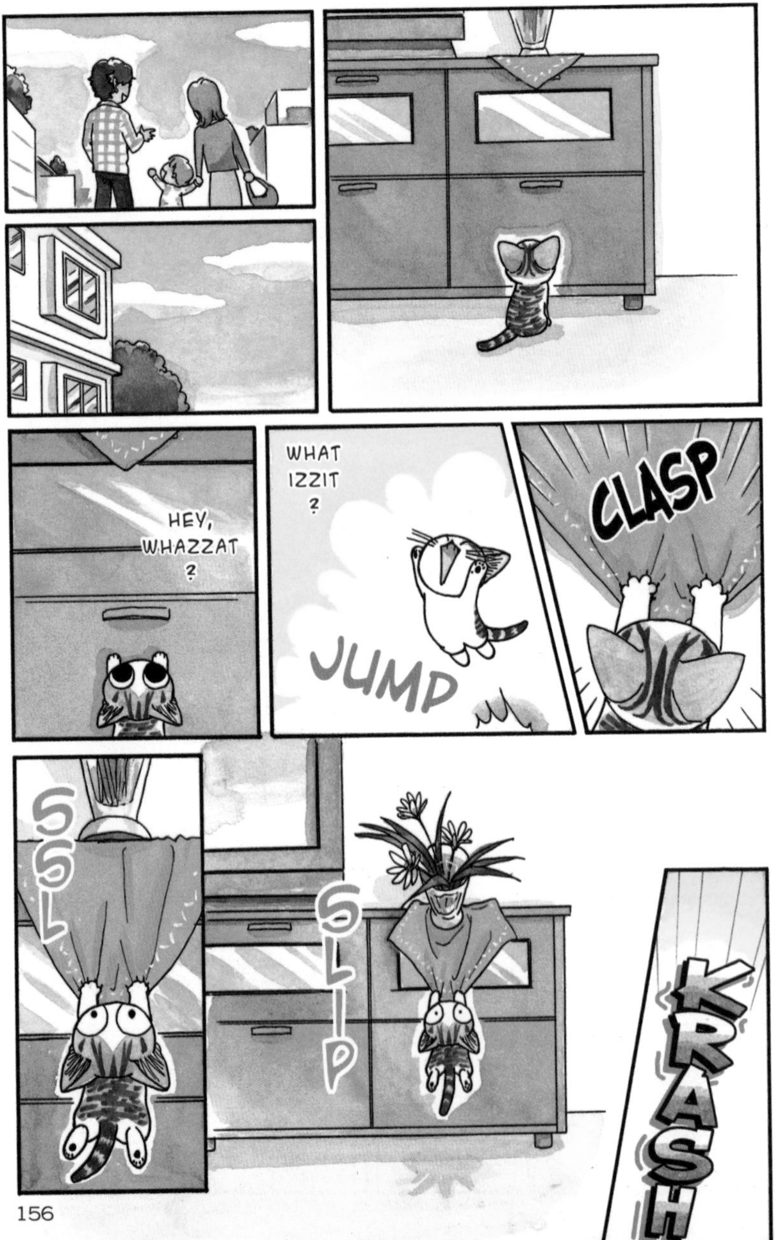
HEY, WHAZZAT?
WHAT IZZIT?
JUMP
CLASP
SSL
SLIP
KRASH

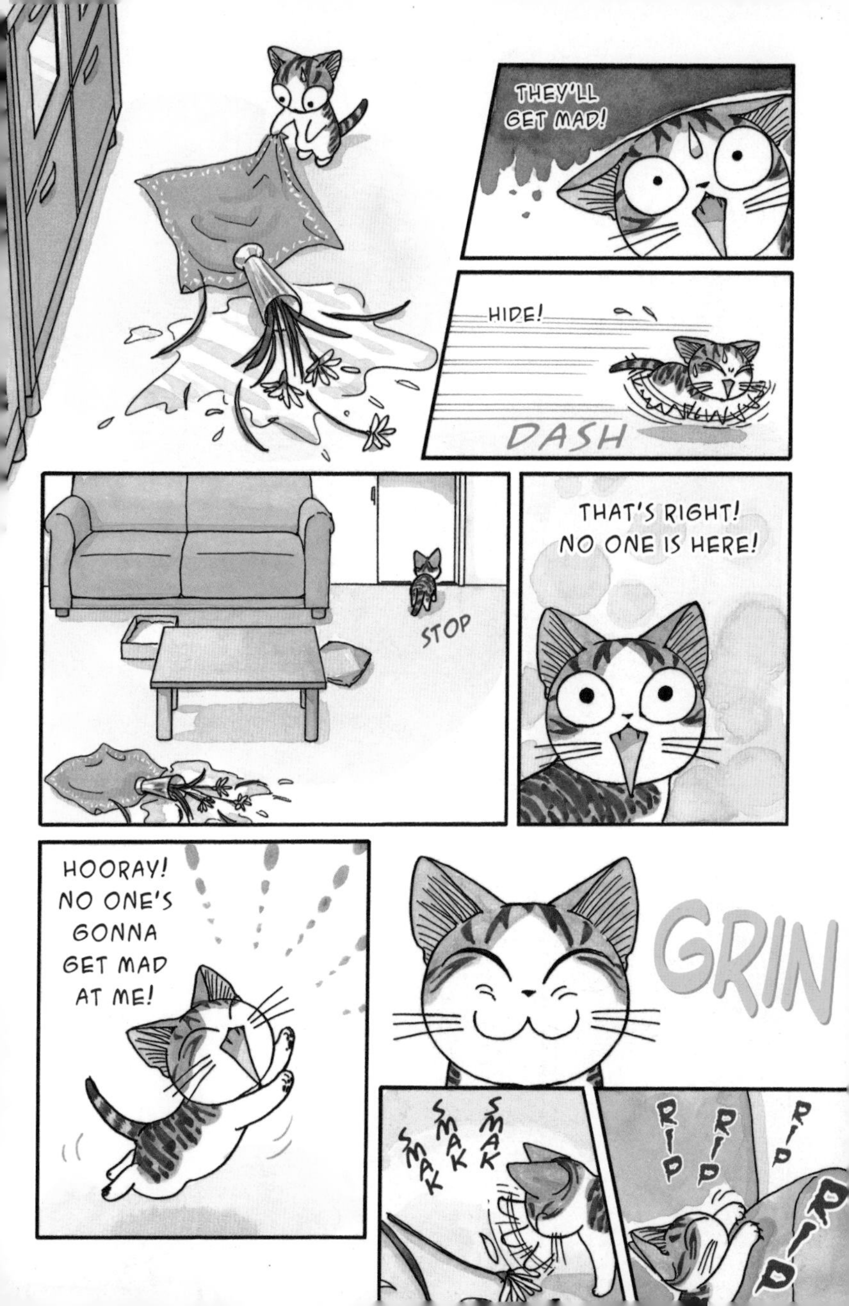
THEY'LL GET MAD!
HIDE!
DASH
STOP
THAT'S RIGHT! NO ONE IS HERE!
HOORAY! NO ONE'S GONNA GET MAD AT ME!
GRIN
SMAK
SMAK
SMAK
RIP
RIP
RIP
RIP

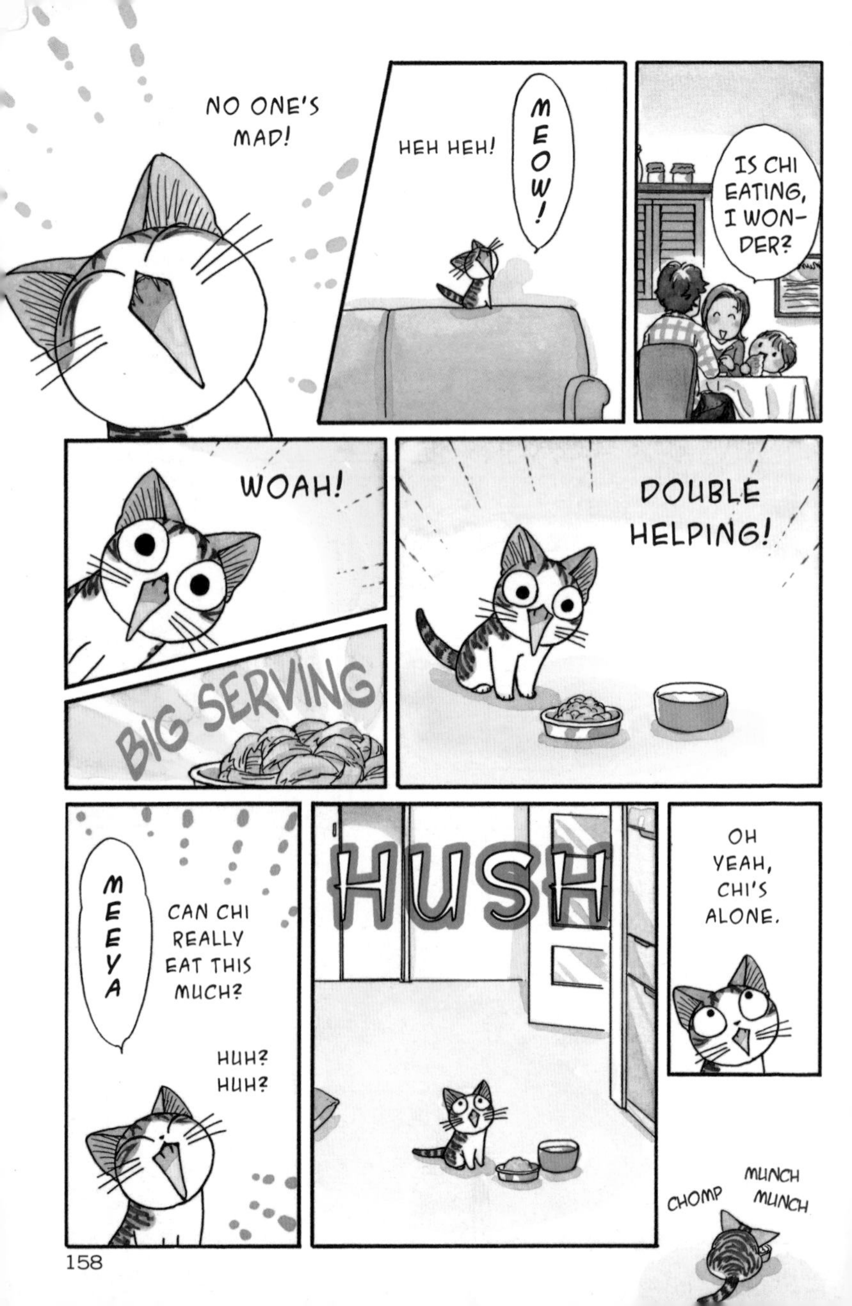
NO ONE'S MAD!
MEOW!
HEH HEH!
IS CHI EATING, I WONDER?
WOAH!
BIG SERVING
DOUBLE HELPING!
MEEYA
CAN CHI REALLY EAT THIS MUCH?
HUH? HUH?
HUSH
OH YEAH, CHI'S ALONE.
CHOMP
MUNCH MUNCH

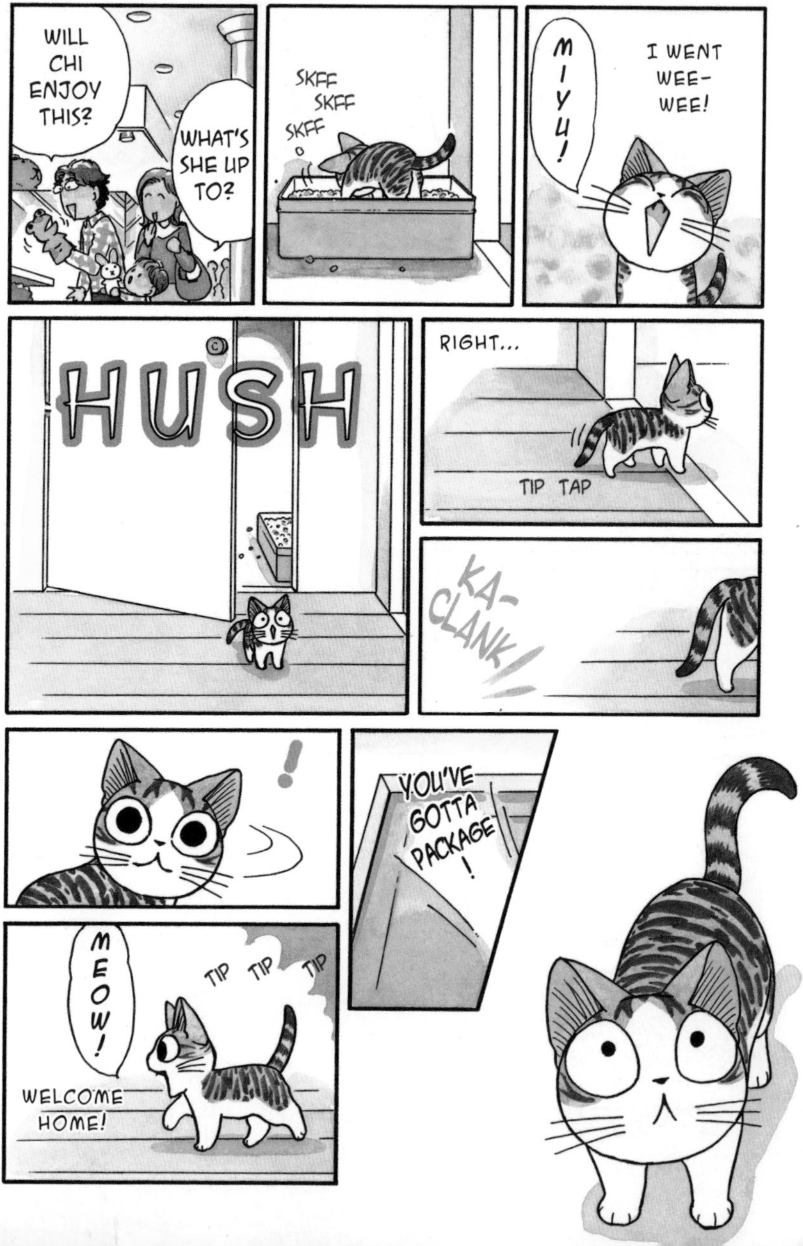
WILL CHI ENJOY THIS?
WHAT'S SHE UP TO?
SKFF SKFF SKFF
MIYU!
I WENT WEE-WEE!
HUSH
RIGHT...
TIP TAP
KA-CLANK
!
MEOW!
TIP TIP TIP
WELCOME HOME!
YOU'VE GOTTA PACKAGE!

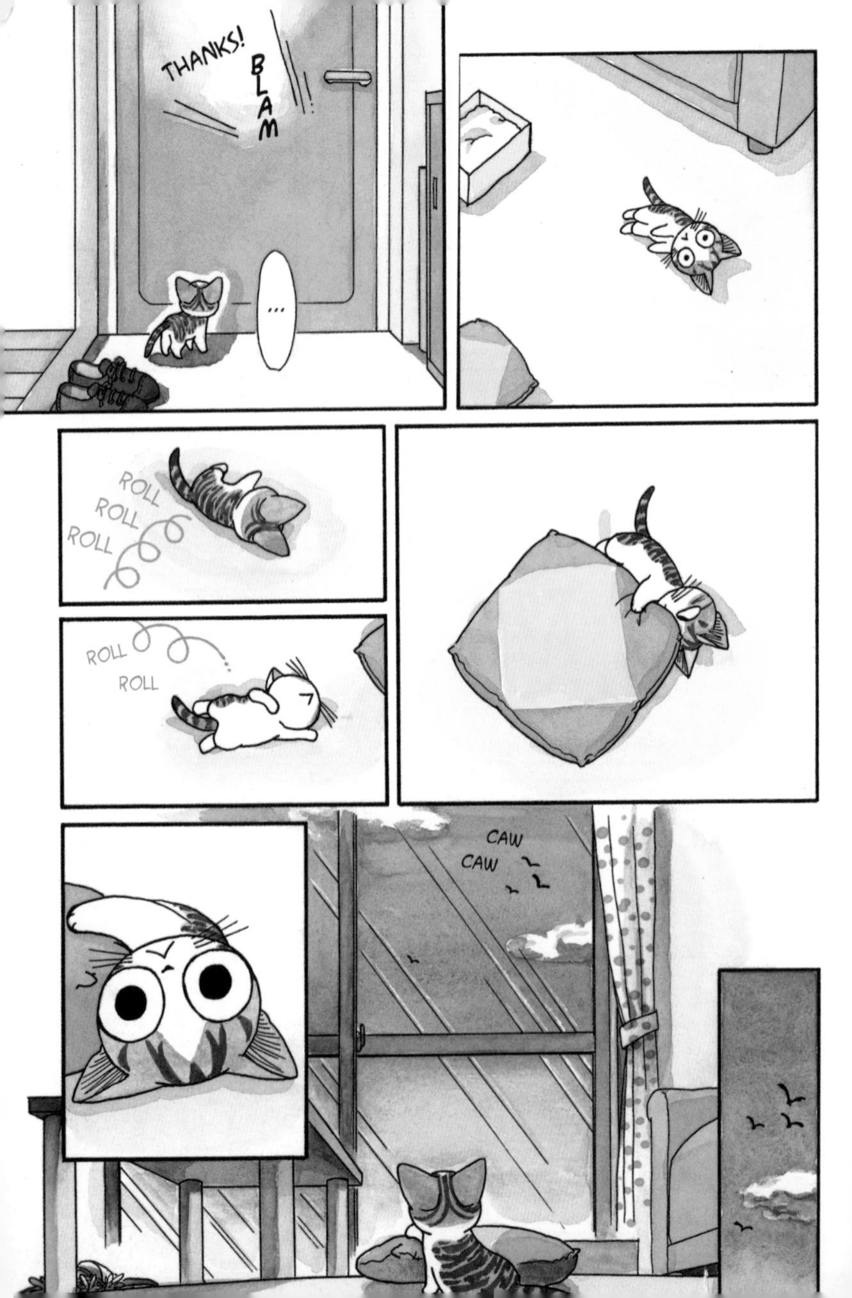
THANKS!
BLAM
...
ROLL
ROLL
ROLL
ROLL
ROLL
CAW
CAW

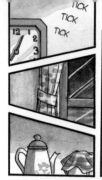

TICK
TICK
TICK

THEY ARE
COMING BACK,
WIGHT?   WIGHT?

GNAW
GNAW   GNAW
              GNAW

TIP TIP TIP

BUT...

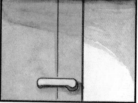

WHAT
IF...

SHAKE SHAKE

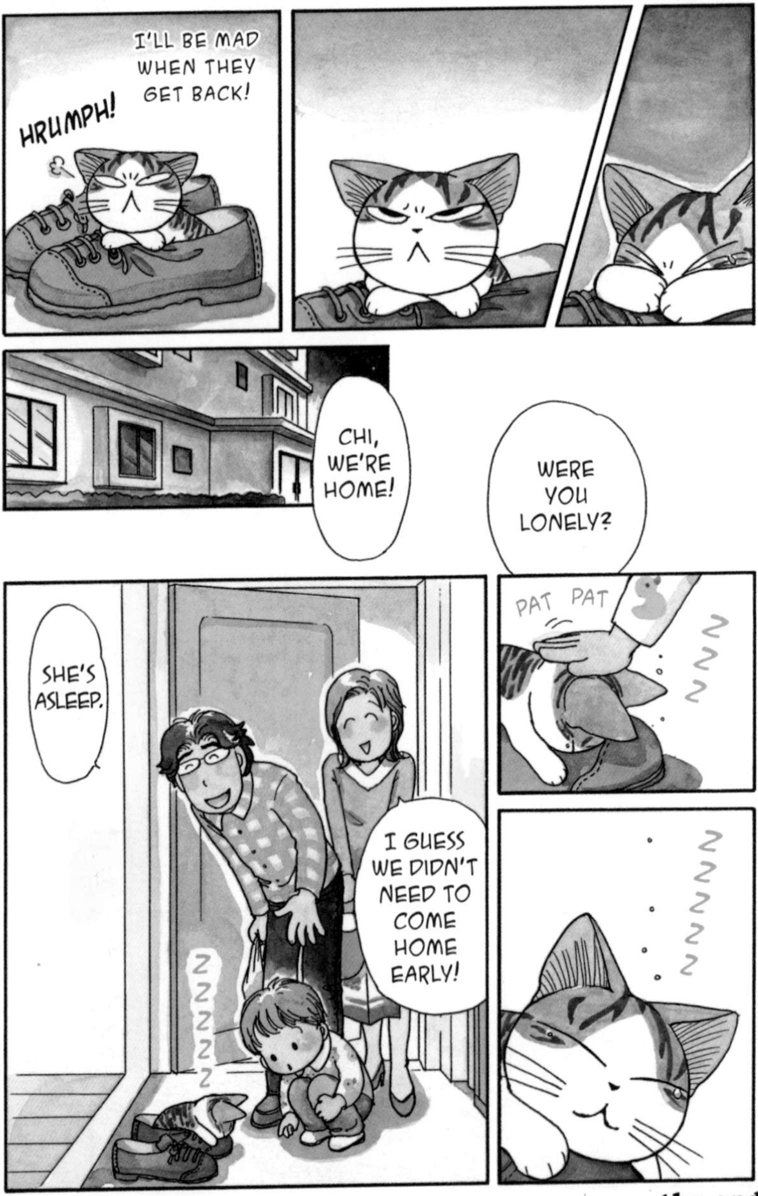
HRUMPH!
I'LL BE MAD WHEN THEY GET BACK!
CHI, WE'RE HOME!
WERE YOU LONELY?
SHE'S ASLEEP.
I GUESS WE DIDN'T NEED TO COME HOME EARLY!
PAT PAT

the end

Introducing **Chi's Home Sweet Home**

America's first detailed look inside
the Yamada family home where Chi lives!

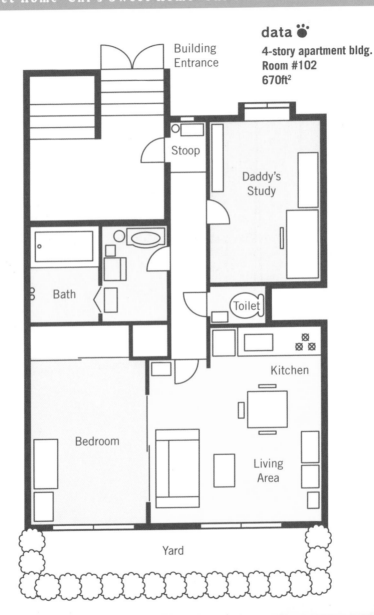

data ⚫

4-story apartment bldg.
Room #102
670ft²

Building
Entrance

Stoop

Daddy's
Study

Bath

Toilet

Kitchen

Bedroom

Living
Area

Yard

Chi's adventures continue in Volume 2!

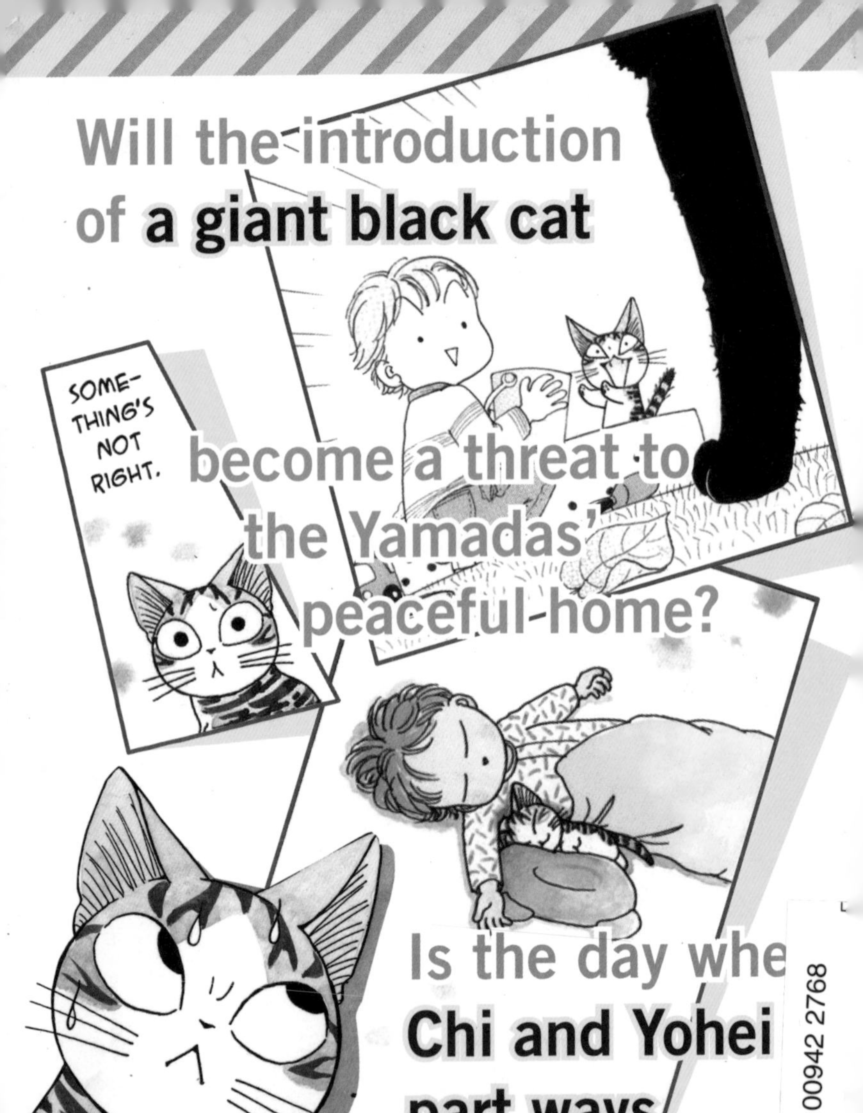
SOMETHING'S NOT RIGHT.

Will the introduction of **a giant black cat** become a threat to the Yamadas' peaceful home?

Is the day when **Chi and Yohei part ways** approaching?!

Find out in Volume 2 of *Chi's Sweet Home*, on sale August 2010!